Praise for *A Fever in the Heartland*

A *New York Times* Bestseller

A *Washington Post* Notable Work of Nonfiction

An NPR Best Book of the Year

A *Kirkus Reviews* Best Book of the Year

A New York Public Library Best Book of the Year

A *Chicago Review of Books* Best Book of the Year

A *California Review of Books* Best Book of the Year

A *BookPage* Best Book of the Year

A *Library Journal* Best Book of the Year

A Goodreads Choice Awards Finalist

Amazon's Best Books of the Year (History)

Barnes & Noble Best Books of the Year (History)

"Powerful . . . As a narrative, *A Fever in the Heartland* is gripping; as a rumination on the moral obscenity of white supremacy—whatever guises it wears—the book is damning."   —*The New York Times Book Review*

"A master class in the tools of narrative nonfiction: high stakes, ample suspense, and sweeping historical phenomena made vivid through the dramatic actions of individual villains and heroes."   —*The Washington Post*

"Egan examines and sorts out the complexities and contradictions of the rise of Stephenson and the Klan. . . . *A Fever in the Heartland* [is] an honest look at what really happened."   —*The Guardian*

"Riveting . . . Egan is a brilliant researcher and lucid writer."   —*Star Tribune*

T0038740

"Masterful . . . This is a fascinating read and revelation of American history." —*The Spokesman-Review*

"A dynamic suspense story." —*St. Louis Post-Dispatch*

"Egan lures us into his narrative with muscular yet agile prose . . . [and] seasons *A Fever in the Heartland* with arresting anecdotes." —*Nashville Scene*

"Egan's riveting page-turner offers profound insights to readers willing to peer into layers of American hypocrisy, intolerance, malignant indifference, and public culpability." —*Library Journal* (starred review)

"Enthralling . . . Egan skillfully leads readers through the horrifying experiences of Oberholtzer and a handful of other beleaguered klan opponents." —*BookPage* (starred review)

"*A Fever in the Heartland* combines Egan's diligent research with his ability to create credible, emotionally gripping scenes." —*Bookreporter*

"With narrative élan, Egan gives us a riveting saga of how a predatory con man became one of the most powerful people in 1920s America, Grand Dragon of the Ku Klux Klan, with a plan to rule the country—and how a grisly murder of a woman brought him down. Compelling and chillingly resonant with our own time."
—Erik Larson, author of *The Splendid and the Vile*

"Timothy Egan's history of the Ku Klux Klan's rise and fall is absolutely gripping. It is also terrifyingly relevant."
—Elizabeth Kolbert, Pulitzer Prize–winning author of *The Sixth Extinction*

"Egan has done it again, mastering another complicated American story with authority and surprising detail. The Klan here are not the nightriders of the late nineteenth century, but a retooled special interest group and unusually potent political power. The influence they wielded over states and policy should put a chill in every American. Bravo." —Ken Burns

"With meticulous detective work, Timothy Egan shines a light on one of the most sinister chapters in American history—how a viciously racist movement, led by a murderous con man, rose to power in the early twentieth century. *A Fever in the Heartland* is compelling, powerful, and profoundly resonant today."

—David Grann, author of *The Wager* and *Killers of the Flower Moon*

"[A] riveting exposé."
—*Booklist* (starred review)

"Riveting history . . . Excellently rendered."
—*Kirkus Reviews* (starred review)

"[A] certifiable page-turner."
—*Publishers Weekly* (starred review)

"Engrossing . . . A valuable work of history."
—*Shelf Awareness* (starred review)

PENGUIN BOOKS

A FEVER IN THE HEARTLAND

Timothy Egan is a Pulitzer Prize–winning reporter and the author of nine other books, most recently the highly acclaimed *A Pilgrimage to Eternity* and *The Immortal Irishman*. His book on the Dust Bowl, *The Worst Hard Time*, won a National Book Award for Nonfiction. His account of photographer Edward Curtis, *Short Nights of the Shadow Catcher*, won the Andrew Carnegie Medal for Excellence in Nonfiction. Egan lives in Seattle.

ALSO BY TIMOTHY EGAN

The Good Rain

Breaking Blue

Lasso the Wind

The Winemaker's Daughter

The Worst Hard Time

The Big Burn

Short Nights of the Shadow Catcher

The Immortal Irishman

A Pilgrimage to Eternity

A FEVER
IN THE
HEARTLAND

*The Ku Klux Klan's Plot to Take Over
America, and the Woman Who Stopped Them*

Timothy Egan

PENGUIN BOOKS

PENGUIN BOOKS
An imprint of Penguin Random House LLC
penguinrandomhouse.com

First published in the United States of America by Viking,
an imprint of Penguin Random House LLC, 2023
Published in Penguin Books 2024

ISBN 9780735225282 (paperback)

THE LIBRARY OF CONGRESS HAS CATALOGED THE
HARDCOVER EDITION AS FOLLOWS:
Names: Egan, Timothy, author.
Title: A fever in the heartland : the Ku Klux Klan's plot to take over
America, and the woman who stopped them / Timothy Egan.
Description: New York, NY : Viking, [2023] |
Includes bibliographical references and index.
Identifiers: LCCN 2022029431 (print) | LCCN 2022029432 (ebook) |
ISBN 9780735225268 (hardcover) | ISBN 9780735225275 (ebook)
Subjects: LCSH: Stephenson, David Curtis, 1891–1966. |
Ku Klux Klan (1915–)—Indiana—Biography. |
Ku Klux Klan (1915–)—Indiana—History. |
Oberholtzer, Madge, 1896–1925.
Classification: LCC HS2330.K63 E43 2023 (print) |
LCC HS2330.K63 (ebook) | DDC 322.4/209772—dc23/eng/20220804
LC record available at https://lccn.loc.gov/2022029431
LC ebook record available at https://lccn.loc.gov/2022029432

Printed in the United States of America
1st Printing

Designed by Alexis Farabaugh

God has no children whose rights may be safely trampled on.

FREDERICK DOUGLASS

CONTENTS

PART THREE

Reckoning

AUTHOR'S NOTE

The following story is true. Dialogue and internal monologue are verbatim from court testimony, oral histories, autobiographies, letters, diaries, and newspaper quotes. See the source notes in the back for further details.

Introduction:
The Quintessential Americans

The most powerful man in Indiana stood next to the new governor at the Inaugural Ball, there to be thanked, applauded, and blessed for using the nation's oldest domestic terror group to gain control of a uniquely American state. David C. Stephenson was sandy blond and thin-haired, with blue-gray eyes and a fleshy second chin much too middle-aged for a man of thirty-three. Charm oozed from him like grease from a sizzling sausage. Everyone called him Steve. But in print, in posters, in letters and telegrams and flyers all over the Midwest, he was known as the Old Man. He preferred that name, and the mystique that went with it, to the only formal title he ever held: Grand Dragon of the largest realm of the Ku Klux Klan the world had ever seen. He was driven to work in a Cadillac, a bodyguard next to him, and never left his pillared white mansion without a revolver strapped to his chest. He looked well fed, well dressed, certainly well satisfied at the reach of an Invisible Empire that was secretive no more.

In his suite of offices inside the Kresge Building, located at the crossroads of influence and history in downtown Indianapolis, he kept seven black telephones and a single white one. The standout was a direct line to the White House, he told guests. Numerous visitors overheard him say, "Thank you, Mr. President, and give my best to Mrs. Coolidge," as they waited for their ration of the Old Man's time. On his desk was a bust of Napoleon. The Emperor was a role model, but even he might blush at the claim that Stephenson made to his inner circle: "I am the law."

You could doubt that, for he had been elected to no office, appointed to no board, hired by no police department or district attorney, named to no court or panel of judges. The only oath he had taken was the one sworn by up to six million men nationwide who donned full-length robes and covered their faces in sixteen-inch conical hoods, formally vowing "to maintain forever white supremacy." Yet a look around the ballroom of the Indianapolis Athletic Club, where 150 of the most influential citizens had gathered to fete the new governor, would leave little uncertainty about who controlled the state.

On this winter day, Stephenson was triumphant, "monarch of all he surveyed," as the *New York Times* described him. It had been barely four years since the reborn Klan moved across the Ohio River and spread north. But now crosses burned all over the state. They burned on the lawns of Black families. They burned near Catholic churches and Jewish synagogues. They burned across the street from police stations. They burned near cornfields at the edge of small towns. They burned after Sunday services and Independence Day parades and Christmas-week sleigh rides. Torching an oversized cross was theater of intimidation, leaping flames on the night horizon, but also a thrilling bond of brotherhood. Hoosiers were joiners. And in 1925, if you were not a knight of the KKK, you did not belong.

The Klan owned the state, and Stephenson owned the Klan. Cops, judges, prosecutors, ministers, mayors, newspaper editors— they all answered to the Grand Dragon. He was backed by his own private police force, some 30,000 men legally deputized to harass violators of Klan-certified virtue. Most members of the incoming state legislature took orders from the hooded order, as did the majority of the congressional delegation. From the low-bank shores of Lake Michigan in the north to the fat bends of the Ohio River in the south, from the rural folds of a county where Abraham Lincoln grew up in a small house that nurtured big ideas, to the window-less shack along the tracks where Louis Armstrong cut his first jazz record, the Klan infested Indiana. All but two of the ninety-two counties had a chapter—the only state with such saturation. One in three native-born white males wore the sheets. And here was yet another plum: Ed Jackson, the Republican whose name had first appeared on membership rolls of the Klan in 1923, had been swept into the governor's office. He owed it all to D. C. Stephenson.

In the golden age of fraternal organizations, the Klan was the largest and most powerful of the secret societies among American men—bigger by far than the Odd Fellows, the Elks, or the Freemasons, and vastly greater in number than the original Klan born in violence just after the Civil War. Gains over the last few years, mostly in the North, had been astonishing. A Klan mayor ruled Anaheim, California; the city was nicknamed "Klanaheim." A KKK chapter was chartered on board the USS *Tennessee*, a battleship anchored off Bremerton, Washington. "The Invisible Empire now has a floating Klan," crowed the order's national paper, the *Imperial Night-Hawk*, which had a larger circulation than the *New York Times*.

In Colorado, an open Klansman, Clarence Morley, won the governorship on the same day that Ed Jackson did in Indiana. He promised to fire all Jewish and Catholic professors at the state's flagship public university. "Every Man under the Capitol Dome a Klansman" was his motto. He joined another Klan-backed governor in the West, Walter M. Pierce in Oregon, who endorsed a voter-approved measure that would essentially eliminate Catholic schools. "Keeping America a Land for Americans" was his slogan. The Klan claimed fifteen United States senators under its control, and seventy-five members of the House of Representatives. Many had sworn allegiance in secret Klan initiation rituals, becoming "naturalized," as it was called.

But the epicenter was Indiana, which was trying to shape human behavior as no state had ever done. At mass rallies, Stephenson and other Klan leaders cited the latest research from influential eugenicists, detailing the skull size, personality deficiencies, and other indicators of inferiority by those not of strict Nordic stock.

The state had passed the world's first eugenic sterilization law, targeting "idiots, imbeciles, and confirmed criminals," as the statute dictated. The Klan was now pushing for a more severe measure, singling out paupers, alcoholics, thieves, prostitutes, and those with epilepsy to be sterilized against their will.

Stephenson's vigilantes assisted the police in enforcing the harshest anti-alcohol laws outside the Muslim world. Prohibition, which Winston Churchill called "an affront to the whole history of mankind," had become the law of the land in 1920. It had long been pressed by the Klan, aimed at Irish, Italian, and German Catholics as part of a crusade against the meeting places and social rituals of immigrants, and at Black men whose lust for white women was said to rise with the ingestion of liquor. Indiana went much further. The state made it illegal to display flasks and cocktail shakers in shop windows, or to sell hair tonic that contained a whiff of alcohol. A new law criminalized possession of an *empty* bottle if it still had the smell of liquor. Punishment was thirty days in jail.

The America of the 1920s was roaring in some quarters but repressive in many others. The first twenty-five years of the new century were the "swiftest moving and most restless time the world has known," wrote Booth Tarkington, Indiana's most celebrated author. In the South, whites had wiped out Black voting rights. They put in place Jim Crow laws that prevented more than one out of every three citizens from owning property in middle-class neighborhoods and from eating, sleeping, traveling, shopping, or going to school with whites. That system was locked down, backed by a Supreme Court ruling with only one justice dissenting. Now the Klan was moving swiftly in its new strongholds in the North to extend suppression of Black families in everyday life.

The twentieth-century Klan was also fighting to close the door on those whose religion, accents, and appearances made them suspect in large parts of the United States—mainly Eastern European Jews, Polish and Italian Catholics, Greeks, and Asians.

"No one can deny that the United States is a white Protestant country," wrote the *Fiery Cross*, the weekly newspaper of the Indiana Klan. Stephenson's press organ was filled with scare stories of those seeking to find a home in a new land. "We receive at our ports of immigration an ignorant and disreputable omnium-gatherum of scorbutic and vicious spawn, people who possess neither blood nor brain, unclean and uncomprehending foes of American ideals." The governor of Georgia, Clifford Walker, told a Klan rally in 1924 that the United States should "build a wall of steel, a wall as high as heaven" against immigrants.

And in these first days of 1925, the ultimate political design was within reach: a Klan from sea to sea, north to south, anchored in the White House. It was an absurd idea only to those who believed that a vibrant young democracy could never be given over to a gifted charlatan. The Klan had been so influential at the 1924 national conventions of both Democrats and Republicans that *Time* magazine had put Imperial Wizard Hiram Wesley Evans on the cover, and dubbed the GOP gathering the "Kleveland Konvention." The Klan got most of what it wanted at both national party meetings. When Evans went to Colorado later that year, he told a gathering of thousands of new initiates who filled a stadium that they had just joined "the most wonderful movement the world has ever seen."

As Stephenson welcomed the fresh crop of politicians under the Klan's thumb today, it was an open secret that Indiana senator

Samuel Ralston did not have long to live. Should he die, the governor would name his successor. And the Grand Dragon of Indiana was the most likely choice to fill the seat, given what Jackson owed him. After that, as Stephenson told associates, "I'm going to be the biggest man in the United States."

Outside, snow showers threatened, the wind was up, and the ground hard. Bare limbs of the big red maples and white oaks, native to this prairie soil, clattered against each other in skeletal gasps. The city was busting at its iron seams, the streets crowded with the clank and cacophony of autos, trolleys, and fine-dressed shoppers eying miracle appliances. Indiana was now as urban as it was rural; for the first time, half the population lived in a city. Many had grown up on farms where they'd pumped their own water, walked behind horse-drawn plows in the field, and rarely traveled more than a hundred miles from their place of birth. Now they had flush toilets and furnaces, toasters and telephones, vacuum cleaners, refrigerators, and the latest marvel: radios, bringing baseball games and music to a wooden box nesting in the family room.

Inside the snug interior of the new Italian Renaissance building, all was aglow with fellowship and praise. Bells rang, ushers shepherded men in tuxedos and white ties and women in evening gowns to their seats. A local writer, William Herschell, was summoned to read a poem he'd written, one of the most popular verses in the state, the closing line familiar to this crowd:

> *Ain't God good to Indiana?*
> *Ain't He, fellers? Ain't He, though?*

The new governor was introduced to a rousing ovation. As secretary of state, Ed Jackson had authorized the Indiana charter of the Ku Klux Klan in 1921. And when he was exposed two years later as the highest-ranking elected official in Indiana to wear "the shroud of the terrorist and the mask of the highwayman," as a crusading Irish American journalist put it, he shrugged it off. As did voters in the 1924 election. Jackson was *one of us*—a neighbor, son of a mill worker, war veteran, small-town lawyer relatively new to the big city, a Disciples of Christ Protestant in good standing, not a shred of ethnicity to him.

When the grandchildren of these leading citizens later discovered hoods in the attic, or membership lists that included their kin, they could not fathom how such a thing came to pass. They knew the Ku Klux Klan was born in the murk of blood-spilling hate, built around a racial order that would find its most ghastly expression in the laws of Nazi Germany. They would tell themselves that the vast Klan of the American Midwest was nonviolent, casually cruel at worst, that its members were hayseeds and dupes and chuckleheads, that one twisted man with a surfeit of charisma had taken over the state without the consent of the majority.

None of it was true.

The Klan dens of the Heartland were not small or isolated or insignificant by any measure. Nor were their members ignorant of the power of their beliefs. They rose to their feet and cheered speakers who called Jews "un-American parasites." They harassed and threatened Catholic clergy and nuns. They passed laws to prevent Black people from moving into their neighborhoods, going to public schools of their choice, or marrying people of another race. They voted overwhelmingly for the Klan slate in state and local elections. On occasion, they clubbed and terrified their enemies, or ran them out of town on a few hours' notice. They bombed homes and set fires. They didn't hide by day and only come out at night. They were people who held their communities together, bankers and merchants, lawyers and doctors, coaches and teachers, servants of God and shapers of opinion. Their wives belonged to the Klan women's auxiliary, and their masked children marched in parades under the banner of the Ku Klux Kiddies.

"I did not sell the Klan in Indiana on hatreds," Stephenson said. "I sold it on Americanism." These people knew what they'd signed up for: that oath before God could not have been more specific about the absolute superiority of one race and one religion and the inferiority of all others.

A handful of Hoosiers were heroic—two rabbis, an African American publisher born enslaved, a fearless Catholic lawyer, a small-town editor repeatedly beaten and thrown in jail, a lone prosecutor. They were aided by a gifted man of letters, a Black poet and Broadway composer who forced an epic national political realignment with his eloquent defiance. Later, these resisters would be nudged from the margins of their time to history's forefront. On this day, they were shut out completely from the orbit of power assembled around the new governor.

"We will stand for the things that are right at all times," Jackson said now, to prolonged applause.

Stephenson settled into dinner at a table in the front of the ballroom. He was with a female companion, one of at least a dozen women he was seen with around town or at the lavish parties he threw inside his mansion. The term of the day was *ladies' man*, for he was surely a charmer, a gift-giver, a note-sender, promiscuous with his praise of women he coveted. But he was much more than that. With an appetite for violent sexual excess, he needed to possess women, to hurt them and make them tremble. Of late, nothing seemed to satisfy him more than a naked woman bloodied by his teeth and begging for her life. His savagery was known only to a few people—it was the great secret of this multiloquent master of the North. But he showed no outward fear of getting caught; law enforcement couldn't touch him. And because the Klan had made him rich, money further immunized him from justice. He earned far more in a year than Babe Ruth. He had a ninety-eight-foot yacht docked at Lake Erie and a private plane with the Klan logo painted underneath, to go with the fleet of luxury cars, a waterfront summer home, and the estate in the most prestigious address in Indiana. One of the men who traveled with him was known simply as "The Bank," and carried enough cash to complete any favor on the spot.

Seated across from him tonight was someone he'd never met, Madge Oberholtzer. She was twenty-eight, daughter of a postal clerk, full-figured, with dark eyes and chestnut-colored hair that she usually wore in a stylish upsweep. Madge had attended Butler College in Irvington, the elegant neighborhood five miles east of downtown Indianapolis. She'd been a member of Pi Beta Phi sorority and fallen in with a passionate group of college Hoosiers trying to get women the vote. She was high-spirited, with an infectious independent streak.

Today, she'd been hired to help set up the banquet, doing table assignments among other duties. She had taken a risk and acted with typical boldness when she seated herself across from the Grand Dragon. Who was Madge Oberholtzer to be at the great and powerful man's table? She still lived with her parents. She'd taught public school for a while, then found a good-paying position with a state literacy program. But that job was on the chopping block. With a single command, Steve alone could fix her problem.

He asked Madge about herself. Her home was just four blocks from his palace of the Klan of the North. She'd walked by the German shepherds and armed guards, the Packards, Caddies, and Lexington Touring Cars, sometimes seeing disheveled revelers spilling out of the house at dawn. Steve himself was a college graduate, or so he said. Hoosier born and bred, he claimed, from an old South Bend family that made its old money in the oil business. Or maybe it was coal. Or banking. He told people he was a war hero, having served in France during the slaughter of the Great War. In business, he bragged of his Midas touch. "It doesn't make any difference what I get into, it makes money for me." His Klan had even tried to buy a college, Valparaiso, envisioning a Harvard of intolerance in the northeast corner of the state.

At the peak of his power, D. C. Stephenson wanted to wipe the dirt of the Midwest from his shoes. He would say goodbye to *Indiano-place, Naptown,* as the swells in his circle called the capital city. This was the year to do it, depending on when that Senate seat opened. All that would stand between him and Klan control over much of the United States was Madge Oberholtzer. She would force a reckoning, a sensational trial of a man who'd enlisted countless Americans to take a pledge of hate. He asked her to dance. And later, he gave her his phone number: Irvington 0492.

A FEVER
IN THE
HEARTLAND

PART ONE

AN EMPIRE OF HATE

1.

Birth and Death of the Klan

When white-sheeted nightriders first appeared in the dark Southern night, many people thought they were ghosts. That was the idea: the souls of those who'd died for a republic of slaveholders had returned from their graves. They were out for vengeance, and they were invisible. They burned houses and churches, stole crops and food, dragged men from their farms and whipped them until they fell, ripped teachers from schoolhouses and branded their foreheads, raped women in front of their children, and shot their husbands at point-blank range. During rampages, they often displayed skeletal hands from beneath their robes, rattled chains, or removed fake heads—all to further the scare of a spectral and invincible force. In daylight, they vanished. The morning after a raid, a victim might come across the man who had torched his barn, the clerk at the mercantile store, and know nothing of his role in the nocturnal horror. But they were not ghosts.

The hooded horsemen were part of the unmoored mass of defeated Confederate soldiers, more than half a million men who'd surrendered on the condition that they not "take up arms against the United States." Though conquered, they were free to return home, free to farm and bank and own property, eventually free to vote and hold office. For the most part, traitors were not tried.

In early 1866, six of those rebel veterans met in Pulaski, in Middle Tennessee a few miles north of the Alabama border, to form a secret club. The market town of 2,000 people was named for a Catholic immigrant from Poland who'd fought for the Americans against the British. Before the Civil War, almost half the county was enslaved. Now they walked the streets—freedmen and freedwomen. They attended schools, held worship services, and made plans to vote. President Lincoln had established a Freedmen's Bureau to help people who'd been held in bondage become people with tools to make a living on their own. His generals had offered reparations—forty acres and a mule, carved out of land seized from more than 70,000 slaveholders. But his successor, Andrew Johnson, had overturned the order just a few months after Lincoln was assassinated. The task of peace, as Walt Whitman had prophesied, would be more difficult than the war itself.

Two of the young men gathered in Pulaski had been Confederate officers. Two were lawyers. One was a newspaper editor. One was a cotton broker. They were adrift, bored, and bitter, chafing at new life in the South after four million enslaved people had been freed, and would soon make up 36 percent of the citizen population. The Greek word *kuklos*, representing a circle, was offered as a name. *Klan* was an alliterative pairing of the first word, and an echo of the clans to which the Old World ancestors of these Scots-Irish Protestants had belonged. A costume came together: a conical top to make the wearer look much taller, a white mask with cutouts for eyes, a long robe with symbols stitched to it. Silly rituals and silly titles were invented. When the first public parade was held in Pulaski, the original six had expanded to seventy-five masked men marching in the street. The local paper printed a story a week about this mysterious new club. What was the purpose? Brotherhood. Mystery. And power. "The first meeting was purely social," wrote James R. Crowe, one of the original half-dozen. "We would frequently meet after the day's business was over in some room or office. We would have music and songs."

His framing of the founding was a not-so-sly bit of myth-crafting. Before long, the music and song had become arson and whipping. In early 1867, a Tennessee paper reported the rise of "some general and unrefined dread among Negroes of a secret order that has recently made its appearance." And that secret order had spread beyond Pulaski. At a regional convention in Nashville, a prominent Tennessean, Nathan Bedford Forrest, declared himself the first Grand Wizard. As a Confederate general, Forrest was notorious for the Fort Pillow Massacre, the execution of about 150 Black Union soldiers who had thrown down their arms and surrendered. On his orders, they were bayoneted, clubbed to death, and "shot down like dogs," one Confederate soldier wrote. Pardoned by Johnson of the war crime, Forrest had trouble making a living in an economy no longer built on human property. Beady-eyed and bewhiskered, he loathed the idea of the Black race standing on equal terms with whites. "The Negroes were holding night meetings, were going about, were being very insolent," Forrest explained in a congressional hearing. "Ladies were ravished by some of these Negroes."

When the South refused to grant basic rights to the formerly enslaved, the region was put under military control and divided into five districts. Reconstruction of a new society was mandated by Congress and enforced by federal troops. Defiant local governments were replaced by law-abiding ones. But now the Klan had a larger purpose: it turned to terror. The silly rituals and silly titles gave way to insurrection. In Tennessee, they started raiding at night, destroying property, breaking into homes, firing shots. Black people who promoted voting were lashed and burned. White teachers in Black schools were dragged from their homes and ordered to leave. One was pistol-whipped and told that "no damn Yankee bitch should live in this county." In Mississippi, the Klan drove out nearly every teacher in a Black school. At the same time, independent Klan units sprouted in California, where migrants from China were nearly 10 percent of the population. Arsonists burned a Methodist church that had housed a Sunday school for Chinese children. The Klan in San Jose issued a threat to farmers in the southern Bay Area: they would destroy all crops of people who hired a single Asian.

Throughout the South and parts of the West Coast, young Klansmen acted with impunity. Their pamphlets were bold and declarative of their purpose, as one proclaimed: "Unholy blacks, cursed by God, take warning and fly." With confidence came arrogance. By 1868, Forrest boasted of a tide of newborn rebels—40,000 Klansmen in

Tennessee, a half million throughout the South, in every province of the former Confederacy. "It's a protective, political, military organization," Forrest told a reporter. When this interview was reprinted in papers around the nation, people were shocked. The North had won the war. The South was winning the peace. And when asked about this assertion, Forrest did not deny it. "If they send the black men to hunt those Confederate soldiers whom they call Kuklux, then I say to you, 'Go out and shoot the Radicals.'"

In July 1866, a white mob backed by police stormed a Black political gathering in New Orleans, stomping men to death, shooting, stabbing, and mutilating others. More than thirty people died and 160 were seriously hurt before federal troops restored order. A similar scene bloodied the streets of Memphis that year—a three-day war that killed forty-six Black people and reduced twelve schools and four churches to ash-heaps. In Arkansas, more than 2,000 African Americans were murdered in the months leading up to the 1868 presidential election. In Lafayette County, Mississippi, thirty Black residents were driven out of their homes and forced to the water's edge, where they were drowned. In the years that followed, people who fished the Yocona River snagged human skulls and bones from the depths.

"The Freedmen are shot and Union men are persecuted if they have the temerity to express their opinion," said General Philip H. Sheridan, whose military district included Louisiana and Texas. A Tennessee authority complained to President Johnson that the Klan rode freely at night, "causing dismay & terror to all—Our civil authorities are powerless."

Johnson was frequently drunk and openly foul-mouthed, a quarrelsome Tennessee Democrat put on the ticket in 1864 by Lincoln as a unity gesture. Just days before he was murdered, Lincoln had become the first president to publicly raise the prospect of full African American citizenship. Johnson, sworn in six weeks after Lincoln began his second term, would have none of his predecessor's vision. He ignored pleas from civil authorities to go after the Klan, and he urged Southern politicians to balk at expanding the Constitution. "Everyone would and *must* admit that the white race was superior to the Black," he said. He vetoed the Civil Rights Act of 1866, a legislative attempt to extend real power to the formerly enslaved, but was overridden by a strong majority in Congress. "This is a country for white men, and by God, as long as I am president, it shall be a government for white men," he wrote that year. He then announced an amnesty proclamation for ex-Confederates, an unconditional pardon, restoring all rights except property ownership of human beings.

Violence escalated: lynching, arson, beatings, a reign of orchestrated bloodshed for the last three years of Johnson's chaotic term. The exact number of deaths has never been fully established, but one military commander, General John Reynolds, reported from Texas that murders of Black citizens were "so common as to render it impossible to keep an accurate account of them." Sheriffs would not arrest their criminal neighbors. Witnesses were intimidated or murdered. "We can inform you that we are the law itself," was the message delivered from a Klan unit to one teacher in Mississippi.

We are the law itself—the same boast would be heard in Indiana, fifty years later, taking flight through the revelations of Madge Oberholtzer.

Johnson was impeached by the House, acquitted by a single vote in the Senate, then rendered powerless. When the Union general Ulysses S. Grant was elected in 1868, he carried most of the North and a handful of Southern states where large numbers of Black men had been able to vote, thanks to the protection of federal troops. A few months into his presidency, he got a letter from a widow, Sallie Adkins, of Georgia; her spouse, a state senator, had been assassinated on the open road by a Klansman. "I am only a poor woman whose husband has been murdered for his devotion to his country," she wrote the president. Grant promised to smash the Klan. There was nothing gallant or noble about these midnight marauders. The president saw them for what they were: killers in bedsheets who were "trying to reduce the colored people to a condition closely akin to that of slavery," he said.

In Lincoln's final days, he had sought to expand the Constitution. What followed was "a massive experiment in interracial democracy," the historian Eric Foner wrote. In the first lightning strike, the 13th Amendment, slavery was formally outlawed in 1865. In the second, passed after the president was killed, a citizen was defined in the 14th Amendment as anyone born or naturalized in the United States. The 15th Amendment, ratified in 1870, prevented states from denying voting rights based on color. Grant called the last of the three additions "the most important event that has occurred since the nation came to life."

The problem for the general who had won the war was that the

Klan was not an organized army with a defined chain of command. Across the South, Klan units would not stand and fight against federal forces. They would not stand at all. They could not be chased across the land or forced to assemble in a defensive posture atop a hill. The enemy was "the most atrocious organization that the civilized part of the world has ever known," Grant's Justice Department declared. After Congress handed him the tools he needed, the president used the Ku Klux Klan Acts to hammer the hooded order. He sent federal authorities, backed by more federal troops, to prosecute what were now federal crimes. He declared martial law in places. He suspended habeas corpus. In the fall of 1869, nearly 2,000 Klansmen were arrested in South Carolina alone. By end of the next year, 3,000 were indicted across the South. A third of them were convicted and sent away with long prison terms. Acknowledging defeat, the Klan formally disbanded under an order from Forrest. He burned all records.

Frederick Douglass had seen the postwar carnage coming. As a manacled young man, he taught himself to read and write, breaking the law and risking the lash, a voracious student of classics, philosophy, and history. As an orator and essayist, he saw his words widely published; by the 1860s, he was the most prominent Black man in America. "The work does not end with the abolition of slavery," he said, not long after Lincoln was shot in the head, "but only begins." When Grant crushed the Klan in the South, Douglass wrote, "The scourging and slaughter of our people have so far ceased."

So far.

2

An Opening in Indiana

1922

T he regular Sunday evening service was just getting under way in Evansville, Indiana, when the doors to Central Methodist Episcopal Church flung open with a bang. The minister was startled. The congregation gasped. A column of white-sheeted intruders, faces veiled but for cutouts over the eyes, marched forcefully up the aisle. The Reverend A. M. Couchman had seen these Kluxers around town for the last year, heard good things about them from fellow ministers, and noticed they had stitched red crosses in a circle over the heart on their robes. Under the vault of the church, the mystery men moved closer, surrounding the white preacher and kneeling at his side. A gift was offered to him, an envelope stuffed with cash, "in the interest of the work you are doing here." Then, just as quickly as they'd swept in, the Klansmen trooped out, filed into cars whose license plates had been covered, and drove off into the mid-American twilight. The minister kept the money, and for the next Sunday and many Sundays thereafter, he spoke of the high ideals of the masked men who had invaded his spiritual sanctuary.

The church lesson of March 26, 1922—front-page news in Evansville—was not lost on D. C. Stephenson, who pored over a half-dozen papers a day looking for clues on what made modern America tick. "It was the first public appearance by the Klan," the fledgling order announced to the press, "but it won't be the last." Money changing hands in a house of God was usually viewed with skepticism. But this bribe of a soul merchant was part of a pattern: the new Klan would build its foundation with the blessing of Protestant clergy.

For Stephenson, it made perfect sense. He was a young man on the make, and a quick learner. His new life in Evansville was a dash and a dodge, just a few steps ahead of the multiple lives he'd left behind. He'd knocked around from town to town, selling linotype parts, stock in a coal company, but mostly selling himself. He could talk a dog off a meat-wagon, as they said in those parts. His smile was toothy and his cheeks dimpled, his eyes blazed, his shoes sparkled, and his clothing was impeccable. He liked heavy food, a good cigar, and many a drink. He looked prosperous, even if he wasn't. He sounded educated, an incontinent user of five-dollar words, even if the college he'd attended changed with each telling. But the truth of his background didn't matter; his swagger was convincing.

The national Klan had sent a recruiter, Joe Huffington, to Indiana in 1921. The goal was to establish a base in the North. As one of his first hires, Stephenson made $12 a week on the Empire's payroll, but that arrangement wouldn't last for long. He joined the Klan because he saw it as a ticket to the top. Small thinking was for losers. Steve wanted the Klan of the North to rise up and come out of the shadows, to show its face and bask in the daylight. The Knights of the Invisible Empire had nothing to hide and much to share.

Stephenson set up a base of operations in the velvety interior of the Vendome Hotel, his residence in Evansville, with its wood-paneled walls, arched entrance, gold-plated spittoons beside black leather chairs. The Vendome was just a few blocks one way from the dockside traffic of the Ohio River, a few steps the other way from the seat of power at the Vanderburgh County Courthouse, a Beaux-Arts masterpiece. Most of the town was white, native born, and Protestant, like Indiana itself. That was the first thing that got Steve's attention not long after he dropped off his suitcases at the Vendome. The other thing was how wide-open the old riverfront burg was for the right kind of people, the ideal setup for Mr. D. C. Stephenson. The fresh-hatched local Klan pledged to clean up all the rot in Evansville even as Steve reveled in it. For those who liked their hypocrisy cut with pleasure, the forbidden vices of a Midwest under moral lockdown were gifts he could bestow.

Sitting flat on a wide bend of the waterway that flows from Pittsburgh to the Mississippi, Evansville was the most segregated city in Indiana, and the third largest, with 85,000 people. Window signs in the business district proclaimed "We Cater to White Trade Only." The Ohio was thick with industrial sludge and the air was heavy with foul-smelling pollutants. On summer days when the sky was hot and wet, when all of Evansville seemed to sweat, Kentucky, just across the river, was barely visible through the haze.

A mob with clubs had chased a group of immigrant miners out of town in 1921. The whiff of socialism was enough to inflame the attackers. Irish laborers had helped to build the city; refugees of the Great Famine dug the ditch that would become the Wabash and Erie Canal, largest in the United States, connecting Evansville to Lake Erie, 460 miles to the north. But because of their religion, they were second-class citizens in the caste system that the Klan exploited in Evansville.

The 6,000 or so Black residents were forced into tenements and shacks in Baptisttown, a shank of the city without electricity or indoor plumbing. They were constantly harassed. Memories of a 1903 slaughter—twelve Blacks murdered and four saloons burned to the ground by a white mob—still haunted. The Carnegie Library, supposedly open to all as a springboard to the world's possibilities, was for whites only. When a white college student working at a gas station during his summer break offered to clean the windshields of Black motorists, he was scolded by the owner. Black people in southern Indiana were not to be served, nor seen in mixed company—an attitude certainly not limited to Evansville.

"The Negro is among us and the race should be encouraged to progress, but that path should never lead to social mingling," warned the *Indianapolis Star* in 1921.

Black innovators were the force behind a burst of cultural creativity, from the poetry of Langston Hughes and the Harlem Renaissance to the crossover dance craze of the Charleston to jazz, the soundtrack of the age—"the tom-tom of joy and laughter, and pain swallowed in a smile," as Hughes called it. But daily life for millions was a reminder that the American promise was not for them. This was even harder to accept for 200,000 Black soldiers who had returned from military service in France and felt entitled to be full citizens. "The great war in Europe, its recoil on America, the ferment in the United States, all conspired to break up the stereotyped conception of the Negro's place," wrote James Weldon Johnson, the literary polymath, a leader of the Harlem Renaissance. Cities erupted in violent attacks on Black property and life. And as vigilante executions by a hangman's noose continued without sanction in the South, Congress could not muster enough votes to pass an anti-lynching law.

Evansville was ripe for the Klan, the perfect place to plant the flag in the North for the second coming of the Invisible Empire. And D. C. Stephenson was the ideal missionary. He had magnetism, unbridled energy, and a talent for bundling a set of grievances against immigrants, Jews, Roman Catholics, and Blacks into a simple unified pitch that made sense of a fast-changing America still dazed by the Great War. Not long after Stephenson joined the hooded order in early 1921, he would eclipse the man who hired him.

"All my friends, a crowd of fine young men, belonged," he recalled, portraying himself as an innocent tugged along by social pressure. "They kept after me, and explained to me that the Klan was not an organization which took Negroes out, cut off their noses and threw them into the fire."

———

Alex Johnson was a bellhop and elevator operator at the Adolphus Hotel in Dallas. It was a swanky place with an elite clientele. He was quick with a compliment. Too quick for some concerned citizens, who spread word that the young Black man was in love with a white woman. On the first day of April in 1921, about the same time that Stephenson swore his oath to the Klan and got his robe and hood, Johnson was kidnapped from his home, gagged, bound, blindfolded, and dragged to the Trinity River bottoms. A noose was tied around his neck. He was whipped, twenty-five lashes. The letters KKK were branded onto his forehead with acid. Half naked, bloodied, and semiconscious, he was dumped at the doorstep of the Adolphus.

The attack on the bellhop was led by a Klan leader from Dallas, Hiram W. Evans, a blank-faced dentist with dark eyes that looked like those of a snowman's ovals of coal. A native of Alabama, Evans studied at Vanderbilt, then set up a practice in Texas, married, and had three children. But the settled life of a family man pulling teeth for profit was not enough for him. Evans smoldered with rage at the changing face of the United States. To Evans, Nordic whites were the only true Americans and the most advanced humans on earth. All others—"Dagoes, Hunkies, Micks, Slavs, Slopes, Kikes," in his vernacular shorthand—were filth and scum. The Nordic race, by which he meant British of Anglo-Saxon blood, Teutonic Germans, and descendants of Vikings from the north, was responsible for civilization. He hated immigrants. He hated Catholics. He hated the sexual freedom of the Jazz Age, in film and in smoky clubs. Above all, he hated race-mixing; physical love, in particular, was abhorrent to him. He urged every state in the nation to "make sex between a white and a black person a crime" punishable by lengthy prison sentences.

Under Evans, the Dallas Klan took off, quickly becoming a national force. These hooded Texans practiced violence and politics in equal measure. A Black doctor who'd been seen with a white woman was castrated. A Jewish tailor was beaten and told to leave town. One month after the attack on the bellhop, the Klan held a large parade in downtown Dallas, marching with banners that read "Pure Womanhood, Our Little Girls Must Be Protected" and "One Hundred Percent American." But the biggest breakthrough was the election of the first open Klansman as a United States senator, Earl B. Mayfield, in the fall of 1922. With considerable help from Evans, he swept the state.

And the abduction and near killing of Alex Johnson? "As I understand the case, the Negro was guilty of doing something which he had no right to do," said Sheriff Dan Harston. "There will be no investigation by my department. He no doubt deserved it." Harston was not only the top lawman of Dallas County, he was a Klansman in good standing. A local judge weighed in as well. "If enough people hear of this it may do some good," said Judge T. A. York. That was the Klan's intent—to publicize its own violent crimes. Evans had even invited a reporter from the *Dallas Times-Herald* to witness a felony in action. The headline of his story was: BELLHOP ACCUSED OF INSULT TO WOMAN.

Evans could oversee an atrocity of that magnitude, boast about it in the papers, and never go to jail, because the Klan of the early 1920s felt invincible—an extraordinary change of fortune from a half century earlier.

The presidential election of 1876 brought the end of Grant's control over renegade elements of the South. The Democrat, Samuel J. Tilden, won the popular vote but fell short in the Electoral College because three states were in dispute. The courts handed the mess off to Congress, which appointed a commission to decide the outcome. As a bargaining chip to get him over the line, Republican Rutherford B. Hayes promised to withdraw federal troops from obstructionist Southern states. In return, he won the highest office in the land by a single electoral vote. His presidency marked the close of Reconstruction and ushered in nearly ninety years of disenfranchisement and segregation for millions of American citizens. Shortly thereafter, Tennessee passed the nation's first Jim Crow law, separating passengers on rail cars by skin color. Starting with Mississippi, ten of the eleven states of the former Confederacy rewrote their constitutions. They made no secret of their intention.

"The new Constitution eliminates the ignorant Negro vote and places the control of our government where God Almighty intended it should be—with the Anglo-Saxon race," said the president of Alabama's constitutional convention. Among the tools of suppression were tests that asked such questions as how many windows were in the White House.

With the abolition of slavery, Black people were no longer

counted as three-fifths but as a full person in the census. Ultimately, that gave twenty-five additional congressional seats to a one-party South that violently suppressed the vote of those newly recognized people. In 1880, 50 percent of Black men in the former Confederacy voted. By 1920, less than 1 percent exercised this fundamental right. Restaurants and grocery stores, drinking fountains and swimming pools, theaters and bars, buses and trains, playgrounds and schoolhouses, even phone booths—all were segregated by race. The Supreme Court backed the electoral disenfranchisement and the lower-class citizenship of millions, finding novel ways around the civil rights amendments to the Constitution. And the federal government walked away, with the tacit approval of the North, allowing two Americas to form.

The Klan was gone but never forgotten, lost but alive in spirit, its mythology braided thick with new narrative threads. Stories were handed down and told over brandies in parlor rooms, stories of honorable men who rose up to restore their rightful place in society. The most skillful promoter of those stories was a playwright and Baptist minister, Thomas Dixon Jr., born in 1864 in North Carolina. In college, he was a classmate of fellow Southerner and future president Woodrow Wilson at Johns Hopkins University. One night, Dixon went to see a stage version of *Uncle Tom's Cabin*. To him, it was a libel on the South, one that he would correct. In 1905, he published *The Clansman: A Historical Romance of the Ku Klux Klan*. The book was a sensation. His Black caricatures were lecherous, slovenly, and criminal. His whites were knights in bedsheets.

The filmmaker D. W. Griffith, son of a Confederate colonel, was obsessed with the novel and decided to adapt it for the screen. In Hollywood, he'd been experimenting with different techniques— longer tracking shots, close-ups and fadeouts, multiple storylines. The filmmaker hired 18,000 extras and used 25,000 yards of white muslin cloth to outfit his cast of Klansmen. His nearly three-hour version of Dixon's book premiered in Los Angeles on February 8, 1915. Later that same year, the twelve-reel epic lit up the East Room of Woodrow Wilson's White House. Wilson had overseen the segregation of the federal workforce in Washington, establishing separate toilets and lunchrooms, with partitions to keep Blacks and whites apart in the governing agencies. Dixon told the president that the film was more powerful than any book or speech—it was "the mightiest engine for molding public opinion in the history of the world." He said the real purpose was not entertainment, but "to revolutionize Northern sentiment."

That it did. Renamed *The Birth of a Nation*, the film played to packed houses, north and south; twenty-five million Americans— one in four—saw it in the first two years of release, the most ever for any picture without sound. The basic storyline was about a young white woman harassed to death by a conniving former slave (played by a white actor in blackface), only to have her honor restored by chivalrous men who lynched the predator. But the larger narrative was an epic fictional rewrite of the first years after the Civil War. The film portrayed Reconstruction-era African Americans as subhuman savages. Black legislators were shown barefoot at their desks, tossing chicken bones into aisles and swigging bottles of liquor. At election time, ballots were stuffed and whites denied the vote. And no alabaster-skinned young lady was safe from over-sexed and liquored-up Black men. The Klan saved the day, riding to the rescue on steeds draped in white. To these fabrications was added one more: the ritual of the cross burning, something the original Klan never did.

Dixon's prediction to Woodrow Wilson was not far off the mark: the film was the most effective and long-lasting source of racial propaganda in American history. And in Wilson, the first Southerner elected to the presidency since 1848, he had his most powerful fan. As a boy of eight, Wilson had seen Jefferson Davis paraded through the streets of Virginia in chains at the close of the Civil War. As a college president at Princeton, he projected intelligence and idealism—traits that carried over into a White House reign that would win him the Nobel Peace Prize. He envisioned a world without war, with a League of Nations to end disputes peacefully. But his was a loathsome soul about race, like much of the country he nudged into the global American Century. Wilson never saw the Black citizens he governed as anything less than inferior. Words from a five-volume history authored by Wilson were used as a title card in Griffith's film, lending presidential authority to this rewrite of a nation. It was music to Lost Cause ears:

"The white men were roused by a mere instinct of self-preservation . . . until at last there had sprung into existence a great Ku Klux Klan, a veritable empire of the South, to protect the Southern country."

Among those who sat through *The Birth of a Nation* over and over was an itinerant Methodist minister and dough-faced alcoholic,

William J. Simmons. Alabama-born, he'd been peddling fire-and-brimstone Christianity in the rural South for more than a decade, never anchored to any one place. In addition to liquor, he had a weakness for pornography and prostitutes. He'd joined the Masons, the Knights Templar, and the Woodmen of the World, and gave himself an honorific—*colonel*, which he insisted everyone use. The film made him weep, made his heart race, and helped to shape the biggest idea of his troubled life: the reborn Ku Klux Klan. His father had been a Klansman in Alabama during Reconstruction. He grew up on tales of how the original terror group "used to frighten the darkies," as he said in a history of the founding. One day Simmons had a religious vision of a uniquely American hate society guided by God.

On Thanksgiving night in 1915, fifty years after the close of the Civil War, Simmons and fifteen other men clambered up the granite monolith of Stone Mountain in Georgia. They built an altar on which they laid a Bible, an American flag, and a sword. The men set fire to a cross and shouted to the heavens an oath of allegiance to the Invisible Empire of a new age. The Ku Klux Klan had risen, Simmons proclaimed, "awakened from a slumber of a half a century."

Simmons modeled his newly chartered Klan after the fraternal orders he knew so well, with codes, secret phrases, hand signs, titles, rituals, oaths, and a constitution. The Klan even had its own calendar and language. The guiding principle was the superiority of white, Protestant, native-born Americans over everyone else. On the point of tribal identity, there was no wavering. "We seek to create, as never before, one grand, glorious America," Simmons wrote in a booklet. "A White Man's nation."

With his other life ventures, Simmons had been a failure. And his Klan, too, despite a burst of initial success, looked to be floundering within a few years. What saved it were two masters of promotion, Edward Y. Clarke and Mary Elizabeth "Bessie" Tyler. Clarke was a cigar-chomping former press agent, quick with a story angle and a scheme a minute. Tyler was the organizer, while also projecting motherhood and piety. Their business partnership had served them well in backing eugenic crusades, harvest festivals, state bans on alcohol, and assorted morality campaigns. They certainly shared with Simmons a hatred of the one in three Americans who were Black, Jewish, or Roman Catholic.

This was a new and expanded roster of enemies for the new and expanding Klan. The original hooded order directed most of its venom against Black people. With Jews and immigrants of an old faith based in Rome pouring into the country, the revived Klan would open up fresh categories of undesirables. Hate was tailored to the region—Asians on the Pacific coast, Mexicans in the Southwest, Mormons in the Rocky Mountains, Blacks in the South, Jews on the East Coast, and immigrants and Catholics everywhere. To this list was added sex—that is, all the new cultural expressions of sensuality.

The Klan operatives didn't need to create resentments—their recruitment pitch fit the times. Bigotry was rarely punished or condemned, even in polite circles in the North. In New York City, wealthy Black residents who owned fine apartments had to take the service elevators in many buildings. At Harvard, Black students were excluded from freshman dormitories. "From the beginning, we have thought it expedient to compel men of different races to reside apart," explained the school's longtime president, A. Lawrence Lowell, in defense of the Ivy League racial barrier.

Tyler said Jews were not even Americans, and Roman Catholics were traitors. Clarke called for sterilizing all Black citizens. But what really drove the pair of promoters into the arms of the twentieth-century Klan founder was money. In 1920, Clarke and Tyler cut a deal with Simmons, granting them a significant share of every new membership. The best way to make their fortune, they realized, was to incentivize local recruiters on the ground by giving them a cut as well. They sold the Klan as a Main Street guardian against immorality, immigrants and their foreign faiths, and African Americans who were rebelling against Jim Crow. In barely a year's time, the number of Klansmen went from 3,000 to 100,000. Texas in particular was such a bright spot that the Dallas dentist, Evans, was brought to Atlanta to join the national leadership and oversee expansion in the North. With all the new money flowing in, Simmons moved into a white-columned mansion on Peachtree Road—Klan Krest, he called it.

At his table inside the Vendome Hotel, D. C. Stephenson plotted a future with Joe Huffington, the Empire's Indiana emissary. The traveling Klansman was concerned about news of the violence in Texas and elsewhere, which had given the resurgent hooded order a run of bad press. The way to win over the Heartland was with a wholesome Klan, a Klan of family and faith and Midwestern values. It would not be the Klan of the whip and the sword, but the Klan of the hearth and the Lord. "It's a clean organization," said Huffington, "standing for the uplift and protection of untainted Americanism."

Steve didn't disagree with the sentiment, though the cynic in him knew better. In his experience, you didn't have to lead a man to hate, just show him the way and he'd do it on his own. But he had much bigger ideas and was already reaching out to Evans in Atlanta. He'd impressed national leadership with his cunning, his guile, and the size of his grandiosity. The United States was full of secretive clubs: Masons, Woodmen, Red Men, Elks, and Odd Fellows, with nearly 40 percent of adult males belonging to a fraternal order. Stephenson and Evans shared a vision: If the new Klan was going to stand out, it needed to be a *player*, and not just when the sun went down. Who cared what a bunch of costumed men did in a basement on Friday night? What about politics? Writing laws and enforcing the rules? Congress? The statehouse? *Real power!*

In the spring of 1922, Stephenson was also running for Congress, scratching the itch of his oversized ambition. But his campaign was going nowhere. For one thing, he was a heavy drinker in a state that embraced Prohibition as the 11th Commandment from God. The most influential political organization in the nation was the Anti-Saloon League, militantly dry and evangelically Christian— riding high at the peak of fundamentalist fury against the ills of alcohol. Without the support of the ASL, he was doomed. For another, he was an outsider. *Who was this guy?* He didn't sound local, didn't speak in Hoosier Twang, the northernmost extension of the South Midland dialect, despite a disciplined effort to talk as if he were from the dead center of the USA. He'd just washed up in Evansville two years earlier, a mystery man with a wife in tow—though Violet Stephenson hadn't been seen with him of late.

What happened at the Methodist church was a turning point. Why run for a seat in Congress, which paid $7,500 a year, when there was a fortune to be made in a movement? In the same week that Klansmen handed the pastor a fistful of money, the papers announced that Stephenson was withdrawing his candidacy for office. He changed political parties, from Democrat to Republican, and pronounced himself an ardent foe of alcohol. If he could repeat the scene from Central Methodist, there'd be no stopping the hooded order. All it took was a small bribe and a bit of Bible talk. The constituency was vast. Evansville alone had seventy-two Protestant churches. In short order, he paid off a dozen or so ministers to evangelize on behalf of the Klan, spreading the word of hate along with the word of God. Those sermons were then widely reported in the Klan's new Indiana weekly, the *Fiery Cross*. In Bloomington one Sunday morning, Reverend Vic Blair introduced Klan concepts to three hundred people in church while waving a copy of its constitution.

"The Klan is not against the Negro, but against social equality," he said from the pulpit. "Not against Jews, but against only the Jews who are trying to gain control of the world; not against the Catholics, but opposed to their systems. It is time for the scum to be thrown from the melting pot. And the Invisible Empire will do the skimming!"

Stephenson presented a plan to leadership: he would conquer all of Indiana for the Ku Klux Klan, not just a bridgehead in Evansville. He'd do it through Protestant churches. He would infiltrate other fraternal organizations, natural joiners. Ministers and Masons— that was the way forward. In the America of 1922, fear of *others* generated a lot of anxious energy. This collective unease had only to be corralled, sanctified, and monetized. For every $10 from a new member, Steve wanted $4. He'd already done the math. He also wanted a big piece of the official uniform required of every Klansman, hood and robes made especially for members, sold only through the Klan for $6. As for using Christianity to inoculate this secret society from the charge of bigotry—it was brilliant! Simmons, the failed minister, had long felt the same way. Surely, an army of righteous preachers could never be impugned as night-riding criminals. When the Imperial Wizard signed the formal charter for Evansville in May 1922—"Klan #1 in the Realm of Indiana"—Simmons's signature was on the top, and that of D. C. Stephenson on the bottom. The new state entity, with Steve now leading the fastest-growing chapter in the North, was formally authorized to go forth and spread "the principles of pure Patriotism, Honor, Klanishness and White Supremacy."

At home, Stephenson had no use for his wife of two years. Marriage was a straitjacket. He told the boys at the Vendome he was unfit for monogamy. *Wasn't it true of all great men?* Violet had tried to make the union work, though her husband was constantly cheating on her and made no secret of it. He said he could get any woman he wanted with the snap of his fingers. Typically, he came home around two a.m., drunk. Or he didn't come home at all. She had no life of her own in Evansville, no family. And what life she had was subject to a side of her husband very few people ever saw. He saved his worst for her. Violet and Steve would split up after a fight. She'd go back to her mother's house in Akron, Ohio, and try to rebuild her world. Then Steve would write a long, loving letter or send an unusually large bouquet of flowers, and she'd return to him, against her better instincts. He was persuasive.

Now, upstairs in his residence at the Vendome, Steve was in a foul mood, and cursed her. The room was hot and stifling, and it shrunk whenever the two of them were together inside. He hit Violet in the face with his fist and she crashed to the ground and nearly passed out. Her fall seemed to encourage his rage. He seized her, tore off her dress, clawed at her body and her cheeks with his fingernails. He kicked her in the rib cage. He grabbed her by the head and pulled out a tuft of her hair. He called her a bitch and a whore and he slapped her and scratched her face until blood flowed onto the floor of the suite at the Vendome. Crawling on the ground, trying to protect herself, Violet was terrified. She knew then that the man she had married could kill her.

3

Men with Badges

Of all the crimes troubling Indiana in the third decade of the twentieth century, stealing a horse was well down the list. Hoosiers had abandoned their steeds and went head over heels for their machines, as they called automobiles. They loved racing them, producing them, tinkering with them, showing them off. They loved honking their horns, polishing their grilles, and letting their kids jump on the running boards. At a time when America made 85 percent of the world's cars, Studebakers rolled out of South Bend, trucks rumbled off the Graham Brothers factory line in Evansville, and assorted small manufacturers purred around the clock in Indianapolis. Anybody with a regular salary could afford a Model T Ford for under $300. In the twenties, the number of autos on the road in the United States more than tripled—from seven million to twenty-three million.

Who would steal a horse? In Indiana, there were four recorded thefts in 1922. But the organization designed to chase down such criminals was still around. Starting in the 1860s, Indiana had allowed people to form vigilante groups, lawfully deputized, for the express purpose of arresting horse thieves. As four-legged transports disappeared, the group declined for lack of purpose. In their collapse, D. C. Stephenson saw an opportunity.

He was the featured speaker in October 1922 at the Horse Thief Detective Association's sixty-second annual convention in the northern Indiana town of Logansport. While seeding Klan dens around the state, Steve had bumped into his share of these middle-aged men playing cops. In his Logansport speech, he played to their fears, their pride, and their boredom. Was there a man among them who wasn't disgusted by the immigrants brewing beer or fermenting wine in their basements? Was there a father or husband who wasn't appalled at women in their short bobs and tapered dresses drinking bootleg gin and dancing to Black jazz—these morality-flaunting, uncorseted flappers? Was there a family protector not alarmed by the sexual promiscuity of the young in their parked machines? Or the filth on their movie screens, films like *Flaming Youth*, whose posters promoted the drama of "youth with its jazz, its flapperism, its petting parties, its reticent disregard for convention"? These pink-faced men seated before Stephenson today could do something about national decline. They could join the Ku Klux Klan, their natural brothers in spirit, faith, and Americanism. *Hear, hear!* Thereafter, the Klan and the private militias would make common cause.

The Klan that spread to the North was steeped in homegrown

Christianity practiced by everyday folks. But instead of love your neighbor, these Klansmen hated many a neighbor. At its core, the new Invisible Empire was a religious organization with alliterative nonsense borrowed from fraternal groups, all the Klaverns, Kleagles, and Klonvocations, the Grand Goblins, Exalted Cyclops, and Imperial Klokards, the robes, rings, and rituals, the secret language and exchanges, the greetings with three fingers signifying KKK. Klansmen held study classes not unlike Sunday school, using a manual as a required textbook. From that guidebook, goals of "preserving the blood purity" of the white race, and "shielding the sanctity of the home and the chastity of womanhood," were drilled into new initiates, along with rituals designed to seal men to each other. And those men had to follow orders. Klansmen were bound by their oath of allegiance to obey all "decisions, decrees, edicts, mandates, rulings and instructions."

The modern Klan rejected modernism—the world was spinning too fast, and they didn't like it one bit. When President Warren Harding, a man of refined mediocrity, was elected in 1920, he'd promised a "return to normalcy." But the twenties were anything but normal, especially among young adults. "Here was a new generation grown up to find all Gods dead, all wars fought, all faiths in man shaken," wrote F. Scott Fitzgerald. The buildings were taller, the stocks higher, the cars faster, the parties gaudier and more excessive. People threw off the cultural remnants of the nineteenth century with abandon, even as others were relentlessly holding back the twentieth century.

Klan members had their own idea of *normalcy* and how to enforce it. And that's where the vigilantes could help out. So the horse thief brigades kept their name, their badges, guns, and power, but changed their mission. They became the Klan's morality police, the might to make right. Their targets were adulterers and young lovers, bootleggers and speakeasies, truants, vagrants, and petty thieves.

Suddenly, members of the Horse Thief Detective Association were breaking up parties and smashing liquor joints. They blocked roads, searching vehicles for bottles, rousting those in passionate embrace. They invaded private homes, looking for alcohol or card-playing. They harassed businesses that opened on Sunday. They served as armed marshals at Klan parades, taking over public streets, directing traffic, menacing the occasional malcontent who booed at the men in white robes. They posted gun-toting sentries outside polling places on Election Day, checking voters as they stepped into schoolhouses and church basements.

"They entered homes without search warrants and flogged errant husbands and wives," wrote William E. Wilson, a white Evansville native, home from college one summer to find a changed Indiana. "They caught couples in parked cars and tried to blackmail the girls. On occasion, they branded the three K's on bodies of people who were particularly offensive to them."

Elsewhere, the Klan encouraged vigilantes on similar morality patrols that took things even further. In Kern County, California, a vast squat of irrigated farmland that had been heavily settled by people from the South, Klansmen kidnapped Dwight Mason, a white doctor, and dragged him to a baseball field for torture. In front of a hooting, clapping crowd of thirty people, Mason was hanged until he lost consciousness, whipped, tarred, and branded. He was targeted because he had filed for divorce. The Klan wanted to make an example of anyone who threatened "the sanctity of the home," as it was put in a statement. He was also said to be performing abortions on the side.

The second-wave Klan could return to its roots of terror because it had survived the kind of scrutiny that would have killed off any other secret society in a democracy. A three-week exposé by the *New York World* in the fall of 1921 had detailed murder, flogging, iron-branding, arson—at least one hundred acts of vigilante violence nationwide. The revelations, many people thought, would horrify most Americans. The series was widely syndicated and prompted a congressional investigation. With cameras clicking and a mass of reporters in attendance, Imperial Wizard Simmons told another story in Washington. "Allow me to introduce myself: I am a churchman."

There was nothing wrong with promoting white supremacy—it was only "race pride," he said. "I cannot see anything anti-American in that." He dismissed the numerous stories of violence as the work of "a paper owned and controlled by a Jew," and imposters trying to take down the Invisible Empire. "Our masks and robe are not worn for the purpose of terrorizing people. I say before God, they are as innocent as the breath of an angel."

At the close of three days of testimony, following a long and impassioned soliloquy, Simmons stood and pointed his finger at his congressional interrogators—they were the ones who should be shamed for going after the family men of his organization. "I call upon the Father to forgive those who have persecuted the Klan!" he shouted. And with that, he fainted and fell to the ground. The politicians folded. Simmons believed the hearing was the best thing that ever happened to the hooded order. "It wasn't until the newspapers began to attack the Klan that it really grew," he said. "And then Congress gave us the best advertising we ever got." Over the next year, the Klan expanded by 1.1 million members.

No longer fearing federal oversight, the Invisible Empire planted new chapters throughout the Midwest, and up and down the West Coast. In Colorado, it was led by a physician, Dr. John Galen Locke, who operated out of the luxurious Brown Palace Hotel in Denver. Like Stephenson and Evans, Locke wanted to package the resentments of the age into a political force. And he recruited heavily among the Denver police. It was an open door.

In Indiana, the local cops were grateful to have a rogue arm of law enforcement to harass offenders of virtue. "They form an unofficial constabulary helping the police," one newspaper wrote approvingly. The numbers of men with tin stars grew in stride with the Klan, from 8,000 deputies to 14,000 in little more than a year. While only those four horses were stolen in all of 1922, the Horse Thief Detective Association added twenty-eight chapters statewide. At the same time, they helped Stephenson swell the ranks of Indiana Klansmen, signing up fellow members of the local horse thief brigade, while distributing stickers for shopkeepers to put in their windows—"TWK, Trade With Klan." With all these new allies, Steve was on a roll, bringing in upward of 2,000 new Klansmen every week.

Potential initiates were usually contacted anonymously. They would receive a note:

"You are being weighed in the balance! The call is coming! Are you able and qualified to respond? Discuss this matter with no one."

A few days later would come another mystery letter, more intriguing:

"You may have heard from us because we believe in you. Are you a real man? Lift your eyes up to the Fiery Cross and falter no more!"

As they moved closer into the Klan circle, recruits had to answer twenty questions from a membership checklist before becoming *naturalized,* including:

"Are you a Gentile or a Jew?

"Are you of the White race or Colored Race?

"What color are your eyes? Hair?

"Do you believe in the principles of pure Americanism?

"Do you believe in White Supremacy?"

Finally, after being properly vetted, a new member donned a pointed hood with a tassel on top, and a white robe, and put his hand on a Bible. For many, it was a thrilling moment, a break from the tedium of daily life.

"I swear that I will most zealously and valiantly shield and preserve by any and all justifiable means and methods White Supremacy. I will seal with my blood by Thou my witness, Almighty God."

Stephenson organized recruiters in all parts of the state and trained them to appeal to three things:

Love of mystery and ritual.

Pride of race and religion.

Hatred.

But first, a sweetener. He suggested that new Klan chapters do something "for the betterment of the community," and make sure the local papers covered it. The winning combination was fabulously lucrative. In advance of a visit to new territory, Stephenson would usually place a print ad or have a pastor promote his appearance from the pulpit. As he entered a church, a town hall, or a school gym to make his Klan sales pitch, he saw every Hoosier head as a dollar sign. "We used to look over the crowd when we first came in and try to estimate what it would net us," recalled his right-hand man, Court Asher. "We'd hire a minister at $25 a lecture and then get their whole congregation to join at $10 a head." The new Klan was not for poor people. That $10 initiation fee was more than the average factory worker made in a day. Plus, there were quarterly dues and uniform requirements. Stephenson got his cut of everything. In a given week, he was taking in five times more than most Americans made in a year. He was well on his way to becoming a millionaire.

The rebranded Klan was an easy sell in the South, playing to Lost Cause sympathies of aging slaveholders who passed on their prejudices to their twentieth-century grandchildren. The North was supposed to be another story. But Stephenson was now proving the skeptics wrong. His instincts told him that racial hatred did not stop at a geographic line in this country, and the top cultural draw of the day was proving him right. *The Birth of a Nation* had done well in the North, just as D. W. Griffith envisioned it would. There were exceptions. People threw eggs at the screen in Boston, and nearly rioted in New York. James Weldon Johnson, the prolific poet and essayist, now leader of the young National Association for the Advancement of Colored People, carried on a campaign against it. Every showing reinforced a monstrous stereotype, he said, causing "incalculable harm" to fellow African Americans. It was "propaganda of the worst and most insidious sort." He was particularly appalled at revived 1920s showings in Washington, DC, for which theaters in the capital were bedecked with flags of the treasonous Confederacy.

In towns across Indiana, masked men rented out theaters for exclusive showings to little or no protest. At the end of the movie, the words of a title card filled the screen:

> The former enemies of North and South are united
> again in common defence of their Aryan birthright.

Though 195,000 Hoosiers had served in the Union Army during the Civil War, the governor had complained to Abraham Lincoln that "no other free state is so populated with Southerners." In attitude and politics, Indiana was the most Southern of Northern states—North Dixie, it was often called—settled by people from Tennessee, Kentucky, and the Carolinas. In its early constitution, Article XIII specifically prohibited free Blacks or "mulattos" from residing in the state. Near the close of the nineteenth century, Indiana's treatment of African Americans was "as inhuman as ever characterized the cotton fields of Georgia or the rice swamps of the Carolinas," said James M. Townsend, who served one term in the statehouse in the 1880s.

There were still men walking the streets of 1922 Indiana who had fought against the slaveholders, and who believed that liberating humans held as property had been the highest calling of their lives. Among them was William H. Stern, a white man raised on a farm north of Indianapolis. When he was nineteen years old, Billy Stern answered Lincoln's call to join an army to crush the South, enlisting in the 39th Indiana Regiment. At the Battle of Stones River, in Middle Tennessee near Murfreesboro, Stern fought in the thick of slaughter that would take more than 20,000 casualties—wounded and killed on both sides—in the first days of 1863. He used his bayonet to stab the enemy, and when the long rifle was knocked from his hands, he wielded his bloodied fists. Stern was captured by the Confederates and dragged off to a freezing POW camp. He later escaped. Now in his eighties, Stern spent his days reminding people what he had been willing to die for. He revered Lincoln. He would never be united with his former enemies in defense of an Aryan birthright.

"The black man that sympathized, worked and fought for this great country of ours during its threatened destruction is a thousand times better than the white man that sympathized, worked, plotted and fought against it," he told fellow Hoosiers in an open letter. But though Stern was a beloved and commanding figure in his small-town community of Hamilton County—his back upright, the huge white brush of his mustache covering his entire lip, his voice a deep baritone—his message was disregarded by thousands of people drawn to the shiny new organization being sold from town to town by D. C. Stephenson. To the astonishment of its leaders in Atlanta, the Klan birthed in Indiana—a state that had lost 25,000 men fighting the Confederacy just a half century earlier—would soon have more Klansmen than any other state.

One of the new horse thief detectives was Steve himself. He was issued a metal badge, on which was imprinted: CONSTABLE, H.T.D. ASS'N. The deputized had powers that local sheriffs did not: they could cross county lines and didn't feel a need to go to court before conducting a home raid. Steve's armed enforcers, his private police force, complemented his spiritual enablers. He called it his military machine—or just the Machine.

Now he instructed his agents to compile dossiers on local public servants, dissenters, and troublemakers. He also ordered them to create a file on every person of voting age, with particular emphasis on those who might be enemies of the Klan. Along with "Bootleggers and Bolsheviks," the edict singled out "All Jews, All Negroes, All Roman Catholics." Across the state, men with badges and no uniforms took to the field as the eyes and ears of a very ambitious Klansman.

By year's end, Stephenson had accomplished something that the initial Klan had not: his vigilantes were part of the system. They operated freely and openly, and their crimes were not punished, just as in Texas. And this time around, there were no federal authorities to interfere. All of it was exhilarating to the men in sheets, as a sociologist found out after reviewing questionnaires answered by individual Klansmen. "Membership in a vast mysterious empire that 'sees and hears all' means a sort of mystic glorification of his petty self," wrote John Moffatt Mecklin. "The appeal is irresistible."

4.

A Coup and a Clash

The talented D. C. Stephenson had proved to be quite the prodigy, as he said so himself. He had the touch and the charm, the dexterity with words and the drive. He understood people's fears and their need to blame others for their failures. He discovered that if he said something often enough, no matter how untrue, people would believe it. Small lies were for the timid. The key to telling a big lie was to do it with conviction. He had once listed himself as a "lawyer" when he joined a Masonic order, though he'd never passed a bar exam. Now he began to describe himself as the world's "foremost mass psychologist." He became a fan of Benito Mussolini, reading up on his speeches and the parallels to his own rise. Even though he regularly disparaged "dagoes," he considered Mussolini somewhat of a mentor. Il Duce was named prime minister of Italy in 1922, the same year Stephenson became a rising national star in the Klan and set his own sights on the highest office in the land. "Mussolini's methods were, to his mind, the model for men of action like himself," one writer observed in a profile of the Klansman from the Heartland.

The national press had started to take note. The leaders in Atlanta were impressed as well. Barely six months after the Indiana charter was signed, Stephenson had far exceeded expectations. Now he promised to work the same magic in Michigan, Kansas, Wisconsin, Pennsylvania, Ohio. His tactics would travel: At rallies, he hired oompah bands and doled out fresh lemonade. His barbershop quartets sang, "If you don't like your Uncle Sammy / Then go back to your home across the sea / To the land from where you came / Whatever be its name."

The mood was festive and forward-looking. All the right people were joining. At Christmastime, Klansmen played Santa Claus and made a show of delivering food to the poor. By the time Steve left Evansville for good at the end of 1922, nearly one in four residents had taken an oath to a cryptic organization dedicated to the dehumanization of fellow citizens. A majority would soon elect a Klansman as their mayor.

The other dynamo behind the far-reaching Klan map was Hiram Evans. In the Dallas he left behind, about 30 percent of white males were Klansmen. The Texas tooth doctor had become more expansive in spreading his narrow views, granting a wide range of interviews. People of different races, he explained, were like different species of animals. One must never breed with the other. His problem with Jews was "racial rather than religious," he said, and thus there should be no mixing of their blood with the white majority. His speeches drew large crowds and his statements were widely distributed in Klan dens and mainstream newspapers. "America must close the door to the diseased minds and bodies and souls of the peoples of foreign lands," he said about immigration. He identified these undesirables as "Italian anarchists, Irish Catholic malcontents, Russian Jews, Finns, Lithuanians and Austrians of the lowest class." Many a United States senator said the same thing.

In Texas, Evans had worked the two avenues of violence and politics. At least fifty people were taken down to the Trinity River bottoms in Dallas for whippings and acid-brandings. Should they call the police, they would be reporting something already known, and even encouraged, within the Blue Wall. For a majority of Dallas officers were now oath-bound members of the hooded order—proof of Malcolm X's later observation that the Klan had "changed its bed sheets for a policeman's uniform."

The flesh burnings and beatings always happened at night. By day, the Klan gave out money to charities and churches, and even built an orphanage—Hope Cottage. The Klan swept the 1922 local elections and put a majority of supporters in the Texas statehouse. The rise of that first Klan United States senator from Texas was heralded in chapters around the nation as a harbinger of American political dominance.

Stephenson was mastermind of a similar play, organizing his forces against Albert J. Beveridge, a former United States senator who had been a Teddy Roosevelt progressive and was looking to reclaim his old seat. Steve's man, the Klan-sympathetic Samuel Ralston, narrowly won—a shock to the political establishment.

Throughout Indiana that year, the Klan had held picnics and packed churches, staged firework shows, parades, rallies. But putting people in office? That was something new.

"What the hell happened yesterday?" a newsman asked the Indiana Republican chairman the day after the election.

"It was the damn Ku Klux Klan," he answered.

In advance of the 1922 fall election, Stephenson had sent a questionnaire to officeholders, asking about their faith and any organizations they belonged to. But he sent his demands only to Catholics and one prominent Jew—a religious test. All were thrown from office after Steve spread the word of their otherness.

"Citizens whose family name contained a Mac or whose first name was Isidore had a hard going at the polls after that," recalled a political reporter at the time, Harold C. Feightner.

With violence, Stephenson was more selective and secretive. He sent a man up to Muncie to muzzle a prickly newspaper editor, George Dale, whose *Post-Democrat* was not showing the usual passivity of the local press to Klan recruiters. Dale was Presbyterian, son of a Civil War veteran, a father of seven. He slouched and sniffed his way around town with a pencil and a notepad, a bent-over and ashen-faced little man in his late fifties with a soggy cigar in his mouth. But he roared in print, even if prone to exaggerations and misspellings. The weekly paper was his life. His weapons were satire and wit. When a local Klan den proclaimed that Jesus was a white Protestant, Dale pointed out that Jesus would have been banned from the Klan—as a Jew and an olive-skinned alien. He mocked the horse thief detectives as "a band of lawless night prowlers." He called a local Klan judge, Clarence W. Dearth, "the most contemptible chunk of human carrion that ever disgraced the circuit bench in the state of Indiana." And he ridiculed any Hoosier of self-professed principle who would hide under a hood. "Isn't it grand to be 100 percent American and wear your wife's nightie and your mother's goose cap around the county at night," he wrote in his front-page column.

On a chilly spring evening in 1922, Dale was out walking along Mulberry Street in Muncie with one of his sons. His paper was working on a story about the Klan's reach into the judiciary, part of Stephenson's plan to get political control throughout the state. A car pulled up and three black-masked men jumped Dale, beating him to the ground just a few blocks from the courthouse. A gun was shoved in his stomach. His son was pistol-whipped. The attack was led by the man Stephenson had sent to town to organize the Klan.

"That man in Muncie must be knocked off," Steve had told the junior Klansman. "It's up to you to see that the job is done right. Send him to the hospital." The editor was badly hurt, ribs broken, face bloodied. But he was unbowed.

"Strange things are happening in Muncie these days," Dale wrote after a young Black man was kidnapped and flogged, but the police refused to look into it. "Hundreds of citizens here, many of them men of high character, are joining the Ku Klux Klan." He was off by perhaps a magnitude of ten. More than a third of white men in town would soon belong. Muncie was not an isolated farm town stuck in the amber of nineteenth-century life. It was deemed so typically American that a pair of prominent social scientists, Helen and Robert Lynd, had chosen it for their landmark study of how people lived in the 1920s, *Middletown*. After scouring the nation, they settled on Muncie as a place "as representative as possible of contemporary American life." In the prosperous city of 40,000, Black people, who made up barely 5 percent of the population, were not allowed into most theaters, schools, or churches. The first suburban subdivision carried a restrictive clause against nonwhites. In Muncie's main public park, Black children could play only in a sealed-off section. When one high school raised the prospect of allowing a Black basketball player on the court for games at the YMCA, it was forbidden. "Well, you know, it's the sentiment here," said an official with the Christian youth group.

But it wasn't just parks, neighborhoods, gyms, and schools that were freezing out certain people. Dale had pieced together one of the Klan's most daring schemes: Blacks, Jews, and Catholics were being excluded from jury service in Delaware County. The levers of this plot were pulled by the local prosecutor and judge—both Klansmen. But Dale's revelation caused barely a stir. And when he appealed to the police to arrest the men who had violently attacked him on Mulberry Street, he ran into another wall of indifference.

The beating was not the worst of it. Dale was thrown in jail by the judge he'd mocked—imprisoned without trial for contempt of court. As he was led away to the state penal farm, Dale overheard the judge say, "They ought to take him out and hang him." The prison was maggot-ridden and freezing. Dale slept on a hard bunk in a wooden shack with more than two hundred other inmates. In his court case, he knew that truth was an absolute defense. The editor said he could prove that the judge had allowed prosecutors to pack a jury with Klansmen during a trial of a fellow member of the order, as Dale had written. Plus, he had every right under the First Amendment to criticize the judge.

Not in Muncie, Indiana, where truth was no defense, and the First Amendment had no force of law.

"Mr. Dale, it is none of your business if this court, the prosecutor, the grand jury and the sheriff belong to the Knights of the Ku Klux Klan," said Judge Dearth when he sentenced Dale to the penal farm. "It is none of your business or anybody else's business." This was a lesson in real power, the Stephenson model in action.

Both Stephenson and Evans had their eyes on an even bigger prize—"control of America by peaceful methods," as one Klan insider recounted. They wanted to stock Congress with members who'd taken dual oaths, one in conflict with the other. In turn, these political foot soldiers would start the process of adding amendments to the Constitution to take away rights given Black people after the Civil War, and to restrict the expansion of certain religions. At least that's what many in the Klan envisioned.

Evans didn't think much of William Simmons, the Imperial Wizard who paraded around Atlanta in a Klan costume of purple silk. The founder was incompetent, buffoonish, couldn't hold his liquor, and lacked vision. He was more of a club man, enjoying the perks as king of the fastest-growing fraternal order in the land. He was standing in the way of the master plan of Stephenson and Evans.

In 1922, Simmons disappeared for six months, allowing internal dissent to fester and his rivals to start plotting. His most trusted pair of subordinates, Edward Clarke and Bessie Tyler, had been arrested for disorderly conduct, naked and drunk when police arrived at a hotel, as the *New York World* reported. Clarke was later indicted under the Mann Act, accused of bringing an underage girl across state lines for sexual exploitation. Criminal debauchery was not one of the Klan virtues the pair of promoters had spread through their powerful propagation department.

A first-ever national convention was called for Thanksgiving week in Atlanta—the seventh anniversary of the founding on Stone Mountain. Simmons thought it would be a glorious affirmation of his power. Stephenson and Evans had other ideas. Klansmen traveled from all corners of the country to fill an auditorium built on a Confederate battleground site. After taking a private train car to Atlanta, Stephenson huddled with Evans on the night before the convention, laying a trap that had been loosely organized in advance. At four a.m., Steve and another high-ranking Klansman arrived at Simmons's mansion and roused him from bed. The Imperial Wizard was groggy from a night of drinking. They wanted him to give up his title. Simmons balked—the Klan was *his*! He'd brought it back from the dead, opened it up to a new range of hatreds, expanded it with the promotional schemes of Clarke and Tyler, saved it with his congressional histrionics. Ah, but this was not a demotion, as Steve explained—*it was a step up*. Simmons would be named Emperor for Life. He'd get an actual white throne inside the Imperial Palace. And he'd get a lifetime salary of $1,000 a month. But in case Simmons still planned to resist, the plotters had leverage—photographs of him drunk and otherwise compromised. He got the hint.

The coup was done. Evans was named Imperial Wizard, and Simmons crowned Emperor for Life. After Simmons was given his honorific, it took some time for him to realize he'd been duped. The Klan now belonged to Hiram Evans and D. C. Stephenson. For his role in the plot, Steve was given control over recruitment of twenty-one states in the North, just under half the country. Klan units were rising every week in this immense territory. And if anything happened to Evans, the upstart from Indiana would get the top job—that was the promise. But Evans would have to watch his back; his partner in the takeover was still hungry, and very impatient. From Indianapolis, Stephenson would oversee a Klan map that stretched from the Atlantic coast to well beyond the Great Lakes, from the Ohio River to the Canadian border. In a candid moment with a reporter, he had said he was "just a nobody from nowhere—but I've got the biggest brains." Now he was a somebody who was everywhere. "He was indefatigable, relentless, revengeful and cruel-natured," a close aide of Simmons wrote in an account of the doings in Atlanta. "He virtually took control of the Klan overnight."

As the longest nights of the year closed out 1922, crosses burned over the pure white snow covering the small towns and prairie stubble of Indiana, and smaller fires warmed the homes of fresh-minted members of the Invisible Empire. The material resolutions for Stephenson's new year included a mansion in the suburbs, a suite of offices in downtown Indianapolis, a lake home in Ohio, a fleet of new cars. He had a staff to hire, a newspaper to run, a military machine to expand, a kingdom in the North. There remained one last building block to this emerging dynasty: women. As Stephenson and Evans envisioned it, the Klan was not just for men. The Empire had vassals in the ministry, in the press, in political office, on the judiciary, and among the ranks of many policemen. All that was missing was the family. Why not give white women a role in fortifying the white race? One of the Klan's core principles was built around "the sacred duty of protecting womanhood." And so a man whose life was a mockery of that principle moved ahead with his most audacious plan yet, a way to control the future. For the hand that rocks the cradle, as he knew from the old proverb, rules the world.

5

Woman of the Year

She was dazzling, born to the pulpit. The mere rumor of an appearance by Daisy Douglas Barr was enough to get working folks to put aside their labors and assemble. She was a Quaker, but a different breed of the Society of Friends. Raised in a patch of low rolling Indiana hills settled by people from Virginia and Kentucky, Daisy preached her first sermon at sixteen after a vision in a woodshed. She told stories, spoke in a simple and direct manner, and was intellectually agile. Daisy married at eighteen, had a child, and after she was ordained at age twenty embarked on a life of revival meetings. She preached in barns and garages, warehouses and theaters. At a time when women had almost no voice in the affairs of Indiana, Barr claimed to speak for half the population—and had no rival in the Midwest. As everyone said, she was *the bee's knees.*

"Easy Daisy, Who's a Daisy, Daisy Douglas Barr!" crowds chanted in affirmation.

At first, her message was moral uplift, resurrection for the ruined. Sex and alcohol were the twin demons of the age and she used her voice to put them on trial. Dance halls were venues of vice. Saloons were dungeons of depravity. She took up the cause of prostitutes and abandoned wives. But liquor was the true home-wrecker. Men spent their paychecks in bars, and stumbled back to house and hearth to batter their wives while their children went hungry. Between 1900 and 1915, the average adult consumed thirteen drinks a week—2.5 gallons of pure alcohol a year. Only with absolute temperance, a radical experiment in social engineering, could society be cured. She joined ministers across the country as a decades-long temperance wave crested with passage of the 18th Amendment. When it was enacted in 1920, Prohibition shut down the fifth-largest industry in America.

"Men will walk upright now," said the most popular preacher in America, Billy Sunday, a former pro baseball player. "Women will smile and children will laugh."

Prohibition, marking the first time the Constitution had been changed to take away a right, was followed one year later with a vast expansion of rights—the amendment giving women the vote in every state. Universal suffrage had long been blocked by Southern legislators who feared arming Black women with electoral power, even within the harsh restrictions of Jim Crow. But the movement to expand the vote also included people who shared the Klan's view of using the newly enfranchised to its advantage, since whites had a far easier time at the polls.

Thus, it was a different Daisy Barr who packed grange halls and coliseums in early 1923. Her belief in voting rights and temperance had evolved into a broader vision of white supremacy maintained by the rising political strength of women. In public, the big heart that had once brimmed with benevolence for fallen humans had shriveled into a raisin of racial animus.

While campaigning against alcohol, she'd fallen in with the Anti-Saloon League, her gateway to the Ku Klux Klan. They shared many of the same values, rooted in a militant evangelism. "The father and mother of the Ku Klux Klan is the Anti-Saloon League," said Clarence Darrow, an assertion that few would dispute. Stephenson modeled his Klan on the well-oiled Anti-Saloon League, using the same Protestant churches as his recruitment base. He envied something else about it—no lobby in America held more power over Congress. And no lobby in Indiana had a stronger grip on the statehouse. They were a moral force that became a political force behind a single issue preached to millions in a nation of dutiful churchgoers. It was "the mightiest pressure group in the nation's history," the historian Daniel Okrent wrote.

The Klan and temperance crusaders formed a perfect team. Any list of Prohibition violators, as Billy Sunday said, "read like a page from the directories of Italy and Greece." Even sauerkraut was suspect because it contained 0.051 percent alcohol. And what happens to a Black man with a head full of liquor, casting his eyes on a white woman? "The strongest argument in favor of prohibition is the imperative necessity of keeping whiskey out of the reckless colored element," said the state's leading dry newspaper, the *Patriot Phalanx.* "The Negro, fairly docile and industrious, becomes, when filled with liquor, turbulent and dangerous and a menace to life, property and the repose of the community," another paper wrote.

All of this was a fine fit for Barr's latest campaign: enlisting women in the fastest-growing movement in Indiana—the female Ku Klux Klan. An adroit assayer of people, D. C. Stephenson drew Barr into his circle not long after he saw one of her sermons. She was better, by far, than the men he'd been paying off to give a spiritual gloss to the Klan. After two decades on the circuit, Barr was an institution. What better symbol of the Klan's drive to soften its image and triple membership than a person known all over Indiana as *Mother*? The Klansman and Mother made a pact designed to enrich both of them. Barr would get a staff of recruiters; they would work the crowds in the stands after she had worked them into a lather from the stage. She received a special robe, cape, and hood, and a title: Imperial Empress of the Women of the Ku Klux Klan.

Barr wasted no time using her new power. She lashed out at immigrants, the wretched masses yearning to breathe free, now unwelcome. From Sicily, an arid and impoverished island devastated by an earthquake in 1908, about 800,000 people had left in the following decade to sail to the United States—among ten million immigrants seeking to become citizens of the New World democracy in that period.

"Formerly, they were from the northern part of Europe, but our immigrants now are from southern Europe and they have not our ideals, either religious or educational," she roared in Rushville, speaking in the largest venue in town. It was the first day of March 1923, and she was in her element. Above her, high overhead, hung a large Klan cross, lit with bulbs instead of fire. "They are idiots, insane, diseased criminals!" As Barr framed the big picture, she said, "This is a struggle for the rebirth of the White Race and the preservation of civilization." Within a generation or two, she warned, white Protestants would be replaced by an inferior breed. The Jews were behind this plot.

Her ideas were backed by influential academics and proponents of scientific racism. Madison Grant, a Yale-educated New York zoologist, had been trying to prove for years that southern Europeans were lesser humans than those from the north; they had low foreheads, he claimed, in addition to being both slothful and oversexed—a seeming contradiction. His book *The Passing of the Great Race* was a favorite of many Klansmen, and was later embraced by Hitler, who called it "my bible."

Turning to other enemies, Barr said it was well known that the Roman Catholic Church was training "100,000 Negroes" to be priests. Jews were war profiteers who'd made a fortune off the carnage of the great conflict, she asserted. There was but one thing the people of Indiana could do to reverse these ominous trends. The men could join the Ku Klux Klan. And the women? Behold, now there was a place for them in the Invisible Empire as well, a new, fast-growing Klan auxiliary: the Queens of the Golden Mask. "They are the best women in the state."

It was true: membership in the female Klan was soaring across the country—not among outcasts, but the "best women," just as Barr said. It was great to belong, to know *your* values were *their* values. "What a thrill when we were told to assemble at a certain place wearing our robes, then marching with others also unknown to us," an Indiana Klanswoman recalled to the author Kathleen M. Blee. "A huge cross, set up in the village, flared up in the darkness, crowds assembled to watch . . . A hush fell on the crowd. They seemed to sense a force of something unknown."

Members took an oath to abstain from alcohol, avoid profanity, keep a clean home, never commit adultery or share the secrets of the organization. Robed and masked, the newly empowered females not only staged parades, picnics, and rallies, but also moved into more traditional rituals—baptisms and funerals, attended while wearing the sheets. Klanswomen were given fashion tips: light on the facial rouge, never show too much ankle below the dress. But they also professed their equality with men—the segregationist as suffragette. "We believe in the mission of emancipated womanhood, freed from the shackles of old-world traditions," stated the Creed of Klanswomen in Little Rock, Arkansas. "We believe that the current of pure American blood must be kept uncontaminated by mongrel strains and protected from racial pollution."

The female Klan of Indiana held its first statewide convention in July 1923, with a parade of white-robed women on horseback, bands and floats, initiation ceremonies, speeches on virtue and temperance, and a cross burning at night. New members were fitted for hoods with cardboard inside to keep the pointy shape over fresh-coiffed hair.

Once a week, Barr spoke to a large gathering in Indianapolis of well-connected Klanswomen. She began these meetings with a call to God, and then another benediction of sorts: reading a roster of retailers, businesses, and service providers who were either members of the Klan or approved by the Invisible Empire. Following Mother's word and guidance from notices printed in the *Fiery Cross*, women of the Klan knew where to shop. They should look for "TWK" stickers in the window. They also knew where *not* to shop, for Barr would also read a list of businesses to avoid, particularly those owned by Jews. "When the women should be as strongly organized as the men," she said to cheers, "there will be no Jewish businesses left in Indianapolis!"

With their livelihoods threatened, Jews and Catholics made common cause with Blacks, who'd long suffered the indignities of being an *other* in Indiana. "Intolerance was everywhere," wrote a lifelong Hoosier, Irving Leibowitz. Jews were a tiny minority, less than 1 percent of the state's population, 23,622 people. The 80,000 Black residents were 3 percent. And Catholics, with 312,000, were 10 percent. More than 95 percent of the population was native born, and 97 percent white. No state in the nation had a higher proportion of that mix.

German Americans also felt the Klan's sting. They had faced the innuendo of dual loyalty during the world war, much of which lingered into the 1920s. German restaurants closed or Anglicized their names. Food was neutered: *Kartoffelsalat* became liberty salad. A prominent Indiana family with German heritage—the Vonneguts, founders of a well-known hardware store—felt shamed. Kurt Vonnegut, the writer, said his parents decided to bring him up "without acquainting me with the language or the literature or the music or the oral family histories which my ancestors had loved."

He said, "They volunteered to make me ignorant and rootless as proof of their patriotism."

Among Jews, there were individual acts of defiance. Louis and Rose Shapiro changed the name of their American Grocery in Indianapolis to Shapiro's Kosher Foods. And just to be clear, they put a Star of David in the window. But others, like the Cohn Brothers Clothing store, were forced out of business. The rabbi of Temple Israel in Terre Haute, Dr. Joseph L. Fink, refused to back down when the Klan sent him a letter demanding his resignation from the community chest. He was summoned to attend a nighttime rally of the Klan at a cemetery. He showed up alone, an elfin figure five feet, two inches tall, to face down three hundred hooded men in darkened mist lit by a burning cross. He told them they were cowards to cover their faces, and un-American for violating the Bill of Rights. He would not resign from public service, and would never hide his faith. He walked away, just as he had walked in, head up high.

Jews had been in Indiana since before statehood, and in the British American colonies since the 1650s. In general, they found less prejudice in the New World than the old. After the Revolutionary War, George Washington had written a warm and welcoming note to a Sephardic congregation in Rhode Island: "May the children of the stock of Abraham who dwell in the land continue to merit and enjoy the goodwill of the other inhabitants." But the flood of new immigrants in the twentieth century prompted fear and hatred in many a native heart. By 1923, nearly two million Jews had come to the United States over the previous two decades. Now they were the object of scorn and harassment. They killed Christ, Klan preachers said. They were behind the Bolshevik revolution in Russia. They cheated Gentiles. They kept their shops open on Sunday. They looked *alien*. And in the darkest caricature, they were lechers and murderers.

Everyone knew about Leo Frank, the superintendent of a pencil factory in Atlanta. One of his workers was thirteen-year-old Mary Phagan. On April 26, 1913, her bloodied body was found in the basement of the shop with a cord tied around her neck. The police seized Frank, the last person who had seen her alive, and charged him with murder and rape. Frank was a New Yorker, a Cornell graduate, a leader of Georgia's B'nai B'rith, one of many Jews who'd moved to newly cosmopolitan Atlanta. Though the evidence was conflicting and inconclusive, he was found guilty and sentenced to death—to the cheers of mobs that had gathered outside the courtroom, some chanting "Death to the Jew." After the governor of Georgia commuted the sentence to life imprisonment, Atlanta blew up. On August 17, 1915, a posse that included some of the leading business and political figures broke into the state penitentiary. With help from insiders, they grabbed Frank from his cell and drove him to a farm. He was strung from a tree and hanged, a slow death by asphyxiation. Among the vigilantes who executed Frank were several of the men who would walk with William Simmons up Stone Mountain a few months later, founding the modern Ku Klux Klan.

What many Americans heard about Jews they got from Henry

Ford, operating out of a Michigan base less than three hundred miles from Indianapolis. His newspaper, the *Dearborn Independent*, was a fire hose of anti-Semitism and reached a peak circulation of nearly one million readers. Every issue of the weekly carried a new episode of a monstrous plan by Jews to control the world. THE INTERNATIONAL JEW: THE WORLD'S PROBLEM was a front-page headline. Ford bound the series into a booklet, and distributed half a million copies to auto dealers throughout North America. A new Model T came with an owner's manual and a tract on the imaginary power of Jewish financiers. Ford saw Jewish tentacles extending to every aspect of life. After biting into a candy bar that tasted slightly off to him, he said, "The Jews have taken hold of it. They've cheapened it to make more money."

Another rabbi, Morris Feuerlicht of Indianapolis, used satire in his sermons and reason in his secular speeches to counter Klan attacks. He was a proud Hoosier, a professor at Butler, the first Jew on the Indiana Board of State Charities. In his scholarship, he wrote of the influence of Judaism on the American founders. In his public addresses, he warned of the rise of a homegrown Klan that wielded "tremendous political power," while relying on "lawbreakers and prominent business people" to do its dirty work. He tried to get the press to wake up to what was happening.

"Public opinion, comments and even news reports of the Klan's doings could not be found" in most of the state's newspapers, the rabbi recalled. One night, a police detective slipped Feuerlicht an undercover report on D. C. Stephenson. It tracked his rise, his connections, his Machine, the politicians in his pocket. One line was deeply chilling to the rabbi: it said that the top Klansman in the Midwest was being carefully "groomed for President."

In the balloons of grandeur that kept Stephenson aloft, the presidency was just a few puffs of helium away. "Boys, I'm not in this for the money," he told his cronies. "You're going to put me in the White House."

He was now a rich man with rich accessories, human and otherwise. After he first spotted the large front porch and three stories of the white mansion at 5432 University Avenue in Irvington, he told an associate: "There is the imperial palace of the Klan of the North." He remodeled it to match his monarchical vision, adding a two-story Ionic portico to replace the old porch. Steve's compound, one of the largest homes in Irvington, was heavily protected. Even the person who mowed his lawn packed a pistol. His wealth gave him entrée into the highest reaches of society. Among his possessions were a half-dozen or so of the leading political players in the state, mindful of his army of informants with their dossiers. By now, Stephenson had embraced the maxim of Machiavelli—it is better to be feared than loved.

The chairman of the Indiana Republican Party, Lawrence Lyons, took the Klan oath, as did Secretary of State Ed Jackson. In an early test of his influence, Stephenson persuaded lawmakers to create a "Klan Day" at the Indiana State Fair. But for all his emerging political strength, he remained a murky character. Even to those close to him, he was a whirl of mystery with a mutable backstory.

Stephenson rented a suite of offices downtown on the third floor of the Kresge Building. He hired attractive women as secretaries and greeters, and posted armed men outside the door. One of the eight phones on his desk, the white one, rang on prompting from Steve to a secretary. He would carry on an imaginary conversation with an imaginary governor, senator, or the president—always in the presence of guests. His base of operations was just a few blocks from the Capitol and Monument Circle, the oversized heart of Hoosier Nation, built around the neoclassical Soldiers and Sailors Monument—a 284-foot tower of Indiana limestone.

For entertainment and trysts, he took several rooms in the opulent Washington Hotel, a Beaux-Arts steel-frame beauty, with giant arched windows on the seventeenth floor.

His top loyalists were losers with enough cunning left in them to want to make another mark. He hired Court Asher from Muncie to be his radar for trouble and his protector. Asher was a short, pleasant-looking man who wore his hair slicked down and his revolver on the outside. He was a burglar, thief, forger, moonshine runner, and ex-con. Asher particularly hated Jews, and he liked his hate delivered with a ready paycheck. "I was making good dough and I saw what a hell of a political organization the Klan could become," he said. He had his skills: he could fix a car, fly a plane, and smell a snitch.

Another hire was Earl Klinck, a beefy sheriff's deputy given to gruff talk, a bit slow on the uptake. Steve had met him in Evansville. After following the top Klansman to Indianapolis, Klinck was deputized to work in the Marion County Sheriff's Office—all while overseeing the sketchier elements of Stephenson's operation, the bribes, bootlegging, and shakedown schemes.

Among Steve's circle, Daisy Barr was the only woman with power. She had moved with great speed in her new role. Together they oversaw another element in the design for a family-friendly Klan: a children's brigade. The Ku Klux Kiddies were issued small-sized robes and masks, recited pledges and songs at regular den meetings, and marched in parades. "This is a godsend to us," one parent wrote to the *Fiery Cross*. "We have a son who is too young to join the Klan, and with this new order he will be able to gratify his wishes to become affiliated with a strictly American organization."

Klan Klubs were established in high schools. Hooded teens soon had their place in yearbooks in Indiana, featured along with the Glee Club or the Debate Society among the accepted extracurriculars.

Steve and Barr also launched poison squads, as they were known on the inside. This was a disinformation brigade—clucks and gossips, but the best-known clucks and gossips in every community, so that false stories could be plausibly true. The fake news originated at the top and was planted at the bottom. It might be a whispered suggestion over a neighbor's fence that a Black family was planning to move nearby. Or that a public servant was a Jew. The Klan prided itself on how quickly it could spread a lie: from a kitchen table to the whole state in six hours or less. The poison served a purpose—to intimidate and frighten certain businesses, as well as local politicians. After a lie took hold, particularly in a small community, some merchants were driven into bankruptcy.

If Reverend Daisy Barr knew in her heart that the leader of the Klan of the North was a soulless man, she kept it to herself. He had made her rich quickly, beyond the wildest—or most perverse—dreams of a Quaker girl from the emptiness of Grant County, Indiana. She also purchased a big house in Irvington and had a closet full of fabulous dresses. But Steve was fluent enough in Bible talk that he may have convinced her they were on the same spiritual team. He had a curious view of the deity at the center of the faith that bonded Klansmen. "I have thought about it many times," he wrote to a friend. "My version of Jesus, the chestnut-haired boy philosopher of Galilee, is a staunch and most practical sociologist and economist."

His letters, fulsome in praise of the recipient, had persuaded Violet Stephenson to give her husband one last chance. It had taken Stephenson's second wife four months to recover from the beating he inflicted on her in Evansville. She had marks on her face from the deep scratching, and lasting emotional scarring as well. During her convalescence, she worked in her mother's dressmaking shop in Akron. She'd also been suffering from a painful sexually transmitted disease, given her by her husband. Steve wanted to visit, but Violet was against it. He had never repaid the sizable amount of money he'd conned out of his mother-in-law. Violet had also been getting notices from Evansville, where her husband had stiffed numerous creditors by kiting checks. He owed the Vendome Hotel $1,000. She knew he was a fraud. But in the best of times, he was a charming fraud. And there was social pressure to keep a marriage intact, even as divorces soared in the twenties.

Now, back in Indiana in mid-1923 for one last attempt at reconciliation, she realized too late that this man she'd pledged to spend her life with would never change. Again, he berated Violet in front of his friends and openly cheated on her. He seemed to revel in her humiliation and her fear of him. His explanation, without apology, was that he was "not cut out to be a husband." If she wanted to stay alive, Violet would have to leave him once and for all—maybe hide somewhere in a different city. He said good riddance and threw her against the wall. He would not let her go without one more beating. She sobbed and tried to defend herself, putting her arms around her head. He slapped her hands away and punched her in the face— a blow nearly strong enough to knock her out. With women, Stephenson never lost a fight. She tumbled to the ground, her vision blurred, her face bloodied. He kicked her in the ribs as he had done in Evansville, putting hard-tipped shoes to flesh, and told her to get out. She grabbed a few possessions and fled. They never saw each other again.

In July, national leaders of the Ku Klux Klan met in Asheville, North Carolina, to celebrate their good fortune and to plan for elections, including the presidency. The year had been one of great success. By the close of 1923, Indiana would have more Klansmen than any other state—north or south. Stephenson had succeeded with an unusual formula for a mass movement: men were the muscle, women spread the poison, and ministers sanctified it all. Nationwide, the Klan had expanded to nearly three million members, and most of the growth was in the Northern states, Steve's domain—Ohio, Michigan, Kansas, Wisconsin, Pennsylvania. Out West, Colorado and Oregon were adding to their Klan rolls just as quickly. The original terror group of the 1860s could only dream of such numbers. The new goal was ten million Americans under oath, though Evans predicted twenty million by decade's end.

The women's Klan had gone from nothing to nearly 250,000 in less than a year's time. Only men were invited to Asheville, with one exception—Daisy Barr. Mother read a poem she'd written for the occasion:

> I am the spirit of righteousness.
> They call me the Ku Klux Klan
> I am more than the uncouth robe and hood
> With which I am clothed.
> Yea, I am the soul of America.

6

The Other Indiana

1923

The genesis of recorded Black jazz took place in the half-light of a gray wooden shed next to a railroad spur in a town thick with members of the Ku Klux Klan. The music was aural energy—alive and original, and it was impossible to sit still while listening to it. After it was captured on wax disc in a small town on the prairie, the world of sound and entertainment would never be the same. But it almost didn't happen. When King Oliver's Creole Jazz Band arrived in Richmond, Indiana, after a six-hour train ride from Chicago, the musicians were lucky to find a place to stay, or even to be allowed to walk through town. The streets were packed with white-sheeted Klansmen from all over eastern Indiana and just across the state line in Dayton, Ohio. The town was hosting the largest gathering of the hooded order in that part of the Midwest. On October 5, 1923, Whitewater Klan #60 staged a parade and cross burnings that would be attended by nearly

36,000—more than the population of the city. On the same day, King Oliver's band was scheduled to press their music into posterity. Playing cornet that day, in a style that seemed to break the sound barrier for the instrument, was twenty-two-year-old Louis Armstrong.

The six Black men and lone woman of the band couldn't stay in any of the proper hotels of Richmond, a factory town built around the gorge of the Whitewater River. They had to find rooms at a boardinghouse in Goose Town, where Italians and Blacks lived, just blocks from the train station and not far from the Gennett recording studio. Even there, they were not free from danger. The Richmond Klan would occasionally torch a cross in Goose Town.

In Chicago, the hot jazz and up-tempo ragtime produced by King Oliver had created a sensation, and made local celebrities of the musicians. Lincoln Gardens, the band's club on the South Side, was so packed that even Babe Ruth was lucky to get a seat when he was in town. "King Oliver and I got so popular blending that jive together that pretty soon all the white musicians from downtown Chicago would come there after their work and stay until the place closed," Armstrong recalled. In the chill of a Chicago winter night, the door would open and out would spill another season—the warmth of music fused to motion.

But in Indiana in the fall of 1923, the musicians were just another half-dozen or so Blacks trying to avoid trouble in a town menaced by men in masks. The Richmond Klan, put together by Stephenson and a local minister's son a year earlier, had become one of his greatest early successes. Nearly 40 percent of white men joined. He recruited out of the churches and a Main Street shop. On that same Main Street, Black customers could no longer buy a cup of coffee from dime stores. Their kids were not allowed to be newspaper carriers or play varsity sports. When a white lawyer tried to help a Black friend join the county bar association, the Klan burned a cross on his lawn and threatened to kill his children. To soften its image, the Richmond Klan gave out Bibles to every public school and made a show of donating money at Christmas to the Salvation Army.

The recording shed was situated out of sight along the hardworking river. For years, it had been a kiln for drying wood to make pianos, a small appendage to a row of smoke-belching brick factories.

"We were all very nervous," said Baby Dodds, who played drums. "Perspiration as big as a thumb dropped off of us."

This was Armstrong's second trip to Richmond, after an earlier visit in May of that year. It was about the same time, and in the same makeshift studio, that Morton, he of the diamond front tooth and fingers that jumped across piano keys like an ersatz gymnast, made the first ever recording of a white jazz band led by a Black soloist. Until then, what played on phonographs in scratchy monotone were mostly classical music bits, Bible readings, Broadway songs, and speeches of politicians like William Jennings Bryan, a regular at the Gennett studio. The first jazz recording ever, in 1917, was by an all-white band. Jelly Roll, who said he was named for a woman's sweet spot, broke the racial barrier with the New Orleans Rhythm Kings. Jelly Roll also claimed to have invented jazz as a child prodigy in 1902, though plenty of people took issue with that boast.

What was not in dispute was the role of one town, in a state that tried to censure human pleasure, in bringing big-time recorded jazz to the world. Known as Harmony Hollow, Richmond was the only place between New York and San Francisco with a decent recording studio. The Gennett brothers, from Italian immigrant stock, ran the large Starr Piano Company. At one point, the seven hundred workers at the factories in the gorge turned out a piano every twelve minutes, feeding consumer demand for an instrument that was at the center of middle-class family entertainment before radio took off. In 1916, the Gennetts started recording music at the former kiln house. They stuffed the walls with sawdust for soundproofing, and tacked rugs to the ceiling. They didn't discriminate. Anyone who could pay could record—cash for sound, no questions asked. They also signed and promoted artists who were shunned by other studios. Jazz came to them in 1923 and would be sold on the Gennett label. So-called race records, though marketed to Black consumers, were showing a large crossover appeal.

King Oliver's band dropped their instruments off in the shed and went to work. When a train rumbled by, they had to stop, wait for it to pass, and start the song all over again. The room was unventilated, the temperature well above 80 degrees, and windowless. The musicians were perched on stools and packing crates. They'd allowed themselves just a single day to record, then planned to get out of town before the Klansmen were set loose after their parade.

In late afternoon, about 6,000 hooded men assembled in a park a mile away. They marched down Main Street, in the direction of the studio. Many carried torches and waved placards proclaiming white supremacy. At least 30,000 people lined the streets to cheer them on. Traffic was blocked by vigilantes of the Horse Thief Detective Association, pistols at their hips. At the front of the parade were Klansmen on robed horses. Close overhead, to the gasp of the crowd, buzzed a biplane with an illuminated electric cross on its underbelly. The marchers were accompanied by Ku Klux Kiddies and at least a dozen bands, including one from Earlham College, where Daisy Barr's son had recruited many underclassmen into the Klan. At the end of the route, several thousand initiates clustered around another park to swear fealty to the Klan—"the oath of Americanism," as the *Fiery Cross* reported.

In the same studio where King Oliver cut his record, the Klan had made several recordings of its own—vanity productions not under the Gennett imprint, which Stephenson hoped to sell across the Midwest. Some of his speeches were recorded as well. Their discs were pressed with red labels and KKK letters and an assurance that all musicians were "100 percent Americans." They did "Onward, Christian Klansmen" and "Daddy Swiped Our Last Clean Sheet and Joined the Ku Klux Klan."

On this October day, the jazz musicians went through some of the numbers that had sent dancers to the floor of Lincoln Gardens. They played "Workingman's Blues" and "Zulu Ball." Armstrong's trumpet was so strong that he was placed near the back of the room, away from the large horn that picked up the music, so as not to dominate the recording. But it was impossible to hide Louis

Armstrong in the fold. He drove "Krooked Blues" and "Alligator Hop," among other songs. Then the musicians packed up quickly and dashed down side streets to get out of town, a circuitous route that would avoid the Klan parade. By dusk they'd made it to the train depot.

Armstrong was still new to lovers of music beyond a few precincts of New Orleans and Chicago, and new to the North by only a year. But when the disc he recorded in Richmond was released, he belonged to the ages.

One of those who heard the record, and then made a pilgrimage from Indiana University in Bloomington to the club in Chicago, was Hoagy Carmichael, a white student of law and disciple of original sound. In 1927, in the same shack, he recorded "Stardust," the song that made him famous. But he always credited the Black performers who came before him. While Daisy Barr was praising the Ku Klux Klan as "the soul of America," Carmichael, one of the most gifted singers and songwriters of the twentieth century, found the soul in places Barr would condemn. It was a small miracle of the times that a uniquely American music, brought to its finest form by people judged inferior from birth, would spread from an off-plumb little warehouse in a city fogged by fear of others.

About seventy miles from Richmond, just blocks from Stephenson's headquarters in downtown Indianapolis, jazz kept underground clubs jumping at all hours on a mile-long stretch of the liveliest street in the state—Indiana Avenue. At least two dozen basement joints fed a need to drink, dance, and hear the most infectious music of the age. Speakeasies had opened in every corner of the country. And in those places, unlike the saloons when drinking was legal, women joined men. The flu pandemic of 1918 and 1919 had taken the lives of 675,000 Americans. The Great War had killed another 116,000. Those who'd been shut in and shut out, who'd rationed food and hope, who became too intimate at too young an age with death, were ready to cut loose and regain human touch. As Willa Cather said, "Nobody stays at home anymore."

The Avenue was a refuge of good times in a puritanical capital city. It was also a bustling commercial center, home for businesses that served the city's 34,000 Black residents. African American restaurateurs, doctors, newspaper publishers, and merchants catered to people who could not get served in much of the city. Their papers carried notices of Sunday sermons and ads for hair straighteners and skin lighteners. The best-known enterprise was Madam C. J. Walker Manufacturing Company, one of the most successful Black business empires in the world. The daughter of a formerly enslaved woman, orphaned at six, married at fourteen, a widow at twenty, Madam Walker started a hair products company catering to Black customers. At the peak of her success, she employed 3,000 people, mostly women, making and selling cosmetics for a population that other companies ignored. She was the first Black woman to become a millionaire, one of the first great female entrepreneurs in the United States. She drove herself around town in a sparkling new Model T and hosted Booker T. Washington after another town in Indiana would not allow him to set foot inside the city limits. For all of Madam Walker's accomplishments, when she went to the Isis Theater and gave the clerk her nickel to see the film, she was told the price for Black moviegoers was five times the amount, and she would have to sit in an isolated area to the side. She moved to New York and died just before Stephenson set up operations in her former city.

The Great Migration—African Americans fleeing one region that denied them basic human rights for another that at least held the promise of full citizenship—had changed the face of the North. The biggest draw was the oldest of American incentives: a chance to move up in life. A factory worker's wage in Detroit, Chicago, or South Bend was three times that of a farmhand in the rural South. In the first fifteen years of the Great Migration, beginning in 1910, almost two million people left their homes for new ones in the North. In Indianapolis, the Black population grew by more than 60 percent. But many whites of the North were as unwelcoming as those in the South.

With Stephenson's move into Indianapolis, the Klan vowed to keep Black residents in a tight geographic box. The city had fifteen African American physicians in 1923, but they were not allowed to attend to patients at the main hospital. Black medical professionals fared no better in their search for homes. When a dentist and veteran of the war, Dr. Lucian B. Meriwether, bought a big house on North Capitol Avenue, neighbors informed him that only whites were allowed to live in that part of Indianapolis. They constructed a fence surrounding his property, ten feet tall, cutting him off from the community. Meriwether sued. The neighborhood hired Stephenson's lawyer and fixer friend, Ira Holmes, who formed the White Supremacy League—founded specifically to keep Black homeowners from white neighborhoods. When a judge ruled for Meriwether and issued an injunction against the "spite fence," as the papers called it, whites defied the order and extended the wooden barrier, further sequestering the family behind a high wall. The Klan posted handbills throughout the city reading "Do You Want a N—— for a Neighbor?" Dr. Meriwether would not budge.

Jim Crow was able to nest comfortably in much of the North because the essential elements were already in place. More than two hundred towns in Indiana, and dozens in Kansas and Ohio, had sundown laws—named for signs at the city limits: "Black Man, Don't Let the Sun Go Down on You Here." This lawless edict could take the form of an outright pogrom. In the little mining town of Blanford, Indiana, just north of Terre Haute, whites told all Black residents in the community that they had until seven p.m. on a winter day in 1923 to leave their homes, after a Black man was accused of assaulting a white woman. The ultimatum was adopted at a hastily called civic meeting. At dusk, cars and trucks stuffed with families and their possessions clogged the main road out of town.

For Black families who stayed quiet and out of sight, for those who didn't push for equality or mingle with whites, the Klan would offer an occasional olive branch. By way of guidance, the *Fiery Cross* ran a piece supposedly written by an African American living in Indiana, under the headline KLAN IS MY FRIEND IF I LIVE RIGHT, SAYS NEGRO.

There were more ominous warnings. One family's home in

Indianapolis was firebombed in 1922, and another's was nearly shattered in 1924 after a grenade was thrown through the front window but didn't go off. When an adult amateur football team of African Americans showed up to play a game in Elwood, just north of Indianapolis, the local paper announced their arrival with this headline: ALL BLACK COONS!

Men talk of the Negro problem," said Frederick Douglass in one of his last public speeches, in 1893. "There is no Negro problem. The problem is whether the American people have loyalty enough, honor enough, patriotism enough to live up to their own Constitution."

Douglass died well before the horror of the Tulsa Race Massacre, when a white mob destroyed thirty-five city blocks in a part of Oklahoma known for its fine homes and businesses—the Black Wall Street. The looting, arson, and murders were sparked by a rumor printed in the local paper, later found to be untrue, that a young Black man had assaulted a teenage white girl. The cause was something much darker and deeper. Roughly 100,000 Sooners had taken an oath to the Invisible Empire. Tulsa was a hotbed of Klansmen. Though there's little evidence that Klan leaders planned the war on their neighbors, they were certainly in the thick of the killings. The marauders burned more than 1,200 homes, five hotels, a dozen churches, thirty-one restaurants, four drugstores, a public library, a hospital, and four doctors' offices. A police detective urged white fellow Tulsans to "get a gun and get busy and try to get a N——." Upward of three hundred people were butchered and hastily buried in the June heat of 1921. A few of the rioters took to the sky, according to witnesses, dropping sticks of dynamite from airplanes—thought to be the first time a city in the United States was bombed by aerial assault. More than 10,000 people were left homeless.

The massacre was a boon for the Klan. By 1923, membership in town was setting new records. That year, more than a hundred people were horse-whipped by Tulsa Klansmen using a cat-tailed leather strap. The slaughter of an entire community, a national Klan lecturer said, was "the best thing that ever happened to Tulsa." As in Dallas, there were no convictions of any of the killers, thieves, and firebombers, no prison terms, no retribution. The Klan of the 1920s had enough control of the legal system to ensure that those who gutted the wealthiest Black community in the United States, a mass murder of American citizens, would not face justice.

7

The Unmasking

1923

On Saint Patrick's Day, a crowd filled basketball-rattled Tomlinson Hall in Indianapolis to hear a fiery Irish American lawyer, Patrick H. O'Donnell. Raised by an immigrant family near Logansport—where Stephenson had first pitched a scheme of vigilantes in service to the Klan—O'Donnell had made his mark in Chicago as a criminal attorney. He was appalled when the Klan started recruiting in the Windy City in 1921. O'Donnell had grown up on stories of the British stripping his people of their culture, their religion, their language, and their civil rights in their native land. Now he saw the Klan trying to do the same thing in the country his family had fled to from Ireland.

O'Donnell organized cops, firemen, priests, Black clergy, and Jewish community leaders throughout the Midwest to make war on the Klan. They founded the American Unity League and started a weekly newspaper, *Tolerance*, which proclaimed its mission was to "smash the Invisible Empire." The paper left no room for nuance: "We hate the Klan and everything it stands for." At an "all races rally" in February, O'Donnell cited Abraham Lincoln's words against the Know Nothings, the political party founded in the 1850s in opposition to immigrants. "As a nation, we began by declaring that 'all men are created equal,'" Lincoln wrote. "We now practically read it 'all men are created equal except Negroes.' When the Know-Nothings get control, it will read 'all men are created equal except Negroes, and foreigners and Catholics.'" The mass meeting was repeated over the next five nights. And in less than a year, 50,000 people in Chicago had joined the American Unity League. There was a huge appetite, as O'Donnell had hoped, for taking down the hooded order.

Klan secrecy, and the oaths never to reveal the names of fellow members, gave O'Donnell an opening. In an internal manual, "Why We Wear the Hood," the Klan had outlined a key to its success: "The secret of our power lies in the secrecy of our members. We can do our best work when we are not known to the public. By this means, we see and hear everything."

Why not go after the "secret" of that power? Why not make the Invisible Empire *visible*, unmasking its members? O'Donnell cultivated insiders, who got him membership rolls. "We feel that the publication of the names of those who belong to the Klan will be a blow that the masked organization cannot survive," he wrote in the inaugural issue of *Tolerance*, dated September 10, 1922. A week later, he made good on the promise and published the first 150 names. The paper cost a dime and sold out quickly. In the weeks that followed, more names were revealed—a prominent bank president, business-men, civil servants. Chicago members of the Klan were listed under the headline WHO'S WHO IN NIGHTGOWNS. In a city where Catho-lics, Blacks, immigrants, and Jews combined were a majority of the population of three million, the revelations caused an uproar. Hun-dreds of families withdrew their money from the bank run by the Klansman. Citywide investigations followed, as did resignations. A week after publication, the city council voted to condemn the Klan and pledged to "rid the community of this organization." It didn't take long for many of the Who's Who to ditch their nightgowns. And within a few months, the state passed a law making it illegal to wear a mask while parading in public.

After his success in Chicago, O'Donnell moved on to other Klan strongholds in 1923. He was an attractive man with a strong jaw, a deep voice—a muscular presence on stage. In Indianapolis on that Saint Patrick's Day, he introduced himself as a proud Hoosier, In-diana born and bred. But what fever, what awful sickness, now gripped this great state, he wondered aloud. He noted that Indiana was number one in a category of infamy: home now to at least 315,000 members of the Ku Klux Klan, "more than Texas, three times as many as Georgia!" The Klan called itself one hundred percent American, but it was "the most un-American organization in the history of the United States," he said. "The Ku Klux Klan is secretly and powerfully assailing every one of the fundamental rights guaranteed to American citizens under the Constitution." And if people did not act now, their city, their state, all of the coun-try could fall into the Klan's hands.

"Mark what I tell you: if they are not exposed and driven from Indiana, they, the Ku Klux Klan, will corrupt your juries, dominate your elections, elect their puppets to power and place, undermine your laws, and violate the principles of your Constitution."

With these words, O'Donnell said what no Indianapolis paper had yet to explicitly say, what no politician of standing would reveal. A Black-owned newspaper, the *Chicago Defender*, had warned of the Empire's political design, running a cartoon of a Klansman grabbing Uncle Sam by the lapel and pointing to the Capitol in Washington, DC. "Listen! I want that building for my private office," was the caption. But O'Donnell had Stephenson's blueprint for total control—the grand plan for the takeover of an American state by an organization rooted in terror—down cold, without a hint of exaggeration. He applied shame, fear, all of his considerable oratorical skills, to get people to rise up against this enemy of a free people.

"You people now live in a Klan republic," he said. O'Donnell drew an analogy between Saint Patrick driving the snakes from Ireland and what people of good will must do now. "We are going to drive the Klan out of Indiana!" he thundered. "We are going to redeem Indiana and re-annex it to the American Union!"

In South Bend, on the same day that O'Donnell spoke, the Klan had a Saint Patrick's Day message of its own: flames for Notre Dame, Roman Catholicism's center of higher learning in America. Unlike most communities in Indiana, the city formed around the southernmost bend of the St. Joseph River was full of immigrant families—Poles, Hungarians, Irish—who found work in the Studebaker factory or one of the subsidiary businesses. Families dreamed of sending a boy to the magical campus just across the river, built around a large golden dome, with a football team coming off two undefeated seasons under coach Knute Rockne—himself an immigrant. O'Donnell had staged several rallies in South Bend, and his paper was well received, especially on campus. "Cheer up, Klansmen—the worst is yet to come," he wrote with typical brio. O'Donnell warned the Fathers of the Holy Cross that the Klan's aim was to destroy the school. The Klan newspaper dismissed O'Donnell as a minor menace who'd soon go away, and characterized his supporters as a "mixture of swarthy Jews, Negroes and foreigners." On the Irish high holiday, the Klan's cross burning in South Bend was a scalding missive from Stephenson: no place in the Midwest was free of the Ku Klux Klan.

After O'Donnell's speech in Indianapolis, people mobbed the stage, asking what they could do to resist. The Klan's enemies needed to join forces, he replied. "The fight against the Klan is not a Jewish fight or a Negro's fight or a Catholic's fight, but an American fight." Within a few weeks, community leaders from all three camps had signed on, opening a new office of the American Unity League—an Indiana foothold inside the Klan of the North. O'Donnell was not bluffing. He would not rest until the Empire was crushed.

In the dark early hours of April 1, two men crept through Klan headquarters in Indy and made their way to a filing cabinet. They knew what they were looking for and where to find it. They hurried out not long after entering, slipping through a back door with a prize: a list of 12,208 names. Later that day, the Indiana edition of *Tolerance* hit newsstands in the city. On the cover was a drawing of fishermen hauling in a large net, above a caption reading "Never mind the minnows: get the whales!" The catch was labeled "KKK senators and judges." The headline was: INDIANA'S REDEMPTION BEGINS. This Who's Who of Hoosiers in nightgowns was only a small sample, seventy names, of what O'Donnell had obtained from the inside. He promised more to come in future issues. The tally included a former judge, law partners, bankers, business owners, Indianapolis police detectives, dozens of well-known Protestant ministers, and one big fish who flipped: Lawrence Lyons, chairman of the state Republican Party. He renounced his membership in a letter written to the Klan and published in this issue of *Tolerance*.

As the names spread around the state, Stephenson raged against traitors and spies inside his realm. He threw things against the wall, stubbed his cigar on the floor, screamed at subordinates until he was out of breath. Even when he wasn't drinking, his anger storms could overturn a room. He moved swiftly into federal court, seeking an injunction to stop *Tolerance* from further publication.

The next day, on Steve's orders, the Klan paper came out with cannons firing: LYONS BETRAYS KLAN OATH. The Republican who'd turned was characterized as a man who was "born in Hell, and inspired by Satan." Three days later, Steve sent a telegram to leading Republicans, including judges, the Indiana treasurer, and the secretary of state, Ed Jackson. "Permit no selection to be made and permit no one to be named to succeed Lyons until I have had an opportunity to confer with you. See that Lyons hands in his resignation at earliest possible moment." He signed it "The Old Man."

And there it was: barely three years after setting foot in Indiana as a friendless unknown from an untraceable nowhere, D. C. Stephenson was telling the state's top elected officials what to do. And they followed the Klansman's every order.

O'Donnell's sources obtained a copy of that telegram, which he printed verbatim in *Tolerance*. He also ran pictures of the two most notable Hoosiers revealed as members of the Invisible Empire—Secretary of State Jackson and E. Howard Cadle, whose Indianapolis Tabernacle was said to be the largest building in America devoted to religious services at the time. It was inside Cadle's domain that the Klan gave one of its largest bribes to a minister that spring—$600. Readers of *Tolerance* could compare that with other Protestant payoffs, a list of preachers who'd been bought by Stephenson to spike the faith with Klan poison, the "subsidized evangelists," as they were called by O'Donnell. Most of the ministers were handed $50 to sell souls on the Klan, but a few were given as much as $250—nearly half a year's salary for a butcher or baker. In his Saint Patrick's Day speech, O'Donnell could only guess at how quickly and deeply the Klan appeared to have taken over Indiana. But now, just two weeks later, he knew precisely; documents from the inside spoke volumes.

The April 1 issue of *Tolerance* also broke news about the Klan's private militia—news, at least, to those who weren't on the receiving end of the vigilantes. "Under the Horse Thief Act, Kluxers in 50 Indiana cities are trying to establish the husky nucleus of a Ku

Klux state constabulary, with power to search your homes and places of business."

A few weeks earlier, that power had been on full display outside the village of Laurel, at the little white farmhouse of Green Gabbard's family. One of Steve's poison squads had spread word that the Gabbards were making moonshine on their property. They were also said to be part of a fledgling group opposed to the Klan's takeover of Franklin County. A judge, the sheriff, and several deputies of the horse thief detectives quickly organized a raid. They stormed into the Gabbard home on the night of February 23, banging down the door, overturning tables and beds, trashing the house. They screamed obscenities at the quivering white family, including a girl of seventeen, newly married and pregnant. She fainted and fell to the ground. The raiders brandished guns and threatened to shoot the young woman's husband. Gabbard pleaded with the gunmen to call a doctor. They refused, instead accosting his son. "God damn him," said the vigilante leader, Judge Cecil C. Tague. Even though no liquor was found, the boy was hauled off to jail and charged with possessing intoxicating drink. Two months later, the teenage girl died—from "shock sustained on the day of the raid," in the opinion of her doctor. The boy was tried in a courtroom overseen by the leader of the raid, Judge Tague, and prosecuted by another member of the invading party. Green Gabbard and his wife, Rebecca, later swore out an affidavit telling of their night of horror, "the unlawful invasion of our home by the Ku Klux Klan." *Tolerance* printed it in full.

O'Donnell was now Stephenson's main target in the press. He

fulminated against "Mad Pat" in the *Fiery Cross*, calling him "an Enemy of America." He ordered Klansmen to burn a cross in the township outside Logansport, where O'Donnell grew up and some members of his family still lived. The May 11 edition of the Klan's weekly published a Who's Who of Catholic businessmen and their addresses on its front page. They were called out as suspect Americans, people to be boycotted and ultimately run into the ground. The ostracized included attorneys, accountants, architects, grocers, electricians, plumbers, and even the "Rome-managed Yellow Taxicab Co."

Fear of Catholics was brought to the American shores by British Protestants steeped in dark conspiracies about the power of Papists. Though many of the colonists were fleeing religious persecution, it wasn't long before some were practicing what had been preached against them back in Europe. In 1644, a mere twenty-five years after the first cargo hold of kidnapped and enslaved humans was brought to Virginia from Africa, the colony passed a law prohibiting Catholic settlers. In the nineteenth century, a convent was burned to the ground in Massachusetts, churches were firebombed and Catholics attacked in a riot in Philadelphia. Thomas Nast, the most influential newspaper cartoonist at the time, stoked loathing of the faith of new immigrants with sketches depicting bishops as crocodiles coming ashore.

Stephenson knew that Klansmen far outnumbered Catholics in Indiana. He sensed that the vast majority of white people in the state would not object to his kicking around a religious minority. It was a safe hunch. Instead of backing down after O'Donnell's revelations, he reloaded. "How dare someone suggest that red-blooded Americans should conform their views with subjects of a power in Rome which is inimical to American ideals," his paper wrote.

The campaign against Catholics was aided by one of the Klan's strangest surrogates: Helen Jackson, who said she was an ex-nun forced into servitude by secretive sisters of the faith. Her book, *Convent Cruelties*, was featured prominently in the pages of the *Fiery Cross*. "Do you ever wonder why so many of our girls are missing?" Jackson wrote. Many had been kidnapped by nuns and taken into cloister, where they were slapped, punched, forced to drink dirty soup and take cold baths, she claimed. O'Donnell put a reporter on the ex-nun's case. The first thing he learned was that Jackson was not an ex-nun, but a former prostitute. Nor was her name Helen Jackson.

At the same time, O'Donnell printed fresh lists of Klansmen in Michigan, Ohio, and smaller towns in Indiana. He devoted an entire issue to an unmasking, more than ten thousand names. But thus far, his campaign did not seem to be hurting the Klan.

Just the opposite.

To O'Donnell's horror, it was backfiring. People looked to see who *didn't* belong, and felt left out. There were no significant resignations beyond the state Republican chairman, no sign that average people had been shamed into giving up their sheets, no great uprising by the citizenry. Instead of mass rejection, there was a rush of new initiates. Rallies were huge—10,000 in Evansville, another 10,000 in Noblesville, just north of Indianapolis.

What should have been shattering news—a Klansman dictating orders to elected officials and leaders of the dominant political party—barely caused a stir. This was O'Donnell's worst fear: perhaps Indiana *really wanted* a Klan republic. At the height of the unmasking, every week, two thousand or more men continued to don hoods and robes for the first time and swear loyalty to a group at odds with the most cherished American values. After his name was printed in *Tolerance*, one defiant pastor in Indianapolis even oiled up a burlap cloth and lit a cross on the front lawn of his church. *Damn right*, he was a Klansman. Proud of it. If all the best people in a community belonged, as Daisy Barr had said, what could be so wrong with the Ku Klux Klan? The banker who held the loan on a house, the grocer who delivered food, the preacher who baptized newborns—this Who's Who was validating, and intimidating. If you weren't a member, something was off, maybe foreign, about you. You were an outsider. Why not be in on the secret while holding the secret? Emboldened by swelling membership, D. C. Stephenson openly proclaimed the very principles that O'Donnell accused the Klan of holding. He turned scandal into virtue. He embraced the hate.

He expanded on "the true principles of the Klan" in the *Fiery Cross* on April 13, 1923, under the headline THE OLD MAN'S MESSAGE. Speaking to "the Klansmen of the Northland," Stephenson urged his 200,000 readers to take on the "amalgamated enemies of America." He didn't have to say who those enemies were, only what the Klan was for: "my countrymen of the White Man's Breed." He lashed out at "the venom and virulence of Mad Pat O'Donnell," and begged God to take him down. That same God had "conse-crated a White Man's Country, a White Man's home, and was ded-icated to a White Man's supremacy in a White Man's realm of honor." The message was signed "The Old Man Himself."

His Klan now claimed 200,000 members in Ohio, and a nearly equal amount in Michigan and Wisconsin. Even Springfield, Illi-nois, hometown for Lincoln during his early political career, had sprouted "one of the liveliest and fastest-growing" Klan units in the country, the *Fiery Cross* reported.

The mainstream press seemed not to care about O'Donnell's revelations or the rapid spread of a closed-door political order, per-haps because it was not uncommon for journalists to join the Klan. As John Niblack recalled, a friend urged him to take the Klan oath not long after he started work at the *Indianapolis Times* for $18 a week.

"How would you like to be naturalized tomorrow?"

"What do you mean, naturalized?" asked Niblack.

"Well, you know, you pay ten dollars and you get naturalized."

"I don't have to be naturalized," said Niblack. "I was born down by Vincennes, Indiana, and I am an American citizen and I have no reason to be naturalized, let alone paying ten dollars. I suppose you're talking about the Ku Klux Klan?"

"You ought to join. Everybody else is joining."

"Well tell me, my friend: what is it with you fellows in the Klan? What do you stand for?"

"We're against the Negroes, the Catholics, the Jews and the for-eigners."

Niblack said there were ten million Black people, three million Jews, and countless Catholics in the country. What did the Klan propose to do? Kill them? Run them out of the United States? "Why don't we live in peace and quiet?"

"You talk silly," his friend said.

"Maybe I am silly. But I'm not going to join because I don't believe in it. I think it's un-American."

That spring, Stephenson opened his office to Niblack and a handful of other reporters, fully confident about spreading the Klan message on multiple fronts. They took note of his charm, his arrogance, the snappy suit jacket draped over the broad shoulders of a man who stood five feet, eight inches, the constant, nervous roll of his fingers on the desk, and all the highfalutin words he dropped into blunt statements of his power. A sign at the entrance read: "All Bearers of Evil Tidings Shall Be Slain." If you wanted a drink, he had the finest stuff smuggled in from Canada or gifted to him from his police allies, not the foul and dangerous white mule hooch, distilled from corn, that reporters and cops passed around in the courthouse pressroom. (It was said that two drinks of white mule would kick you into the police station, three drinks into a hospital, and four into your grave.) And certainly he didn't have to muck around with the dehydrated blocks of grape juice sold by mail to poor lovers of wine, who added yeast, water, and sugar to bring their brick to liquid fermentation.

Steve was a name-dropper, well connected, mentioning the finest people, judges, politicians, and newspaper editors he knew. When asked about the bust of Napoleon in his office, he offered some accurate-sounding quote from the Emperor. He'd memorized enough aphorisms from history that he could sound authoritative at times. The Klansman's personal ornaments—the attractive women out front, the pistol-packing protectors hovering around him— made a strong impression. Steve needed only to snap his fingers and Klinck or one of his other armed acolytes would jump.

He was vague about his plans and even more opaque about the Klan's intentions. It was a God-fearing, law-and-order-loving, woman's-purity-enforcing, patriot-heart-beating, white-supremacy-upholding, Christian-based fraternal club with chapters in every part of Indiana—certainly nothing any respectable citizen should fear. But stay tuned: the Klan had big things in the works for this year. Big things for Indiana. Big things for the Midwest. Big things for the nation. About his own background, Steve repeated some version of the narrative that had carried him so far in so little time: Hoosier native, college educated, war veteran, a descendant of seasoned wealth. Single. And then, upon further reflection, he elaborated on an earlier answer. "I am the embodiment of Napoleon." He gave no sign he was kidding.

8

Creating D. C. Stephenson

I n the selective biography that he rationed to the press and friends in high places, the verifiable details of Stephenson's life story usually began in 1920. He had no past before then. No parents. No siblings. No wife or children. No friends from high school. No college chums. No former army buddies. No business associates. Where was he from? *Nowhere*, or on a rare occasion, *somewhere*. But his enemies, who were growing inside and outside the Klan, were starting to piece together the true story. The Old Man was not a Hoosier native, but born in Hill County, Texas, on August 21, 1891. His father was not a banker or keeper of old money, but an itinerant laborer, working as a sharecropper throughout hardscrab-ble parts of the High Plains. His mother was dead to him; from an early age, they never got along. He was embarrassed because she was gray-haired and stooped, *like an old lady*, by the time Steve was ten. The family had moved from place to place in a covered wagon and lived for a while in a dugout—earthen floor, six feet or more belowground, with walls of plank board and black tarpaper. At one point, Steve was enrolled in a Catholic elementary school. He had a talent for talk and inventing stories about himself, and a good memory. His formal schooling ended in eighth grade, which he left just before he turned seventeen. It was the same year, 1907, that the former Indian Territory of Oklahoma became a state.

Early on, he spent more time with girls than boys. A trick of his was to grab a girl's breast and fondle it in front of others. The shock effect gave him power, and revealed to him at a young age that he could get away with things as others could not—simply because he dared to cross a line. He left home not long after dropping out of school and never went back. He would erase his past and blot out his family, re-inventing a dirt farmer's kid into D. C. Stephenson, a refinement from town to town. It helped if you looked the part. In reaction to his mother's shabby clothes and his father's soiled overalls, Steve strutted around Oklahoma farm towns in a full suit. His prominent accessory was a gun. After he got his first pistol, he was never without a firearm. Words were his passport upward. He could talk a line of silk-spun bullshit and he could write, both aided by drink. After a few pops of liquor, he had courage enough to start giving speeches—on street corners, in school gymnasiums. In one town he spoke of the evils of socialism. In another, he praised socialism. He found work in small Oklahoma newspapers, which was a way to meet women, and to ingratiate himself with the local power structure.

When he was twenty-three, Stephenson started wooing Jeanette Hamilton, a merchant's daughter who went by "Nettie." He was going places, he told her, with *big, big, big plans.* Together they could forge a magnificent life. Nettie was delighted when the newspaper in Hugo, where Steve worked as a typesetter and writer, presented her in its pages as "The Most Beautiful Girl in Oklahoma." Steve could brag about that, and now had the photo and clipping to prove it. They married in Tishomingo, Oklahoma, on March 26, 1915. His parents were not invited. "He was the most ambitious, hardworking young man you ever saw," said Nettie. "I thought we had a great future before us. He had the flash of a genius and I believed in him."

But he couldn't hold a job. He refused to pay his bills. He lied by way of respiration. He even stiffed the barber in one of the towns where he briefly touched down. He was frequently gone, spending nights with other women in the wind-raked towns of central Oklahoma, rolling in like a tumbleweed and out like a dust swirl. Just after the wedding, the couple was living in Madill, south of Oklahoma City, where the owner paid Steve $20 a week to run the weekly. He was free to print whatever he wanted. Five months into the job, Steve wrongly accused a man of a crime in the pages of the paper. This time, his lies cost him. He was fired. The Stephensons moved back to Hugo, eighty miles east, and another newspaper job. Nettie was pregnant. Her husband didn't like the swollen belly or the cramps or the burdensome future that a child presented. One night, he exploded, slapping and punching the most beautiful girl in Oklahoma. When Nettie showed up at the paper with an eye blackened and a cheek reddened and swollen, the pregnant wife of D. C. Stephenson admitted that her husband had battered her. But he suffered no consequence. He could always beat a woman, especially if that woman was his wife.

Six months after the wedding, Stephenson deserted Nettie. He said he was going away to look for work and would summon her. He promised to send money. As her pregnancy advanced, Nettie feared for the months ahead. Her family had warned her about this man; they saw him as a person without character. He proved them right when Nettie was taken to a hospital in Oklahoma City to give birth. From her bed in the maternity ward, she wired her husband, begging him to come to her side, to help out. He said he was unable to travel the few hours on a flat road to the city. He sent her $5—the only money she ever saw from him during the pregnancy. He told her he was still planning to move back with her, and that things were going well in Cushing, the latest town as he bounced around Oklahoma. But when Nettie and her baby girl showed up, unannounced, she found a man who'd created a fictional alternative life. He hustled her over to a run-down hotel and shook her violently. He had no more use for Nettie, and none for a screaming infant. Besides, he'd wanted a boy.

"Don't tell anyone we're married," he said. "Don't tell anyone!"

She was stunned.

"I said, 'Don't tell anyone you're my wife.' I don't have a wife."

At the time, he was living with another woman, the bookkeeper at the local paper, in an apartment above a garage. He'd told everyone in Cushing that he was a single man. The next day, he fled. It took a while for Nettie to track him down. But after months of sending letters begging for child support, she finally got a response from her husband, the only time she ever heard from him after he'd abandoned her. "You must not try to find me," he wrote. He would not see the mother of his only child for eleven years.

Facing the draft when the United States entered the war against Germany in 1917, Steve joined the Iowa National Guard. He gained a reputation as a carouser, a gasbag, a petty thief. He borrowed money and never repaid it. He stole flasks of liquor from beneath the pillows of other men. His fellow soldiers hated him so much that they petitioned their superior officer to transfer him out of their unit. He was moved to Camp Devens, Massachusetts. After being discharged, he returned to Iowa, working as a traveling salesman. He told people he was a war hero, an officer, and a gentleman. In fact, he had never set foot overseas. It was then that he met his second wife, Violet, in 1920. Not long afterward, he borrowed a large sum of money from her mother. When he married Violet, he wrote on the Ohio marriage certificate that he had no prior wives.

In the months before Stephenson nearly killed Violet with his fists, she came to the conclusion that he had married her only to get at her mother's cash. She never saw empathy or regret from him. He was a cipher.

Just because he never went to college didn't mean that Stephenson, or his Klan, couldn't *own* a college. What the American race needed, he believed, was a place to turn out purebloods with a solid academic foundation. It would be a factory of sorts, shaping young men who were in some way duplicates of the D. C. Stephenson he had created from scratch. He set his sights on Valparaiso University, sixty miles from Chicago and equally distant from what was emerging as the Klan's biggest institutional enemy in Indiana: Notre Dame. The Gothic-towered, cobblestoned lanes of Valpo, as it was called, were ideal. The school had a storied history: founded by Methodists in 1859, admitting women well before most colleges went coed, and second only to Harvard, at one time, in rankings of largest private school enrollment. But the world war drained Valpo of young men, and it ran into further troubles with accreditation. By 1923, the university was nearly bankrupt, and the board of trustees considered shuttering the school.

KLAN WILL TAKE OVER
"POOR MAN'S HARVARD"

The headline from the *Daily Republican*, in Rushville, Indiana, was still aspirational, but not by much. The story noted that "the institution will be non-sectarian, but Negroes will not be admitted." The Klan promised a "one hundred percent American" curriculum. Stephenson sent his man, Milt Elrod, editor of the *Fiery Cross*, up to the northwest corner of the state to seal the deal. The city of Valparaiso was already Klan friendly. When Stephenson had tested the waters with a rally in May, the Klan parade drew 5,000 ghost-sheeted marchers and another 30,000 spectators. No doubt, the turnout was aided by the appearance of tight-wire walkers, bronco-busting Texas cowboys, twenty brass bands, and a massive barbecue. Steve knew how to throw a hatefest. Every Friday night throughout that summer, a hooded horseman would lead a column of Klansmen from Main Street downtown to the Porter County Fairgrounds, where a rousing round of race-baiting and immigrant and Catholic bashing was followed by the lighting of a large cross. In other towns, a rally might be designed around a high-dive competition, men jumping into a net from a hundred-foot tower. He also staged baseball games, burning a cross while fans ate hot dogs and slurped sodas after the games. He may have picked up this idea from Evans, whose Texas order had fielded a baseball team with *Ku Klux Klan* stitched across the front of their flannel uniforms.

Flush with money, the Klan dangled $350,000 before the keepers of Valpo's withering flame—enough to fend off creditors. As Steve envisioned it, his college would not be a two-bit, backwater school, but a prominent national university, "a monument to American ideals and principles," and not a poor man's Harvard, as the headline had it, but a serious rival.

He still had to get Imperial Wizard Evans to sign off and pony up the rest of the money. That could be a problem. As united as the two most powerful Klansmen were in staging the coup in Atlanta, they were now fighting over the spoils of the expansive and wealth-generating machine of the new Ku Klux Klan. Evans was leery of Stephenson's lordship over his own private college. Already, Steve's territory was becoming an empire within the Empire. They arranged to meet in Washington, DC, at the Willard Hotel, the temporary residence of many a president-elect while waiting to move a few steps over to the White House. The setting would give Stephenson a prime view of the place he hoped to call home one day.

In mainstream quarters, the press reception to Klan U was not favorable. A newspaper in New York imagined a slogan across the school's gateway arches: "Abandon All Brains Ye Who Enter Here." They envisioned a commencement where degrees were awarded in "Jew-hating" and "fanaticism," and classes in whipping, lynching, tar-and-feathering. "What a fine bunch of imbeciles will this college turn out each year with a faculty made up exclusively of Kluxers," wrote George Dale in his Muncie *Post-Democrat*. Even after his lockup on the penal farm, and facing a boycott that was killing subscriptions, after vandals stole ink from his printing press and tried to foul the typesetting machine, Dale kept pounding away. "God pity the helpless youth of Indiana whose nutty parents contemplate sending them to this proposed insane asylum."

While Evans mulled the proposal to buy a college, Stephenson staged a show of force in Dale's hometown. A massive parade of slow-moving vehicles and horses bedecked with flags took over the main streets of Muncie on a warm spring night—"the largest crowd ever to gather" in the city, the papers noted, about 40,000 people. It wasn't the usual Klan festival, heavy on kitschy entertainment and Americana; this one had more menace. Burly men in masks walked beside the cars, eyeballing the crowd from behind their hoods. They ordered all male spectators to remove their hats as the parade passed by. An army captain, John O'Neill, a veteran of the Great War, refused to comply as he watched from his parked car. A gang of Klansmen yanked him from his vehicle and threw him to the ground. He was pummeled into unconsciousness, his face bloodied. It took a dozen stitches to sew up the gash in his cheek.

Dale was watching it all with his daughter, terrified by the ugly display of force. Of late, the editor had been receiving death threats. When he walked down the street, women of the Klan would spit on him—as ordered by Steve. He looked spindly and frail. "He can't weigh more than a hundred pounds at most," a visiting reporter wrote. "Any husky 14-year-old boy could knock him down." His house was vandalized, rocks thrown through windows, his seven children heckled and bullied. One gunshot had been fired into the Dale home. When a Klansman in the parade spotted Dale, he barked out an order: "Go get him!" Hooded men surrounded the editor and ordered him to remove his hat. A Klansman reached beneath his robe for his gun. Another one slapped Dale in the face. Dale turned to a nearby cop who'd witnessed the attack. He demanded that the officer arrest the man who had just assaulted him.

"He told me that I ought to have known better than to stand around and thus invite trouble when a Klan parade was going by," Dale wrote. With a snicker, the cop said that the editor could always take his complaint to higher-ups—Muncie's chief of police or the Delaware County sheriff, both Klansmen who'd recently passed by in front of them. Or he could go directly to the prosecutor, the one hidden by mask and robe at the head of the Klan parade. "Muncie is now in a state of civil war," Dale wrote. "An armed, masked and secret organization has taken over the government."

On a sultry June night in 1923, two sheriff's deputies on motorcycles were patrolling the roads outside Columbus, Ohio. Around midnight, they spotted a Cadillac coupe parked just off the highway. They pulled up beside the car and approached with flashlights. In the back seat, two people were untangling from each other, a man with his suit pants down and a woman with her dress scrunched above her breasts.

"What's going on?" asked the deputy, Charles M. Hoff.

D. C. Stephenson hastily pulled his pants up, slicked his hair back, and sat upright in indignation.

"Nothing's going on," he said.

"It looks like there's been *something* going on. What are you doing there with your pants unbuttoned?"

He protested. This was an affront to a powerful man, and an insult to the young lady's honor. "I'm going to marry this girl," he said. She was twenty years old, hired by Steve two months earlier as a stenographer. She was reluctant to talk.

"I don't care if you're married now," the officer replied. "You have violated the law. You don't have no headlights or a taillight."

He ordered Stephenson out of the car and said he was going to place him under arrest for indecent exposure and parking a car on the highway without displaying the proper lights.

Steve was furious. But he held his anger in check, smoothed his clothes, and tucked in his shirt. He approached the officer outside the car and motioned for him to step away.

"Can I talk to you alone?" Again, he told the cop he was a prominent man, well known throughout the Midwest, and couldn't afford the publicity of an arrest.

"Is there anything that can be done?"

"What's your official capacity?" the officer asked.

"It doesn't make any difference."

"What's your name?"

He refused to identify himself, lingering in the dark for several minutes, steaming. Ohio was a second home for Steve during the warm months. He'd purchased a showcase at Buckeye Lake, where many of the wealthy and powerful of the state passed their summers. He could count on Ohio judges, prosecutors, politicians as friends of the order. Youngstown, 170 miles from the site of the police encounter, was about to elect a Klan mayor.

At the same time, the morality patrols, those peripatetic Klansmen deputized as horse thief detectives, had announced new campaigns to clean up vice. In Hammond, an Indiana city on Lake Michigan, the Klan took to monitoring dance halls, music clubs, and movie theaters for violations of clean living, most having to do with sex. "Automobile parties, stalled on county roadsides, are to be particularly watched," wrote the *Fiery Cross*. Of course, the crusade didn't apply to Steve's automobile party on a county roadside.

Still, the cops were unmoved by the fast-talking, fleshy-faced man they'd found with his pants down in the darkened back seat of a Cadillac at midnight.

"If you don't want to give me your name," said Officer Hoff, "I'll drive you down to jail and we'll find out what your name is there."

He shined his light on the license plate and started writing up the account for the arrest record. Steve made one last appeal.

"I'm a special deputy myself," he said.

"Let me see some identification."

Steve opened his wallet and pulled out an official-looking card with his name on it and a metal badge, showing him to be a deputy of the Horse Thief Detective Association. This link to the brotherhood of blue was enough to keep Steve out of jail and the incident from the papers. The wall between the private D. C. Stephenson and the public man was intact—stronger than ever, as Steve interpreted the roadside encounter in the heat of a summer night. What could hold him back? At this point, certainly nobody in law enforcement.

9

A Master Race in the Midwest

1923

At a night rally in the summer of 1923, Stephenson gave a long speech on eugenics before a somewhat baffled crowd of coal miners. He had taken up the cause of racial purity by legislation with the confidence of a man whose convictions were shaped by the uncomplicated concision of crackpots. He claimed that ethnicity was fate: millions of people were doomed in utero to become degenerates or castoffs. "In reference to feeblemindedness, insanity, crime, epilepsy, tuberculosis and deformity, the older immigrant stocks were vastly superior to the recent." The new Americans were "dregs from putrefied vomit," parasites, illiterate, dumb, lawless, with overactive sex drives. Nor would young immigrants ever improve with schooling. For they are "citizens of a lower class, just as the Negro is a constant menace to the standards of civilization which Americans hold dear."

With Prohibition on the books, and Jim Crow expanding beyond the South, the top objective of the new Klan was stopping the flow of people who could never be idealized Americans. Fixation on designing a more perfect white citizen had become an obsession of the 1920s Ku Klux Klan. At one end of life, the hooded order supported "Better Baby" contests at state fairs. There, not far from pens holding prizewinning hogs and oversized gourds, were exhibits explaining how proper breeding could lead ever upward, refining the race while keeping it pure. From animal husbandry to ideal infants—it made sense. Babies were judged on a scorecard, with points taken off for unusual ear size, the shape of a child's head, or eyes that didn't shine. The good-looking, glowing, exclusively white babies were awarded ribbons. Black babies and babies of immigrants were excluded from the competition. As the Indiana director who ran the contests explained: "We cannot make a silk purse out of a sow's ear, nor can we make a citizen out of an idiot or any person who is not well-born."

On the adult side of their campaign, the Invisible Empire joined forces with experts who issued studies on the dire threat to a race of diminishing thoroughbreds. Led by a eugenics committee, Congress was drawing up a bill to close the door on nationalities debased from birth.

Well ahead of the rest of the nation, Indiana had already put some of these ideas into law. For sixteen years, the state tried to keep those who were demonstrably stupid, sickly, disabled, or prone to criminality, vice, or drink from ever having children of their own. Starting in 1907, with passage of the world's first eugenic sterilization law, Indiana attempted to cull undesirables from inside its borders—"bad seeds." The preamble of the law stated: "Whereas heredity plays a most important part in the transmission of crime, idiocy and imbecility . . ." The words were a direct contradiction of the ones Hoosiers would recite on the Fourth of July, the self-evident truth that all men are created equal.

By the dawn of the 1920s, about 2,500 people in the state had been sterilized against their will. More than half of those forced into a procedure to end their bloodline were labeled "mentally deficient," a term broad enough to include "idiots, imbeciles, and degenerates" but also "epileptic persons" and the highest grade of legal inferiority—"morons." The law was finally struck down by the state supreme court in 1921, though a new statute was drafted soon thereafter and became a top priority of the Klan.

Both Stephenson and Imperial Wizard Evans liked to cite well-credentialed men of science to bolster their claims. Stephenson quoted extensively from the work of Dr. Harry H. Laughlin, the chief eugenicist guiding the anti-immigration forces in Congress. Laughlin came from Iowa, where he immersed himself in the mechanics of breeding livestock. Allowing strong, healthy animals to cross with weaker ones, he concluded, was no way to run a farm— or a country. He created a model human sterilization law, building on the pioneering work from Indiana, that was drafted by more than thirty states. Ultimately, about 70,000 people across the United States would be forcibly sterilized. A special category of "degenerates" was added in many of these states in order to sterilize homosexuals. Laughlin's law also drew strong interest from a circle of proto-Nazi scientists in Germany. Laughlin himself would later praise Hitler for understanding that "the central mission of all politics is race hygiene."

Among Dr. Laughlin's colleagues, the subordination of the Black race was a settled question. The debate had moved on to whites with a shade of color. If the United States were to become "darker in pigmentation," as the influential eugenicist Charles Davenport explained, the typical American would eventually be "smaller in stature, more mercurial, more attached to music and art, more given to crimes of larceny, kidnapping, assault, murder, rape and sex-immorality."

It was too late to keep out immigrants who would help shape the American Century. Rudy Valentino, a heartthrob filling movie theaters across the nation, had been born Rodolfo Pietro Filiberto Raffaello Guglielmi di Valentina d'Antonguella in Castellaneta, Italy. He passed through Ellis Island in 1913, after leaving one of the poorest parts of hollowed-out Puglia. Irving Berlin, born Israel Beilin, fled pogroms aimed at Jews in the shtetl where his family lived in the Russian Empire. Among the songwriter's contributions to his adopted country was "White Christmas," the most-recorded holiday song in history and the best-selling single of all time. Another Jewish composer and songwriter, George Gershwin, born Jacob Bruskin Gershowitz, came from a family in Russian Ukraine. His *Rhapsody in Blue* was created in 1924, the year Congress was finalizing legislation that would prevent millions of Jews from fleeing a Europe soon to be tyrannized by the Nazi Holocaust.

About the same time that Stephenson was giving his speech on the inferiority of these new immigrants and disparaging American Blacks as a "constant menace" to Western civilization, James W. Johnson drew a packed house to his lecture inside the colored YMCA in Indianapolis. His title: "The Negro's Contribution to American Culture." A poet, Broadway lyricist, composer, educator, and columnist, Johnson was a big part of the swell of African American artistic expression sweeping the nation. He was also now well into his tenure as the leader of the fast-growing NAACP. As a field organizer, he'd helped to plant new branches across the country. Indianapolis had an active chapter, run mostly by women. They had been able to block one Klan rally in the city in 1922, and were fighting new efforts at enforcing residential segregation. Johnson was the embodiment of Black success, throwing off one institutional tether after the other. He was the first African American to pass the bar exam in Florida. As part of President Theodore Roosevelt's informal Black Cabinet, he was a special ambassador in South America. As the first Black executive secretary of the NAACP, Johnson used both muscle and his fluency in diplomacy in the job.

But culture was his ongoing passion: it was the best argument—by example—against everything the Klan preached. He cowrote a comic opera. Hundreds of his songs were performed on Broadway. He crafted verse in Black dialect and old-fashioned iambic meter. One poem, lauded as a work of genius when it was printed in the

New York Times, tried to take in the entire sweep of Black history in the New World, as this sample stanza demonstrated:

> *This land is ours by right of birth,*
> *This land is ours by right of toil;*
> *We helped to turn its virgin earth,*
> *Our sweat is in its fruitful soil.*

Johnson urged his audience of Black Hoosiers to be evangelists of culture, to shout it from the rooftop of the segregated Y. He reminded them that African Americans had given the nation its "most distinctive form of art" in the new century—jazz. Indiana, with its recording studio by the tracks in Richmond, had played a big role in bringing this sound to millions, as his listeners well knew. At a time when cities were closing off their neighborhoods, their public schools, their shared spaces to Black citizens, Johnson was amazed at the spectacle of underground clubs packed with white people "doing their best to pass for colored."

With Johnson in town, Indiana Avenue was alive with fresh indignation and racial pride. But the eugenicists had all the political momentum. Immigration panic was in the air. So was ethnic trepidation. One club, the American Breeders Association, had nothing to do with horses; its eugenics committee was headed by a man who'd been president of Indiana University, and the first president of Stanford, David S. Jordan. He taught that the human race could be improved only by preventing the disabled or certain nonwhites from reproducing. At the very top, President Harding endorsed *The Rising Tide of Color: The Threat against White World-Supremacy*, a bestseller about fears of diminishing racial superiority, written by a Harvard PhD, Lothrop Stoddard, who was also a Klansman in high standing. Harding's vice president, Calvin Coolidge, had penned a piece in *Good Housekeeping* saying that "biological laws tell us that certain divergent people will not mix or blend." The article was titled "Whose Country Is This?"

The Klan could not have framed it better. In Colorado, the Klan referenced "scientific evidence" as proof that "descendants of savage ancestors or the jungle environment" along with certain immigrants were unfit to ever govern the United States. Under their Grand Dragon, Dr. Locke, the newly powerful Klan of the Rocky Mountains urged passage of a forced sterilization law similar to the one Indiana had pioneered. Edward Clarke, the marketing genius hired by Simmons, had long advocated sterilizing Black men and women. Now here were university presidents and other men with advanced degrees to give these ideas a boost from on high. Testifying before Congress, Dr. Laughlin said sterilization laws would lead to lower taxes, lessening the burden of society to take care of people with epilepsy, the blind, the deaf, and the mentally disabled, not to mention the high cost of jailing criminals prone to music and art.

As Stephenson neared the end of that night's speech, he summarized what was at stake when "members of inferior races" were let into the United States. "This is a struggle to save America," he said.

"It's a struggle perhaps even more serious than that between the states in the Civil War." The hundred percenters from the Heartland were at the forefront of a war to prevent "the inevitable destruction of what may be called the American race."

His speech was reprinted in the main Klan newspaper and circulated in chapters throughout the North. It didn't take long for the message from that night, crafted with half-baked statistics and questionable allusions to history, to take an even harder turn.

"I want to put all the Catholics, Jews and Negroes on a raft in the middle of the ocean and then sink the raft," said a Klan speaker in rural Whitley County, just outside Fort Wayne. His suggestion was met with wild applause.

10.

Independence Day

High in the Fourth of July sky over Kokomo, a small biplane came into view at midmorning, a speck in the stonewashed blue of a still and stifling day. On the ground, a mass of white-sheeted men and women, the largest crowd ever gathered in the history of the Klan, craned to get a look at what was dropping from the heavens. They had come from all over the Midwest, and their parked machines clotted roads for seven miles outward— spokes of solidarity radiating from the belly of Indiana. The hazy humidity made people sweat beneath their sheets, but few bothered to disrobe. They were one under their hoods, a prairie of white. The plane was the color of an oriole, black and orange, with two open cockpits, canvas wings, and a cross and inscription on its underside: "Evansville K.K.K. No. 1." For an instant, it looked like the plane was going to crash, veering low to the ground and nearly clipping a tree. The crowd gasped. But then it looped upward, to applause and cheers, and climbed high enough to give the great and powerful sovereign of the Indiana Klan another look at his subjects. Of course the plane would never crash; D. C. Stephenson was indestructible.

Steve could see knee-high cornstalks wilting in the July heat, the spires of Protestant churches, the big yards of clipped grass, baseball fields and fairgrounds, a business district of hardware stores with barbers, butchers, banks, and the crowd—oh, the immensity, pilgrims of prejudice as far as the eye could see. To Steve, it was a perfect picture of small-town America on the nation's birthday. Fully half the town of 30,000 belonged to the Klan, including mayor, prosecutor, police force, and school board. The local chapter took out ads in the *Fiery Cross*, bragging that the city had a higher proportion of Klansmen than any other community in Indiana. And the daily newspaper printed notices of upcoming Klan events on its front page, alongside the weather forecast.

It was the averageness of Kokomo—"the dead level typical-ness of the town," as one native son who was there on that day recalled— that made it an ideal host for the hate group that had taken over the Heartland. The Klan made life less dull; it gave meaning, shape, and purpose to the days. Folks got their news from editors loyal to the Klan or from a gossip chain that started with a Klan poison squad plant. They took their moral guidance from preachers in the pocket of the hooded order. They were good people, or so they told themselves, of the same faith and same race, with the same fears and the same goals—though they were modest only to a point, as this showing of self-congratulatory sentiment made clear. The few who did not look like them were no trouble in Kokomo. The town mandated segregation in 1919, ordering all Black children, no matter where they lived, to attend a school set aside for nonwhites. In the chill of winter, some of the students had to walk miles in freezing weather, passing much closer schools to get to their racial cloister.

The Fourth of July gathering was advertised as "a monster rally" to discuss "the conditions of our country." It was held along a vale of grass and shade trees around Wildcat Creek, owned by the Nathan Hale Chapter of the Ku Klux Klan. Visitors slept on prairie turf, in tents at the park, in hotels with people packed ten to a room. They carried flags, bunting, and signs that read "America Is for Americans." They threw money into a huge pot—$50,000 at day's end—for construction of a Klan-exclusive hospital, because members didn't want to be treated at the city's only hospital, run by Catholic sisters. On Independence morning, they marched in a parade with floats depicting Klansmen protecting women from predatory Blacks and lecherous Catholics. Then they moved on to the creek-side park, where each person had to utter a password to proceed. The Klan was still a secretive organization, after all. Reporters covering the event had to pledge not to name any of the speakers, except for a handful of well-known national officers. The hooded masses bowed their heads in unison to receive a group benediction from a Protestant minister, and then they were treated to brass bands and speeches that were equal parts uplift and condemnation.

The Klan's official estimate of the assemblage—200,000 KLANSMEN MEET was the *Fiery Cross* headline—was surely an exaggeration.

But even a low guess of about 100,000 by the *Indianapolis Star* gave credence to the Klan paper's assertion that Kokomo had hosted "the biggest crowd of one-hundred percent Americans that ever assembled in any one place at any one time." It was "a throng beyond the comprehension of the human mind."

Up in the air, Steve got one last look at the multitudes. His pilot was his bodyguard, the jailbird and bootlegger Court Asher. Coming in for a landing, the plane was bouncy and uneven. Asher was a thrill devil, and the Klan plane was his favorite toy. It rumbled a few times on the hard ground before coming to a stop, the engine throttled. Steve bounded from the rear cockpit.

The crowd roared as he approached them, waving and smiling like the pope greeting the pious inside St. Peter's Square. Many fell to their knees.

"The Old Man! It's the Old Man!"

He mounted a platform draped in flags, red-white-and-blue bunting, and letters on a string of lights spelling out "WELCOME STEVE."

"Some of them stretched out their arms to him like they were praying," said Asher. "If he had told them to sprout their wings and fly, half of them would have tried it."

He paused for several minutes, soaking it all in, mass adulation for a man who'd led a life without friends, a life devoid, by his design, of contact with the family that had raised him and the family he'd created and abandoned. He needed to be told that he was loved, that the world would know he was loved, even if the love was dictated by his own hand.

The crowd could not know that their illustrious leader was a drunk and a fraud, a wife-beater and a sex predator, a serial liar and an unfettered braggart, a bootlegger and a blackmailer, caught by police barely a month earlier in an act that these very people were crusading against. They could not know that he had left behind a family in rags and distress, whom he still refused to support; that his own mother, an impoverished and widowed waitress in Oklahoma scraping by on tips at a luncheon counter, had been begging him for money. That he had stiffed merchants from Oklahoma to Kansas to Iowa to Indiana. "I have yet to find any person that had a good word to speak of him," an investigator wrote later. "He usually left a trail of grief behind him."

But even if the Fourth of July celebrants in Kokomo knew about the Big Lie of Stephenson's life, would it have mattered? They believed because they wanted to believe.

"My worthy subjects, citizens of the Invisible Empire, Klansmen all—greetings!"

This Fourth of July was his coronation. For as of today, D. C. Stephenson was finally given the crown he'd been promised by Imperial Wizard Evans after the coup in Atlanta one year earlier, his payback for his part in ousting Simmons. Though he oversaw a Klan confederation of twenty-one states, Steve had not been given the formal title until now. Evans was on hand to mark the high occasion. "I have come to see what is the cause of this remarkable growth of the Klan spirit in the realm of Indiana," said Evans. He could easily have made the same boast in Colorado, where Klansmen climbed to the top of 14,115-foot Pikes Peak on the same

Fourth of July to initiate new members in a state they would soon control. Or in Oregon, where thousands of Klansmen strutted through towns in Independence Day parades. But nothing could match what was happening in the center of the country. As the *New York Times* noted, "In no other state of the union, not even Texas, is the domination of the Ku Klux Klan so absolute as it is in Indiana." Stunned at the breadth of Stephenson's makeover of the Midwest, the paper put the number of Hoosiers in hoods at half a million.

Was all of this the doing of D. C. Stephenson? Or was it a winning gamble by a few visionary Klansmen who bet that the same hard-heartedness that stirred the men on Stone Mountain in Georgia could be found in abundance in Middle America? As the Klan philosophy took hold in the North, it was polite at first, often expressed in codes and winks. "We solicit the patronage of 100 percent Americans, who prefer being served by 100 percent American workers," as a local Ford dealer in Indianapolis worded his ad. And then, more forcefully—as when the main bus company in Indy started refusing service to Black transit users. Today, Evans praised the Machine, the vigilantes with badges, for its "wonderful accomplishments in the interest of law enforcement." As the crowd hushed, the Imperial Wizard read a proclamation that made D. C. Stephenson the Grand Dragon of the Realm of Indiana.

Steve followed with a long and tedious discourse on pure Americanism and the problems of an "inflexible" Constitution. Were the Founders to return today, they would surely insist on a rewrite, he said. The Supreme Court, for one, should be reined in by new amendments giving Congress power to override judicial decisions. On and on he went, second-guessing Hamilton, Madison, and Jefferson. It was good that the masses were kept hydrated by 70,000 bottles of soda that had been trucked to the rally. Even with liquid refreshments, many people fainted or were treated for heat-related stress. When Steve finally ran out of wind, a feast of epic scale was presented: more than six tons of beef, 2,500 pies, seven wagonloads of watermelon. The Klansmen and Klanswomen and Klan Kiddies could at last take off their masks and enjoy a picnic among their tribe in the shade along Wildcat Creek.

As the crowd dined, Stephenson went back into Kokomo's business district and took a break at the best hotel in town. After he started drinking, he eyed one of his secretaries who'd made the trip from Indianapolis. For press, his handlers had screened three reporters in advance: a Catholic from the *Indianapolis News*, a Klansman from the *Indianapolis Star*, and John Niblack of the *Indianapolis Times*. The Klan journalist got drunk on white mule and was too wasted to conduct an interview. The Catholic got spooked by the size and sentiment of the crowd and decided to stay in his room. That left young Niblack as the sole reporter. After making his way past several armed guards, he found himself face-to-face for the second time with the Old Man, whose nose was reddened from the sun and drink. He asked him about the ultimate plan for treatment of Catholics, Jews, and Blacks—the same line of questioning he'd raised when a friend had tried to recruit him into the ranks of the Invisible Empire.

"Do you intend to kill them, run them out, or live with them?"

Stephenson didn't answer. He sat, grim-faced, rattling his fingers on a desk.

"What is the ultimate objective of the Klan?" Niblack followed up. "And how much money have *you* made out of all this?"

The last question set off the newly crowned Grand Dragon. No one spoke to him this way. But Niblack had raised an overarching and obvious issue: following the Klan's agenda to its logical end, what *was the plan* for the nation's thirteen million African Americans, three million Jews, and eighteen million Catholics?

"Just stop right there," said Stephenson. "You're part of a national conspiracy to upset the Klan."

Conspiracy? Niblack said he answered to nobody but his editor and his readers. He belonged to no organization but that of the alumni association of his school, Indiana University in Bloomington.

"I can see that you are not for us," said the Klansman, now visibly angry. "You are against us. Get outta here!"

As darkness fell, the crowd size swelled even more in anticipation of a fireworks display equal to the occasion. A parade of men on white horses that had pranced down Main Street assembled for the show. They sang "Onward, Christian Soldiers."

Back at his hotel, Steve was now drunk. He ordered his secretary to join him on an errand in the car. He drove a short distance, found a hideaway. Parked. Undid his pants. He crawled atop the woman and tried to rape her.

In covering the Kokomo rally in the *Fiery Cross*, the Klan had offered another one of its tributes to independent women. The paper saluted "fair damsels of the women's movement for the distinguished service you are rendering to Anglo-Saxon American womanhood." All Knights of the Klan were indebted to them. And one day soon, the Klan paper editorialized, "the rights of women will no longer be a strange sound to American ears."

Stephenson's ears, at that moment in the car in Kokomo, were filled with the screams of the woman he was attacking. Primed with adrenaline and drink, he tore her dress, tugged at her panties and shook her, the smell of whiskey and cigars all over her. She bolted from the vehicle, walking quickly in a daze in the dark. At the time, she was too traumatized to go to the police and report a felony committed by one of the most powerful men in the state. And besides, what good would it do? The Kokomo cops were Klansmen. But later, she told investigators her story. "He tried to have intercourse with me," she said. "He was a beast when he was drunk."

An hour after the sun went down, a giant wood cross was draped in oiled burlap and set afire. Drums rolled and Klan anthems were sung throughout the evening and into the night. "Kokomo has seen with its own eyes the class of people who comprise the Klan," the *Fiery Cross* wrote in its report of the biggest day in the history of the Ku Klux Klan. "It saw staunch American farmers with their wives; merchants of repute; bankers of integrity; honest and hard-working mechanics, and ministers and devout church members."

Robert Coughlan, a ten-year-old boy from a Catholic family,

had watched the white-sheeted invaders take over his town, alternately fascinated and frightened. He saw them exchange cryptic, ritualistic greetings and wave at each other with three middle fingers of one hand, that secret salute of the KKK. At day's end, he was sitting on his front porch when a member of the Klan walked up the steps of a house nearby and plopped into a chair on the veranda. Once the mask was off, the boy could see that the now visible congregant of the Invisible Empire was his neighbor, Mrs. Crousore. Coughlan's family had been anxiously vigilant for two years, fearing an attack. There were rumors that their pastor at Saint Patrick's Church would be killed, that the few Jewish merchants would be run out of town by a mob with flaming crosses, that Mr. Coughlan, a Catholic teaching at a public school, would be fired because of his faith. These fears did not take the form of their neighbor, the kindly Mrs. Crousore—until that night.

Why, Coughlan wondered later as a writer trying to come to grips with what had happened to his neighbors, "did the town take so whole-heartedly to the Klan?" His answer was rooted in "the deadly tedium of small-town life," a militant religious fundamentalism "hot with bigotry," and "American moralistic blood lust that is half historical determinism, and half Freud." These people needed to hate something smaller than themselves as much as they needed to have faith in something greater than themselves. The Ku Klux Klan "filled a need," Coughlan concluded, "a need for Kokomo and all the big and little towns that resembled it during the early 1920s." But then it metastasized. "It first appealed to the ignorant, the slightly unbalanced and the venal," Coughlan wrote, "but by the time the enlightened elements realized the danger it was already on top of them."

Steve's pilot and wingman, Court Asher, always keen to a new con, had a more cynical explanation for the Klan's takeover of the Heartland and beyond. No man is a hero to his own valet, as the saying goes. But Asher marveled at his boss's talent for mass manipulation. "Billy Sunday was a great spellbinder. Steve was a better one." He was particularly amazed at how many preachers he'd been able to fool, concluding that men of God were easy marks. "Sometimes we'd leave a wild party, slip into the robes, and go into church to pray with a bunch of new Klansmen," he said. "Stephenson would kneel down and pray as convincingly as any minister." He knew the Old Man's true character. He'd seen the violent rages, the battered and bloodied women who fled hotel rooms in tears and torn clothes, the Grand Dragon passed out and smelling of bourbon and tobacco. Steve could flip on a dime, from benevolent shepherd of a vast crowd to an intoxicated monster. "It was the damndest thing I ever saw, how this guy could spread the bunk and make the hicks eat it up."

Those he disparaged, the many thousands who'd donned a hood and put their hand on the Bible in solemn ritual, would likely disagree. They did not consider themselves hicks. And what they swore to uphold was not bunk, but something close to gospel.

11.

Governors, Guns, and God

1923

Just weeks after the coronation in Kokomo, Stephenson basked in the glow of political sycophants aboard his latest possession—a ninety-eight-foot yacht, the *Reomar II*. The Grand Dragon now had a floating palace on the Great Lakes to go with his chandeliered mansion in Irvington, his summer home in Ohio, and his private transport above the clouds. He was as far from the Oklahoma dugout of his youth, with its dirt floor, tarpaper walls, and leaky roof, as he could be. It was laughable, a mere two years earlier, when a drifter in a fine suit first appeared in Indiana and told people he was going to be the biggest man in the United States. Few doubted him now. He had paid more than eight times the average price of a new American home for a vessel that had been built for an auto magnate. He anchored his latest luxury on Lake Erie, at a yacht club in Toledo, Ohio. Steve had no interest in sailing.

He bought the big boat to impress. A sister ship was owned by Al Capone and used by the gangster for the same purpose.

On this day in early August, some of the most influential men in the Midwest—the governor of Ohio, a United States senator from Indiana, judges, mayors, and congressmen—had answered Steve's engraved invitations to a lavish party aboard the *Reomar II*. They were there to plot next year's elections, and for the prospect of depravity after hours. Stephenson's Klan had just renewed its call for a Constitutional Convention to establish "the racial destiny and define a wise, safe and true Americanism" for the United States. Steve was indeed proficient at "getting the hicks to eat his bunk," as Court Asher had put it. But he was equally skilled at catering to a different crowd—people of wealth, title, and education who believed that they were superior, the leading men of the leading race.

A few days earlier, on August 2, President Warren G. Harding had dropped dead at the age of fifty-seven, taking his last breath inside San Francisco's Palace Hotel. His wife was reading a piece from the *Saturday Evening Post* to him when his heart stopped at 7:30 p.m. Four hours later, Calvin Coolidge was awakened by his father at the family homestead in Vermont and sworn in. After taking the oath of office by kerosene lamp in a house without electricity, President Coolidge went back to sleep.

Harding's death was a shock, instantly fueling rumors of assassination by poison. He'd been on a tour of Alaska, British Columbia, and the Pacific Northwest, a hardy and hale presence on the stump. He had a deep summer tan to go with a bald eagle's head of silver hair, enhancements of an affable Ohioan who'd been elected in part because he looked like a president. A stroke was initially said to be the cause of death. This was followed by reports of food poisoning, to which many people added: at the hand of his long-suffering wife, Florence. The president, who also liked his Prohibition-era scotch and soda, had carried on a lengthy affair with a married woman, and other dalliances as well, including one with a woman thirty-one years younger than he. Their trysts sometimes took place in a large White House broom closet. But as a later medical analysis found, Mr. Harding was not murdered by Mrs. Harding. He was most likely done in by a massive heart attack.

The Klan had tried to claim the president as one of their own—a lie, but an excellent recruiting tool, considering he'd won the presidency with 60 percent of the popular vote in 1920. A year after getting elected, Harding gave a speech in Alabama, calling for the end of lynching and racial inequality, putting him at odds with the Invisible Empire. It was lip service from a president who allowed the Klan to flourish on his watch. As a tribute after Harding's death, Stephenson's Klan burned a cross on the banks of the Ohio River in Evansville, and sent a five-foot-high bouquet of lilies spelling out the initials KKK to his funeral in Marion, Ohio.

Now, to pick a president in 1924. A Klan favorite was Henry Ford, the most prominent anti-Semite in the nation. But the titan of the Model T was a tease, issuing contradictory statements about his plans. He was also considered somewhat of a dim bulb, outside his expertise at factory precision. One potential candidate, Senator James "Sunny Jim" Watson, was on board the *Reomar II*. Steve kept a letter from Watson, assuring the Grand Dragon that he was "glad to help along the cause." The Klan wanted Sunny Jim to be Coolidge's vice president. Another politician aboard Steve's floating party, Indiana secretary of state Ed Jackson, was known to everyone as an oath-bound Klansman, per the disclosure in O'Donnell's *Tolerance*. He was being groomed by the Klan to run for governor next year. One of the tasks the Grand Dragon had in mind for Jackson was to bribe the current governor of Indiana, paying him to appoint a Klan-backed prosecutor in the largest county in the state, covering Steve's base of operations. The plan was still taking shape.

The presence at the party of the Ohio governor, Victor Donahey, was further proof of Steve's political control of the Midwest. There were nearly as many Klansmen in the Buckeye State, where it had been growing steadily in tandem with its neighbors, as in Indiana. Summit County, covering the booming tire factory town of Akron, was home to almost 50,000 members, including the mayor. A group of Klan nightriders known as the Battalion of Death had been harassing students and faculty at the University of Dayton, a Catholic college. They held a noisy rally, burning a three-story cross, jeering at students and insulting the faith of those who walked by. One night, forty carloads of hooded men rolled up to the campus and spread out. They planted twelve bombs, which went off without killing anyone. They also bombed their own headquarters— and blamed it on Catholics.

Just across the border in western Pennsylvania, the Klan came out of the shadows with a series of fright moves. The hills and hollows of that part of the state, rich with veins of coal and wells of oil, offered new life for people fleeing poverty in Poland, Italy, and Ireland. These aspiring Americans were predominantly Catholic, and were welcomed by Jewish merchants, most of them newly arrived as well from places like Russian Ukraine. But the settled order of white Protestant families was unsettled by the surge of immigrants. They also complained about the young Black people who'd recently moved to this stretch of the industrial North for factory jobs. With all of the change, the Klan had plenty to work with, and they were forceful in pressing fear out the door—issuing threats, publishing names of people under surveillance, and physically attacking others. A cross was lit on the lawn of a Black family in Erie, Pennsylvania, with a note pinned to the door. "The Kluxers have paid your disorderly house its first visit to warn you and the rest of your kind to close up and get out," was the message. "Now listen up, you black violators, close your place and go. Erie doesn't want you." The threat was backed by "8,000 White American Men"—a healthy sliver of the state's Klan. Within a year, it would claim about 125,000 members.

As overlord of expansion in the North, Stephenson urged Klan units of western Pennsylvania to become more political, part of a boundless movement, not just a network of local fraternal orders. In New Wilmington, 5,000 ghost-costumed men marched with torches under a full moon. In Punxsutawney, 1,000 Klansmen assembled not far from Gobbler's Knob, home to a prescient winter groundhog. Five thousand Klansmen paraded through New Castle. Fights broke out, with volleys of bottles, rocks, and gunfire, when the Klan tried to torch a cross near an Italian immigrant neighborhood in Steubenville, just across the border in Ohio. A six-year-old boy, part of a family from the mountainous Abruzzo region in Italy, escaped without harm. It would be some time before the lad, Dino Paul Crocetti, would make his mark as the singer Dean Martin.

This flurry of fights, rallies, and undisguised threats had to please the most exalted guest aboard the *Reomar II*—Imperial Wizard Evans. After giving Stephenson his title in Kokomo, the Klan capo had decided to stick around and take a long look at the vibrant heart of the Empire. But there was now considerable tension between Stephenson and Evans, which they'd managed to keep under wraps in Kokomo. The Imperial Wizard had decided to reject the plan to buy Valparaiso University, infuriating the Indiana Grand Dragon. He also thought Steve might be making too much money from his significant skim off the top of robes sold, initiation fees paid, and annual dues levied. For his part, Stephenson was chafing at limits to his power set by the one man who could still give him orders. But the two leaders agreed on the larger aim: The Klan did not exist for neighborly lodge meetings and fraternal gibberish; it *was* a vast movement, political in scope.

And it was still violent and criminal when necessary. A few days before the Kokomo rally, Klansmen kidnapped a minister, Reverend Oren Van Loon, from just across the state line in a small town in Michigan. He had criticized fellow Christians, saying from the pulpit that "the cross should not be used as a symbol of terror." Days after he disappeared, the minister was found, unconscious, with the letters KKK branded on his back.

Two weeks after the Fourth of July, a mob of 5,000 Klansmen hurled rocks and bottles at firemen trying to extinguish a burning cross in Indianapolis. Open fires were prohibited in the city; the Klan's main ritual was no exception. But Stephenson was defiant. In violation of the ordinance, his followers torched a massive cross on a hot night. When police arrived, they drew their guns and ordered the hooded rioters to stand back. Only under armed escort could the firemen leave the scene. The Hoosier Klan had shown Evans how fierce they could be.

"I want people to be afraid of us," he said with satisfaction.

The Imperial Wizard was even more impressed by the turnout at Buckeye Lake, a favorite getaway for people living in nearby Columbus. Even Steve had not expected upward of 75,000 people to show for a rally at the lake on July 12—the biggest Klan gathering in Ohio history.

Three days later, Stephenson stumbled down his Buckeye Lake compound to a cottage that housed some of the women who worked for him. It was 3:30 a.m. He was naked but for his underpants, and so drunk he could hardly stand. He barged inside and went to the bedroom of his stenographer, a nineteen-year-old from Indianapolis who'd been an employee since April. She jumped out of bed, terrified at the sight of the glassy-eyed Klansman staggering toward her. He grabbed the girl and tried to kiss her. He was her boss; she was told when hired that she should never cross the Old Man. He threw her to the bed and lowered his underwear. As he tried to pin the woman, she squirmed out of his grasp.

"Get out!" she said. "I'm going to scream!"

Her threat, which would have awakened others, saved the young woman from the assault. It was the second time in less than two weeks that Stephenson had tried to rape someone. As in Kokomo, the police were not summoned.

If Evans knew that the co-architect of the blueprint for Klan control of the United States was a violent sexual predator, he never let on as the two men schemed on the deck of the *Reomar II*. They pored over a list of Klan-backed candidates for high office next year—governors in the West, the South, and the Midwest, senators from ten more states, and the presidential ticket. About seventy members of Congress were faithful to the hooded order, by the Klan's tally. It had sympathetic governors in Georgia, Alabama, and California. John C. Walton, the Oklahoma governor who had declared open war on the Klan, was facing impeachment from a legislature dominated by the Invisible Empire. After Black residents were butchered in Tulsa, after a Jewish merchant was stripped and beaten to a pulp in the same city, after a bootlegger was killed at his home in Ardmore and the vigilantes found not guilty, after Klan "whipping squads" were unleashed, the governor had put the entire state of Oklahoma under martial law and called up the National Guard. But the Klan was superior, in numbers and influence. They forced Walton out.

In Oregon, the Klan had put their candidate, Walter Pierce, in the governor's mansion in 1922. The same year, a majority of his state's voters approved of a centerpiece of the hooded order: an amendment requiring all children to attend only public schools, meaning Catholic ones would dry up. As governor, Pierce also backed a proposal that would make it illegal for an immigrant to own land, and a second act to end the Columbus Day holiday. The property prohibition statute was aimed at Japanese immigrants; the anti-Columbus bill was an attack on Oregonians with Italian heritage.

"Every one of my ancestors has been a Protestant, for three hundred years," said the new governor.

The Klan had taken root in both the rural side east of the Cascade Mountains and the metropolitan areas in the west, up and down the Willamette Valley. The first American town founded west of the Rocky Mountains, Astoria, at the mouth of the Columbia River, elected a Klan mayor in 1922, and hosted a convention of the order two years later. Ten thousand people attended. Reuben Sawyer, a Portland pastor and a student of Henry Ford's tracts against Jews, filled churches in the Beaver State with anti-Semitic rants. "In some parts of America," he warned one crowd, "the kikes are so thick that a white man can hardly find room to walk." Speaking to 6,000 in Portland, he said Jews were trying to establish "a government within the government." In the same city, another top Klansman told an audience that "the only way to cure a Catholic is to kill him."

What most Oregonians knew of African Americans and Jews did not come from personal experience. Like Indiana, Oregon had only a small number of these minorities. The state's racial animus dated to at least 1844, when the provisional government ordered all Black people out of the territory. After Oregon became a state in

1859, it banned nonwhites from living there. Following the Civil War, Oregon was one of only six states to refuse to ratify the 15th Amendment, which granted full voting rights to all male citizens, regardless of race. By the mid-1920s, there were more Klansmen, per capita, in Oregon than any state but Indiana.

Colorado was not far behind. Rocky Mountain Klansmen kidnapped two prominent attorneys—one a Jew who defended bootleggers, the other a Catholic whose crime was his faith—then clubbed them nearly to death. They tried to force a Black family out of their home in Grand Junction, warning that if they did not leave, their lives would be in danger. But the violence did nothing to curb popularity. The Klan mayor of Denver, elected in 1923, named fellow members of the Invisible Empire as police chief and city attorney. One night alone, the Klan set seven crosses ablaze throughout Denver. They would soon be "the largest and most cohesive, most efficiently organized political force in the state of Colorado," wrote the *Denver Post*.

As Evans and Stephenson envisioned things, it should be impossible for anyone in America who opposed the Klan to be elected to high office. By sheer numbers, the Klan could use its bloc of power as a wedge to get its way. As for the issues, weren't most Americans behind the Klan's campaign to outlaw alcohol in every square foot of the United States? Didn't a majority want to keep the races separate and unequal? Wasn't there a consensus to slam the door against new immigrants? The country was 90 percent white. Consider the millions of potential *new* recruits, those open to an appeal to ethnic vanity and racial panic.

"There are millions who have never joined, but who think and feel and, when called on, will fight with us," Evans wrote. "This is our real strength, and no one who ignores it can hope to understand America today."

The Klan leadership had not yet settled on a presidential candidate, though William Gibbs McAdoo, son-in-law of Woodrow Wilson, was saying all the right things on the Democratic side. McAdoo was born in Georgia in the midst of the Civil War. He shared his father-in-law's sympathies to the Lost Cause and was quick to wall off Black workers in the Treasury Department he oversaw after Wilson segregated the federal workforce. He'd even allowed a cage of a sort to be assembled around one Black worker who needed to interact with his white colleagues. Coolidge, the new president, had not spoken out against the Klan, implying by his trademark silence that he would make no trouble. The party on Lake Erie ended with numerous pacts between Steve and his political lackeys, and big plans for the coming year. The Klan would be a major force at the national conventions. No one on board the *Reomar II* doubted that the future of the country belonged to an organization of shrouded men clinging to the past.

Imperial Wizard Evans had one more stopover before summer's end. He led a Klan march into Carnegie, a small town of mostly Irish Catholic steelworkers just outside Pittsburgh. On Saturday night, August 25, about 10,000 Klansmen gathered on a hill over-looking the town, cheered the initiation of another thousand into the hooded order, and burned an enormous cross. If the blaze on the hillside was meant to provoke, it had its intended effect. As darkness deepened, people poured out of their houses and gathered on a bridge where they would make a stand against a torchlight mass of Klansmen.

The white-sheeted army moved on to another bridge, a span ob-structed by a truck. They pushed the vehicle to one side. But now enough of the townspeople had arrived to block this entrance into Carnegie. They threw rocks and bricks and sticks and lumps of coal at the men in masks. The Klansmen hurled objects back at them. Glowing KKK letters were ripped from a car. A sheriff climbed atop his auto and ordered the Klansmen to disperse. They hooted at him. Evans was not going anywhere. His masked men started singing "Onward, Christian Soldiers" and vowed to take the town. Linking arms, they surged forward, spreading out quickly along the main street. In the stampede, one deputy nearly fell off the bridge. Another was trampled. From corners of darkness and chaos came bursts of light and gunfire, bullets zinging in both di-rections. Now it was a full-scale riot. Klansmen pulled guns from beneath their robes and fired them at residents of Carnegie. In the exchange, one man in a sheet was shot in the head and died on the spot. Only then did the crowd begin to disperse.

Stephenson showed up the next day to begin making a martyr of the murdered man. "Mourn, Klansmen, a brother has died," read the tribute in the *Imperial Night-Hawk*. "He died because he was an

American." There would be no cooperation with police; the code of silence born in the initiation rite would prevail. Without witness help, the authorities could not charge any member of the Invisible Empire for firing weapons within the city limits. They did arrest a Carnegie undertaker, Paddy McDermott, for shooting the Klansman, but an inquest jury could not find sufficient evidence to charge him. This gave the Klan even more fodder. A decent one-hundred-percenter had died at the hands of an Irish Catholic mob in the Klan's telling—all the more reason to keep these murderous immigrants from American small towns. At the same time, "Jewish, Catholic, Italian and Negro peoples" were allowed to march in Pittsburgh unmolested, Evans complained.

Back in Indianapolis, the Grand Dragon ordered up boldfaced headlines of the riot, claiming one hundred Klansmen had been injured, and offered a reward of $5,000 to help convict Paddy McDermott. Stephenson would use the Machine if he had to, and the uniformed police who took orders from the Klan, and all his new political minions, to bend the institutions of civil society to his will. As Asher observed, "There was no power that Stephenson feared at this time."

PART TWO

MONSTER OF THE MIDWAY

12.

Lord of the Manor

It was an eight-minute walk from the Stephenson compound at one end of University Avenue to the home of Madge Oberholtzer at the other. Their fates and that of the Klan would soon be entwined; for now, four long blocks separated them. The air was cleaner in Irvington than the capital city's factory haze, filtered by thick-armored hardwood trees that had taken up residence centuries ago. One native oak was nearly four hundred years old, and had such a leafy hold on the sky that it was given landmark status. Every house on the broad, winding lane had a story to tell, just like the village's namesake, Washington Irving. The writer of "The Legend of Sleepy Hollow" and "Rip Van Winkle" was honored with a bust in a hushed circle off the avenue. Surely unknown to Stephenson, he had chosen to live in a town with a heritage of open-mindedness. Irvington was founded by abolitionists. After the Civil War, Black and white students attended school together. Irvington's pride and joy, Butler, was one of the first colleges in the Midwest to enroll women, and to hire them as faculty. Catholics worshipped at Our Lady of Lourdes, a church of Gothic grandeur, soon to be a target of the Klan.

If you were lucky to live on University Avenue, with its mix of Italianate, Victorian, and Colonial Revival houses, you would never aspire to another home. The Oberholtzer residence was built for a doctor. After he died, a postal clerk at Union Station, George Oberholtzer, bought the three-floor Arts and Crafts–style house for $13,000, using his life savings and his wife's inheritance. Inside were a massive rock fireplace and built-in cabinets. Outside, the porch was a wonderful perch, situated to catch the evening breezes.

After graduating from Manual Training High School in Indianapolis, the only daughter of George and Matilda Oberholtzer enrolled at Butler College and pledged a sorority, Pi Beta Phi. She could walk from her house, passing the Irving bust in that peaceful garden circle where she used to stage impromptu plays as a girl, to the college's twenty-five-acre campus. Madge was bright, quick-witted, and strong-willed. She had dark, greenish eyes and was athletic—seemingly in perpetual motion. She loved dogs and made friends easily. She had shown talent as a painter, her skills honed during a scholarship at the Herron Art Institute. In college, she was mentored by suffragettes who argued in "Indiana nice" that denying women the vote deprived democracy of the wisdom of mothers and grandmothers. She was the opposite of a wallflower, as the Butler yearbook noted in a sarcastic write-up of her in 1917: "Madge is a timid little creature with a baby voice, who allows professional gruffness to frighten her into speechlessness, but once outside of the depressing influence of classroom walls she waxes adjectivorous and verbiforous and is able to hold at bay the most fluent masculine word-artist on the campus."

Madge spent three years at Butler, leaving at the end of her junior year, in June 1917. Just three months earlier, the United States had declared war on Germany. Time, which had moved so slowly in Indiana, took off in a gallop. Boys left Butler to become men in the war machine. Women assembled socks for soldiers in a classroom converted to a small knitting factory. At home, Madge tilled a victory garden, contributed her share of handmade hosiery for the troops *over there*, and took Red Cross training. At the end of that year, she took advantage of a wide-open wartime job market and was hired as a high school teacher in a small town. At the close of the school term, she moved back to Indianapolis, where she had her pick of employers—better options than returning to school. She worked as a clerk, an office manager, and a state employee.

Madge didn't need a husband or a church to tell her how to live. She dated frequently, and was selective, in no hurry to marry, though she was apparently engaged at one point. She was a woman of her age, pushing back against centuries of caged convention, game for a party, but serious about building a life of her own. In this decade of change, she could vote for a president. She could run for office. She could own property without needing a man's permission. She could order a drink at an underground club. She could even choose when to have children (a primitive cervical cap had been available for a decade).

In 1923, Madge bought a Ford Model T coupe and taught herself how to drive. The car gave her real independence. She gave up her job and talked her friend Ermina Moore into joining her on an adventure—a slow drive across the United States to California. There was no guarantee of following asphalt all the way. The new Lincoln Highway, stitching one coast to the other for the touring motorist, was continuously paved only from New York to Iowa. They would camp at night or find rooms in roadhouses. Women drivers were still rare. And even more scarce were women traveling half the length of the country on their own. Madge's sense of daring was matched by a cautious sense of invincibility. She pointed her way west in a machine she fired up every morning by a hand crank. She knew how to change a flat, return a steamed radiator to operation, read a bad situation at a late-night stop. The cross-country trip was exhilarating.

Two months on the open road of America drained her savings. She was much relieved, upon her return from California, to land a good job with the Young People's Reading Circle, in the state Department of Public Instruction. She rose quickly, becoming manager of a lending library for poor school districts. And it paid well, nearly $4,000 a year. Still, to save money and help out at home, Madge lived in a big room upstairs in the dream house her parents had bought in Irvington. Her father had assumed more mortgage than he could afford. To meet the monthly bill, he took in other boarders as well.

But now Madge's job was in jeopardy: her department was going to be eliminated by the legislative assembly. The times had gotten tougher, with a farm recession roiling businesses throughout the Midwest. In her walks, Madge had passed by the armed sentries, police dogs, and luxury cars clustered around Stephenson's compound. She had even been inside the place, back when another sorority held pledge parties there. Of late, the big house was a source of mystery and intrigue, the drapes always tightly drawn, people coming and going at all hours. The owner did nothing to clarify things; he was not exactly neighborly by the social standards of Irvington.

The *Indianapolis Star* had recently carried a lengthy profile of the Grand Dragon, based on a story that first appeared in a New York paper. "Mr. Stephenson is beyond doubt the ablest and most picturesque leader the Knights of the Ku Klux Klan ever had," the paper wrote. He was fabulously rich, as the article explained in some detail, born to wealthy parents. A college graduate. Went to law school as well. "With money to gratify any desire to entertain his retinue of friends, he enjoys his bachelorhood enormously." Madge hit on an idea: perhaps the solution to saving her job, and keeping the income that allowed her parents to hold on to their home, was the man inside the manor at 5432 University Avenue.

The Klan, on one level, represented nearly everything that Madge had been raised to reject. Her church, Irvington's Methodist Episcopal, supported missionaries abroad and aided poor women at home. At Butler, she had classmates who were Catholic, Black, and Jewish. Among the 304 students enrolled her freshman year were members of fourteen different faiths. She wasn't afraid of the New America; she lived it. And she certainly had no intention of lending support to the Invisible Empire. Her plan was strictly to ask for a favor from the man who controlled the state, who also happened to be an Irvington neighbor. Still, he *was* the leader of a violent hate group. The profile in the paper had painted the Grand Dragon as the relatively benign boss of Indiana, with Stephenson asserting that his "Klan is not based on racial, religious or other prejudice." That was a preposterous claim, easily disproven by a simple reading of the Klan oath. But Madge, like much of the state, like the fawning newspaper profile that dwelled on how "able" and "picturesque" he was, like those leading citizens and Bible-clutching pastors whose sleep was not disturbed by what had happened to Indiana, chose to do business with the Klansman rather than fight him.

Madge couldn't just knock on the door and barge into the mansion. Well, she could try, and had the bravado to consider it, but she would never make it past the guards and police dogs. Someone had to make an introduction. That someone was Stanley Hill, another state worker, a man she had dated but now considered a friend. Hill had talked to Steve a couple of times about Florida real estate opportunities, a side interest to both men. And he knew a guy who knew a guy who could help them. All she needed was a foot in the door; she could take it from there. After some thought, Madge Oberholtzer decided to try to talk her way into the inner circle of the Grand Dragon of the largest Klan realm in the world.

The parties were bacchanals of bad taste, and Stephenson spared no expense. Once through the classical columns of the mansion's white portico, guests left behind everything they professed to stand for in anticipation of a night like no other in Indiana. The evenings started out classy. White-gloved servants handed out drinks and finger foods. There were proper toasts and proper introductions. Troupers from a musical revue entertained and a small orchestra played in the ballroom. You were sure to see politicians, perhaps a federal judge, or someone from the Indianapolis baking company that claimed it had introduced sliced loafs to the world—Wonder Bread, as it was called. Among nearly seven hundred Protestant ministers who were honorary members of the Indiana Klan in 1924, a few of them could be found inside as well, minus their clerical collars. For drinks, Steve had anything you wanted— *anything.* Supply was unlimited and there was no need to fear a raid of the best-dressed and highest-standing lawbreakers in Indianapolis; the police had not only given Steve a pass on Prohibition but often served as his protectors.

While still sober and standing, the Grand Dragon would offer a tour of the palace he'd purchased in 1923. The Colonial Revival house was built in 1889 on a two-acre lot. Steve added the Ionic columns to make it look more like the mansion of a Southern plantation, and built the biggest garage in Irvington—a four-car brick detached unit with a second-floor apartment. The floors were golden oak, buffed to a diamond sheen. Stained-glass windows allowed a rainbow of light to pour in during the day. A grand piano was the centerpiece of the main parlor. Only the best people lived among these leafy lanes—a college president and bank owner on one side, a newspaper publisher or prominent doctor on another. *Now, look*:

here was an Oriental rug, worth more than the average American home, Steve noted. Upstairs, on the second of three floors, were five bedrooms, including a master with a brick-faced fireplace, and a guest chamber with walls of peacock blue and velvet drapes.

Steve liked to give speeches at these parties, though they could be hard to follow as he slurred his way through an inebriated oration. Guests remembered him predicting "a great revolution" soon to come, with Klan values dominant throughout the land, a Klan-altered Constitution guiding the country forward, and Klan politicians in control of government at every level. As the night wore on, the music got jumpier, the guests louder. Middle-aged men of privilege could be seen on corner couches in the embrace of somebody not their wife. Steve usually had a photographer circulating, given free access by his boss to take pictures of the most intimate situations. The photos proved very useful and helped to ensure that those in the know would not turn on their political master—a conspiracy of silence that proved remarkably successful. Late into the night at one party, a five-foot cake was brought in on a massive silver tray carried to the living room by four buff-looking men. Steve clapped his hands and asked the guests to circle around. After he cut the cake, a nude woman popped out.

"I saw girls and young married women dancing all but unclothed, their dresses torn from them, ripped into rags and tatters amid wild streaks of glee and maudlin attempts at song," one guest recalled. "The house rang with drunken shouts, abandoned laughter and wild outcries. Anything went."

At another party, Steve disappeared for an hour or more. Then the Lord of the Klan's Palace of the North reappeared in the form of a mythic satyr—his chest and sizable white belly bare, an animal's tail pinned to his behind. A circle dance formed. Naked women designated as wood nymphs pranced around Steve as he whipped them with a light lash. This went on for some time, until only a single nude was still standing. She would be his prize for the night.

"These parties would have shamed Nero," said Court Asher.

The new man in the big house unsettled many a nerve in Irvington. For a neighborhood that projected restrained elegance, it was jarring to have a strong-armed vulgarian move into one of the most prominent residences. People were never sure if one of their neighbors had taken the dark oath. When Klansmen were spotted in Irvington, they were impossible to identify. "They always had a hood on their head," recalled Bernice Glass, a student at Butler College whose family home was a block from Steve's mansion. "Nobody ever told you whether they were a member or not."

Early on, Butler had welcomed Black applicants. One of its former students, the musician and composer Noble Sissle, had produced a hit musical in 1921, *Shuffle Along*, before eventually teaming up with Eubie Blake and Lena Horne. He was a classmate of Madge's in 1915. "You didn't think about that colored boy being at Butler—he was just one of us," said Glass. But by the time Steve was staging his blowout parties late into the Irvington night, the Klan had infected the neighboring college, and had burned a cross of terror at the nearby Catholic church, Our Lady of Lourdes. In 1924, for the first time, the few Black students were not grouped alphabetically with all others in the Butler yearbook. They were relegated to a separate section in the back. Shortly thereafter, the school adopted a quota system, restricting Black enrollment to a tiny minority.

For Stephenson, the late-hours debauchery at his oversized home was political theater, a demonstration of his independence from the moral order his Klan dictated for everyone else. Ever since his groping of schoolgirls in Oklahoma, he'd been pushing the boundaries and getting away with more horrific behavior. Now he carried on with women he barely knew, while engaged to be married to several women at the same time. It required him to practice duplicity and charm in equal measure, something that had served him well since he'd set foot in Indiana. But in the spring of 1924, one of his fiancées found out about his multiple entanglements.

"It's a dangerous thing to have two engagement rings out at the same time," she wrote him. "I would like to know just how many girls you are keeping and just how many times a week you have them out to your house. A year ago you said, 'How would you like to be my girl?' Doesn't it get monotonous when you use that on so many?" She had discerned a pattern in his life of deception. After a few dates with a woman, he would propose marriage and purchase an engagement ring. He felt that this gave him license to have sex, or to be protected from legal challenges to his predations—as he tried to show when caught by the deputies at the roadside in Ohio. "Steve, you lied to me about getting married. You lied to me about being divorced. You lied about buying me a car." She considered telling the newspapers about the Old Man's true self, or going to the authorities about his links to bootleggers.

His binge drinking was also catching up with him. He checked into a hospital for treatment. A few days in, he started shaking, shivering, and sweating, with an irregular heartbeat—all symptoms of delirium tremens. At about the same time, he struck up an affair with Clela Hull, a dark-haired aspiring doctor. She was charmed by Steve, by the regular deliveries of roses and written compliments, the promises and outward generosity, but also strangely drawn to the dangerous elements of his character. He always kept a gun at his bedside. He told her he "controlled every court in Indiana." For $30, he could get someone to sign an affidavit to anything he dictated, he boasted. For $50, he could get a man killed.

Soon they were engaged as well. "I would like to go some place where there are not so many people who know me—Chicago, etc.—and just let loose," she wrote in a late-night letter to Steve. "I am so tired of being a good little girl as I have been all my life." In her months with the Grand Dragon, her view of humanity and the future had dimmed. "I have decided there isn't much in life anymore so why not get all we can out of it." But a day later, she changed her tone. "That letter was not me at all. I could never be the kind of person I said I wanted to be. I guess the devil got hold of me when I wrote that . . . Steve, I really do think a lot of you in spite of the fact that you deserted me, but unless you return the feeling I do not want to see you again. I would also like to have my umbrella I left in your car."

One night Steve drove one of his stenographers to the house of another off-and-on girlfriend, Margaret Reynolds. He gave the young woman pills that he said would make her feel happy. Instead, she felt faint.

"Don't let him do anything to me if I pass out," she said.

She did pass out, and woke up alone the next morning, her clothes on the floor, strange bite marks on parts of her body and some dried blood. *What was this?* She wondered if Stephenson had chewed on her. He may have raped her while she was knocked out, she told investigators a year later. "I don't know whether or not he had intercourse with me while I was unconscious," she said. But at the time, she was too scared to do anything. His reach into the cops and courts, he told her, was beyond anything she could imagine.

As the Invisible Empire approached the apex of its power, Stephenson was becoming ever more violent and sadistic. The Wizard of Indiana's Oz, who gave long speeches on the inferiority of other races and the superiority of white Protestants, was a creation that existed only on stage or in the pages of the *Fiery Cross*. The half-naked satyr, the rapist, the drunken flesh-chewer, the gangster and political dictator was the true and more brazen self. And with each passing month, he felt more unrestrained and less likely to keep up the mirage of a decent man.

At the start of 1924, Steve checked into room 931 of the Deshler Hotel in Columbus, one of the premier guest palaces in the Midwest, just off the square and steps from the bustling Ohio headquarters of the Klan. He started drinking whiskey late on that morning of January 5. His companions were two men, one a former officer with the Columbus Police Department. Around noon, Steve picked up the phone and asked if he could get a manicure. He wanted it done in his room, by a woman. The hotel sent up a young manicurist. She was taken aback by what she saw when she walked into room 931. All three men were drunk. Steve was in soiled pajamas. The room had been overturned, the bed unmade, wet towels on the floor. Three half-empty whiskey bottles—quart-sized—were on a table. When the manicurist entered, the two other men stepped outside the room, leaving Stephenson alone with his prey. He told the woman to have a drink. She refused. He patted the bed forcefully, held out one hand.

"How about that manicure?"

As she tried to back away, he lunged for the woman and held her tight. He wanted sex, and he wanted it now. She squirmed and yelled no. He said he would pay for it—$100 cash, on the spot. She gathered her things and tried to leave. Visibly angry, Steve screamed at her.

"You little bitch!"

He stumbled over to a table to get his gun.

"You'll have sex with me or I'll kill you."

She fled the room, running into the hallway in tears. She found a bellhop and told him what had happened. The guest in room 931 had tried to rape her, and would have assaulted her at gunpoint had she not escaped. The bellhop went to have a look. Once he was inside, Stephenson struck him in the face with his fist, knocking him to the ground. He continued to beat him as he crawled around. The bellboy got away and immediately notified security. A house detective called the police. When they arrived, he and three officers rushed upstairs to the ninth floor. The room was a mess. A large glass mirror was shattered into pieces. Chairs and bottles were smashed. The bellboy, who'd been waiting in the hallway, had welts and cuts on his bloodied face and was woozy from the whacks to his skull.

"He was as intoxicated as any man I ever saw," the security man said of one D. C. Stephenson. "He was standing by the bed with a death grip at the foot of the bed." The cops struggled to arrest Steve. Despite his diminished capacity, he forcefully resisted, screaming at the officers that he would not be taken; he was a powerful man, there would be hell to pay. At one point, he waved his gun at the hotel security officer. He threatened to sue the Deshler, to bring down the greatest luxury property of Columbus, Ohio. *He*, not the manicurist, was the victim.

The Grand Dragon spent twenty-five hours in the Columbus city jail. He vomited, passed out, wobbled back and forth, ranting and raving from behind bars. He summoned a big-time lawyer, the mayor of nearby Newark, Ohio—a prominent Klansman. His first task was to spring Steve from jail, quietly. The lawyer paid a $180 bond, and his client was released. Next the lawyer went to the Deshler and tried to ensure that none of this would get out. But it was too late. On January 6, stories of the drunken sexual assault and melee were splashed across the front pages of the Sunday editions of two Columbus papers.

Imperial Wizard Evans was furious—not so much at the criminal act of his fellow commander, but at what the story would do to the image of an organization that claimed to stand for protecting the purity of women. He ordered an internal investigation and a secret tribunal.

Because of Stephenson's prominence, his actions "caused the public to look down upon the Klan," Evans's men wrote later. "He was understood, in the state of Ohio, to be the absolute authority of Klan activity and the man in whose hands the entire future of the organization rested."

But once again, Stephenson's crime went unpunished. He tried to silence the manicurist; it was an old habit by now, buying off his victims. Without her testimony, the case would be hard to prove. He sent a man, who said he was a doctor, to explain things away to the woman. *You see*, he said, it wasn't Mr. Stephenson, but the booze. "He is a dandy fellow and he would not have done what he did had he been sober." Steve offered to pay his victim a month's salary if she would write a statement saying he had not attacked her. She refused. But because she was engaged and worried about what her fiancé would think if she had to go through a trial with a man who would try to destroy her, she backed off.

The case disappeared. Instead of prison, the Grand Dragon went back to Indianapolis to expand his power and resume his old habits. Once again, Indiana embraced him, even after news of his assault had made its way into the state. Stephenson said it was a setup by his enemies, a smear. The papers had it all wrong. Ministers did not give up their Klan robes or turn on their leader in Sunday sermons. Elected officials did not distance themselves from their political master. Most newspapers did not condemn. Membership in the Invisible Empire did not decline. Cross burnings did not stop. All the right people did not turn down invitations to parties in Irvington. Hoosier Klansmen were not repulsed by his behavior, at least not outwardly. Many chose selective amnesia, in service to the greater good of the Invisible Empire and what it stood for. Some were even impressed. For here was a man liberated from shame, a man who not only boasted of being able to get away with any violation of human decency for his entire life, but had just proved it for all to see.

13.

Rage of the Resistance

One man and his newspaper could have, most certainly would have, pummeled the Grand Dragon for what he did in Columbus. He'd have called out the political class, the evangelical supporters, the silent editors and pillars of the community. Patrick O'Donnell's crusade to crush the Klan had become his life. But he was out of business in 1924, his paper shuttered after barely two years of operation. The year before, he had run a string of fresh exposés, revealing Klan membership throughout the Midwest under a recurring feature: "Is Your Neighbor a Kluxer?" The answer to that question drove subscriptions—*Tolerance* reached a peak circulation of 150,000. O'Donnell's informants inside the highest reaches of the Klan were bringing him meaty stories and new lists of members.

"I had a conference with people who are helping me to overthrow the Ku Klux Klan," he wrote the president of Notre Dame, the

Reverend Matthew J. Walsh, in mid-1923, warning of threats against the university. "I have obtained the most secret document that has yet been obtained by any agency and it reveals the startling strength of the Klan," O'Donnell told Walsh in another letter at year's end. The report was from minutes of a meeting of the Klan's other Grand Dragons, organized by D. C. Stephenson. And indeed, the numbers were staggering, even if exaggerated or counting women—nearly 400,000 Klan in Indiana, more than 200,000 in Michigan and Ohio, 75,000 in Minnesota. His sources told him that Stephenson was planning to "pull loose from the Evans crowd" in Atlanta and make the national Klan his own. Though Steve and Evans were feuding, the rift remained an inside secret. But O'Donnell caught wind of the clash that would split Klan leadership at its highest level. The Imperial Wizard's refusal to purchase Valparaiso University had incensed Stephenson. He would not let it go. He started disparaging Evans around other Klansmen. The college was crucial to his dream of an empire in the North. It fell to the Lutherans to save the vine-covered school from bankruptcy and the clutches of Steve's Klan.

O'Donnell warned Father Walsh that *his* college was still very much on the minds of Klan leadership: it was a target of a future terror attack. Through poison squad plants, the Klan was laying the groundwork, claiming that the university had a cache of weapons hidden under the campus—guns for the assault on pure Americans by papal forces. O'Donnell told the school president about a document he'd seen outlining plans to blow up Notre Dame's Golden Dome by dropping a bomb from an airplane.

Even in South Bend, with its large number of Catholics and

immigrants, Stephenson could count on thousands of Klansmen. The rallies and cross burnings near the campus increased, as did the campaign to bring down O'Donnell. The *Fiery Cross* published a pamphlet: "Intolerance: An Expose of Patrick H. O'Donnell." That didn't stop O'Donnell. It only made him more determined.

But what did stop him was the nation's best-known chewing gum magnate, William Wrigley Jr. He'd made a fortune selling his own Juicy Fruit and Spearmint gum for pennies a pack. In 1920, he bought the Chicago Cubs and built a towering landmark on the north bank of the Chicago River, the Wrigley Building. In 1923, O'Donnell was handed a Klan initiation form with a signature of William Wrigley at the bottom. He rushed it into print. It was sensational news. Thousands stopped purchasing Wrigley's gum and vowed to stay away from Cubs games. But the Klan form was a fabrication. O'Donnell had been tricked. Wrigley sued him for $50,000. After O'Donnell's source admitted in court that the signature was forged, the anti-Klan crusader was doomed. *Tolerance* was forced out of business. O'Donnell lost his credibility, his money, and his voice. He was a broken man. "The opposition," wrote the *New York Times*, "now appears leaderless."

Having defeated his most persistent enemy, Stephenson decided to make a move on Notre Dame. He called for a three-state show of Klan strength in South Bend in the spring of 1924. The Grand Dragon felt it was vital to crush the remaining pockets of resistance. "The fiery cross is going to burn at every crossroads in

Indiana as long as there is a white man left in the state," he said. He was also livid after Evans had conducted an internal investigation into his behavior, and wanted to show him that the boss of the North was not to be challenged.

The school had been founded by six priests, four of them Irish immigrants, in a clearing above the St. Joseph River in 1842. The chaplain of the storied Irish Brigade in the Civil War, Reverend William Corby, expanded the college, adding the nation's first Catholic law school during his years as president. By 1924, Notre Dame had a campus enrollment of 1,600 students, including many veterans from the Great War. Its football team under Knute Rockne lost just a single game in 1923 and set a goal of going undefeated this year. Catholics throughout the country followed every contest. Tuition was $100 a semester. The clerics enforced mandatory morning and evening prayers on their all-male student body, and insisted on lights-out at ten p.m. The Golden Dome, rising nearly two hundred feet over South Bend, glowed throughout the night.

Klansmen started pouring into town on Friday evening, May 16, many wearing their white robes as they stepped off the train in South Bend. A group of Notre Dame students pointed them into dead ends and out toward the edge of town, deliberately misdirecting them.

"Are you here for the parade? This way."

The Klansmen were free to assemble, but not to stage a march through town; fearing violence, the police chief had denied a permit. Father Walsh had sent out a memo confining students to campus for the weekend. He wanted no trouble. But the appearance of so many masked invaders who had slandered these young men, their faith, and their school had roused the Notre Dame student body to defy Walsh's order.

On Saturday morning, a day darkened by brooding clouds, the Klan gave notice that they intended to stage a parade—permit be damned. The police chief notified the governor, requesting help from the National Guard. Steve showed up before noon. With two bodyguards on either side of him, he gave a speech in a park by the river, unleashing his usual churn of contempt, with an extra dose of anti-Catholicism. Then it started to rain, drowning his words and dampening the robes of the Klansmen. At midafternoon, about 2,000 wet men in white milled through the streets of downtown South Bend, passing by the memorial to those in St. Joseph County who'd been killed by the Confederacy in the Civil War. Before the Klansmen could get much farther, a flying wedge of Notre Dame students sliced into them, causing panic and knocking dozens to the ground. Guns were fired in the air. Fistfights broke out. The students tore off Klan robes and waved them high as trophies. They took the hoods and put them on their own heads—dunce caps, they said, chiding the Klansmen. One student was knocked to the ground by a baseball bat. The panicked Klansmen dashed to their headquarters in the city, a turreted building at the corner of Michigan and Wayne. They bolted the doors and rushed upstairs to the third floor, behind an electric cross lit with red bulbs. By this time, Steve had fled, making a beeline back to Indianapolis in his touring car.

At the base of the building was a small grocery store. The students purchased two bushels of potatoes as weapons. They hurled the spuds at the windows, trying to break the glass, or to put out the lights of the Klan's symbol. Irish American boys rioting with the iconic food of their tribe—it was enough to make some laugh at the image. Catholics had put up with years of abuse; they'd been called un-American and told they didn't belong in this country, and certainly not in the state of Indiana. They'd been shunned as dupes of a Roman plot, and slaves of the pope. Now they had their tormentors surrounded, hiding and fearful. The Klan had planned to force Notre Dame into submission, to let these Catholics know that even here, in the safety of their campus, they had much to fear and nowhere to hide. The opposite had happened. It was said by those in the crowd that Notre Dame's star quarterback, Harry Stuhldreher, one of the vaunted Four Horsemen, lobbed a perfect strike upward, his potato scoring a direct hit on one of the bulbs lighting the Klan cross. A roar followed. A group of Notre Dame men broke through the door of the building and charged upstairs. Only when met by a Klansman with a drawn gun did the students retreat. By dusk, the police had made eight arrests and were able to disperse most of the crowd. The Sunday edition of the *Chicago Herald and Examiner* carried the news in a front-page banner, as if touting an upset win by Rockne's footballers:

STUDENTS ROUT KLANSMEN

On Monday, about five hundred students gathered outside Klan headquarters as the building emptied. Klansmen waved their guns and threw bottles and rocks at the kids. The students heaved them back. Father Walsh put himself between the two sides. He mounted a Civil War memorial cannon, called for calm, and ordered the Notre Dame enrollees to turn the other cheek and return to campus. "Whatever insult has been offered to your religion, ignore them," he said. It was a gutsy move by a war veteran and priest who had much to be aggrieved about after the continuous insults of the Klan. His appeal for calm didn't prevent a flow of nasty letters to him threatening the school and deriding the campus as a haven for "mackerel-snapping anarchists."

"Not even a Negro has done what you Roman Catholics have done to disgrace the flag," wrote one man, who signed his letter "A Klansman."

Another informed the school president that the college was lucky to be intact. Next time, "we'll wipe the Notre Dame buildings off the face of the earth."

"You dirty, un-American skunks will pay for your mob actions in South Bend," threatened the *Fiery Cross*. The paper urged lawmakers to take away the school's tax-exempt status and warned of sanctions to come. "We showed you a few tricks at the recent primary and we are going to show you more at the election in the fall."

News accounts of the riot would give rise to a story that still lives, that the "Fighting Irish" nickname was forever set by the clash of Notre Dame against the Ku Klux Klan on May 17, 1924.

It is a fact that few Hoosiers dared to stand up to the KKK," wrote Irving Leibowitz, the midcentury Indiana historian. And yet there were several people who continually battled the Invisible Empire at the height of its power. In Evansville, the freshman congressman William E. Wilson spoke out forcefully. He'd been warned by Senator Ralston that if he expected to stay in office, he damn well better take a vow and bow to the Ku Klux Klan. Wilson told his son that his defiance would kill him at the polls.

"A lot of good, honest but misguided people have turned against me," he said. But why, his boy wondered, after all he'd been able to do for his district, including bringing home federal dollars for a bridge across the Ohio River.

"It isn't what I've done that counts. It's what I refused to do."

"What's that?"

"Join the Klan." The congressman's home had been vandalized and its windows broken. Callers threatened his life and that of his family. Neighbors shunned him. People he thought he knew had shown a streak of ugliness. "We've gone a long way in this country," he said to his son. "But apparently we haven't freed men and women of their suspicion of each other, their prejudices, their intolerance. I think it's going to be a big battle in this century. My little fight here in Indiana is just a preliminary skirmish."

Black Hoosiers who'd come to Indiana as part of the Great Migration warned that the skirmish, as the congressman called it, was entering a dangerous new phase. Indiana was fast becoming the Alabama of the North. But maybe, some pointed out, it had long been the Alabama of the North, and it was wishful thinking to expect otherwise simply because it was outside the old Confederacy.

The NAACP drew a red line. James W. Johnson, the national secretary who'd given that rousing speech on Black culture a year earlier in Indianapolis, wrote a strong letter to Coolidge. He demanded that the president denounce what was going on in Indiana. The Klan, as he noted later, was now "blot[ting] the light from the skies for the Negro" and must be stopped before it could grow by another hooded man. As a boy growing up in Jacksonville, Florida, Johnson had first shaken the hand of a president, reaching out to touch Ulysses S. Grant during a parade in 1877. He'd considered Teddy Roosevelt a friend. He despised Woodrow Wilson for turning back the clock on progress for African Americans, and found him stiff and hypocritical in person. Coolidge was colder still, and their only meeting had been awkward.

"I was expecting that he would make, at least, an inquiry or two about the state of mind and condition of the twelve million Negro citizens of the United States," Johnson wrote, "but it was clear that Mr. Coolidge knew absolutely nothing about the colored people."

Johnson had been trying, without success, to get Congress to make lynching a federal crime. The NAACP had compiled a grim record of these executions. They found that Black citizens had been hanged for "talking back to whites," and "not driving out of the road" to let white motorists pass. Among the victims over a thirty-year span were more than fifty Black women. The nation was at a hinge moment, he felt. "At no time since the days following the Civil War had the Negro been in a position where he stood to make greater gain or sustain greater loss in status." For more than fifty years, Black voters had been the most reliable Republicans. It was time for a Republican president to do something in return—even if all it amounted to was a statement of disgust over the reach of the Ku Klux Klan.

"Colored people throughout the United States, but especially in the North, are waiting for an unequivocal statement from you as head of the Republican Party on the Ku Klux Klan," Johnson wrote Coolidge. The president ignored his plea. Still, Johnson would not give up. With each passing day that Coolidge remained silent, Johnson alerted the press, keeping pressure on the White House. If Coolidge continued to shun him, Johnson was ready to make the larger move—using the leverage of the Black vote to show politicians at the highest level that they could not take African Americans for granted.

In Muncie, George Dale would not give up his part of the fight. After his time in prison, after getting assaulted twice by Klan thugs, his family threatened, he continued to tangle with the mighty octopus controlling Indiana. Dale was nearly bankrupt, his credit no longer good at the grocery store, his paper running on fumes. He'd been forced to sell his home to stay afloat. In Muncie, the "Constitution had ceased to function," wrote the *Chicago Tribune*, after the Klan had established a "super-government" not based on the rule of law. But so long as Dale still had an ounce of ink to spill, he spilled it on the Kluxers, as he called them. His latest target was Daisy Barr. Mother was unassailable going into 1924, just like her mentor Stephenson. Women of the Ku Klux Klan had grown to more than a million members nationwide.

Taking a page from Steve's book, she had cut a side deal with Imperial Wizard Evans that paid her $4 for every initiation fee from a new member of the women's Klan. That, plus a big part of the female robe sales. Word of her windfall got out after she was sued by a rival Klanswoman and investigated before a grand jury for embezzlement. Dale broke the news: Mother's morality campaign was a big grift—like the Klan itself. The Muncie editor blasted out a series of headlines on how Daisy Barr had fleeced women in the Midwest. She became a millionaire, he wrote, as "an imperial nighty peddler." He made fun of her in a front-page poem:

> *Perhaps you think that Daisy's flighty*
> *But she got it all at ten per nighty*
> *A million bucks she got, 'tis said*
> *And gave to the wizard nary a red.*

At the same time, Rabbi Morris Feuerlicht, who'd been rallying the small community of Indiana Jews to fight back, went after Barr and other anti-Semites. He was fed up with attempts by the Klan to make life unbearable for Jews—from petty shaming to "brazen terrorist tactics," as he called the burning crosses of intimidation. The Klan led a successful boycott of a hit film playing in Indianapolis theaters, *Potash and Perlmutter*, because the leading characters were Jews. Worst of all were the continued campaigns to force Jewish-owned retailers out of business. In Muncie, the rabbi and the editor joined forces, backing a leading lawyer to take on the

Klan judge in an upcoming election. But that judge, Dale's enemy Clarence Dearth, made a direct appeal to Indiana's worst instincts in the campaign:

"Do you want a miserable Jew to sit in judgment upon you?" he said. The answer was no—the Klan judge won easily.

Feuerlicht was more successful against Barr. The state had proposed building a hospital in Indianapolis for exclusive use by white Protestants; it would be named the Daisy Barr Home and guided by a board of directors appointed by Women of the Ku Klux Klan. As the first Jewish member of the Board of State Charities, Rabbi Feuerlicht led a public campaign to prevent it from going ahead. The furor he generated was strong enough to stop the Daisy Barr Home before a single brick was laid. That defeat, Dale's constant ridicule, and revelations about how much Mother made from every woman she ushered into the Klan sent Barr into retreat in 1924. She left the state the next year and never returned.

The Klan resistance missed one of the biggest stories during the Empire's rule over Indiana. Stephenson and his dutiful secretary of state, Ed Jackson, had been plotting a move on the governor, Warren T. McCray, ever since the party on the yacht in the summer of 1923. McCray was a wealthy farmer and cattle breeder, but by 1923 he was broke and deep in debt after the farm recession. He used his leverage as governor to borrow money and dig himself a deeper hole, one a grand jury would soon be looking into. Jackson was the odds-on favorite to replace McCray in 1924. But why not get something from the wounded incumbent before he left? With his nose for exploiting human weakness, Steve cooked up a scheme to bribe the governor with $10,000 in cash. What he wanted was simple: a Klan district attorney in Marion County, the state's most populous.

"Ten grand is a lot of money," said one insider after the Grand Dragon outlined the plan.

"I know what I'm talking about," Steve replied. "I have an organization in this state so complete that I can tell you today what any man you can name does tomorrow."

Stephenson sent the secretary of state to the governor's office with a suitcase stuffed with cash. But McCray, soon to be indicted for embezzlement, showed surprising steel.

"You can take your money back to your office, Ed," he told Jackson. He'd lost everything, he said. He was a ruined man, destitute, likely bound for prison. "But I will never surrender my integrity. Take your money and get out."

Instead of naming a Klan prosecutor, the governor appointed William H. Remy, a graduate of DePauw University and Indiana Law School, a war veteran. Remy had planned to be a book editor. But after his discharge from the army, he visited the centers of publishing in the East and didn't like what he saw. "On Christmas Eve I went to Boston," he wrote in his account of the times, "and hardly a word of English was spoken." He said Slavs, Jews from Hungary and Russia, Poles, Italians, and "many Irish" were pouring into the country after the war. He struggled with his own feelings. Back home in Indiana, people who were "predominantly Protestant, white, gentile and native born" had developed "a great resentment" against the aspiring new Americans. He understood why they joined the Ku Klux Klan—they were deeply afraid of change. But after seeing the world beyond Indiana, Remy had resolved to live with it. He was thirty-two when appointed prosecutor. The Klan quickly tried to co-opt him. Stephenson sent the party chairman to visit Remy, a fellow Republican, with a list of Klan-approved lawyers to appoint as deputy prosecutors. Remy wouldn't even look at the list.

"I am going to drive you out of politics in Marion County," Remy told the Klan emissary. *Well then*, this upstart wouldn't last long in office, the chairman replied. Remy was no longer welcome at party headquarters or party meetings, and certainly not at any of the lavish parties at the mansion in Irvington. He had no future in Indiana. Stephenson would see to that.

14.

The Klan on Top

1924

By mid-1924, seemingly nothing could slow the march of the Invisible Empire across the United States. In cities big and small, North and South, the blazing cross had become as much a part of life as the soda fountain and the barbershop pole. More than 10,000 turned out for a Klan picnic in Colorado. The Klan terrorized Jewish, Italian, Black, and Latino neighborhoods in Denver, and could count on brothers under the sheets in law enforcement to avoid arrest. "They paid ten dollars to hate someone," said a Denver judge, "and they were determined to get their money's worth." Thousands flocked to a Klan rally in Washington state, where a speaker said the order was now "the biggest, best and strongest movement in American life." In Kansas, two years after the governor had warned of "the curse that rises out of unrestricted passions of men governed by religious intolerance and racial hatred," Klan membership hit an all-time high of 60,000 people.

There, the Klan vandalized Catholic cemeteries, threatened to attack Black families who moved into white neighborhoods, and got a high school instructor fired for teaching a class in jazz dancing.

For Indiana, Stephenson wanted to prove that the Klan could win an election without masking its intent. Thanks to his horse thief brigade, the Grand Dragon now had files on nearly every voter and politician. These dossiers were given to the Klan's county leaders, who made house visits pushing the hate slate. The first big test of the Machine's ability to control the state was in the May primary. For governor, of course, the Klan's man was the Klansman— Ed Jackson. But another Republican, Indianapolis mayor Lew Shank, was rallying what remained of the anti-Klan forces in his party.

The Klansman won the primary in a rout. There was no subterfuge, no hidden message; it was all out in the open—a straight choice, "for or against the Klan," as the *Indianapolis Times* wrote.

"It seems the people want Klan rule," said Shank, the defeated Republican. "So we'll give it to them."

Nationwide, when members of the secretive society opened their daily newspapers they found that their prayers to a discriminatory God had been answered. The last of the big three issues that had driven membership to unprecedented heights was resolved in the Klan's favor. Congress passed an immigration measure that slammed the door on those who could never meet the Klan's definition of one hundred percent American. Strict quotas on shunned countries slashed new arrivals from eastern and southern Europe to a bare trickle, shutting out Jews and olive-skinned Catholics. The new law made it impossible for someone from Japan to come to America legally, and tightened the already harsh ban on Chinese. Africa was shut out as well. After all the speeches and essays about eugenics and human imperfections, after the crusades against the criminality of the *mongrel hordes*, the hooded order got everything it wanted. The National Origins Act of 1924, a Klan-blessed master design for the future of America, passed in the House by an overwhelming margin and sailed through the Senate with only six dissenting votes. Though historic moments often slip by without notice at the time, this huge plot point in the national narrative was marked by a banner headline in the *New York Times*:

AMERICA OF THE MELTING POT COMES TO AN END

The law's quota system was based on the census of 1890, before most southern European and Polish Catholics, and Jewish refugees from pogroms in the East, had crossed the Atlantic. As it happened, the best way to build a wall was to turn back the clock. America would be replenished with people who looked like the ethnic face of Indiana—a blueprint for a bloodstream. The effect was immediate and dramatic. In 1921, nearly a quarter million Italians had fled their country for the United States. By 1925, that number fell by 90 percent. About 200,000 Russian Jews arrived on American shores in 1921. A year after passage of the Immigration Act, only 7,000 were let into the country. Greeks went from 46,000 in one year to a few hundred. Left behind in Poland were 3.5 million Jews who would be targeted with mass execution in little more than a decade. Also among those denied entry because of restrictions on Jews was the family of Anne Frank.

The law would shape the face of America for much of the twentieth century. Though the Klan took credit for "wielding a mighty influence" in Congress, they had plenty of help from people who never took the secret oath. Voting with the Klan was the easy thing to do, for the backlash against immigration had reached a point where a majority in office was ready to close the gates.

Now it was on to the presidential election. The Invisible Empire would be anything but hidden as the two major parties nominated their candidates. A Klansman in the White House was perhaps out of reach for now. Stephenson's personal timeline called for him to run in 1928. But a Klan insider for vice president was possible. Steve invited a few of his favorite politicians to join him on the *Reomar II*, sailing from Toledo to the Republican National Convention in Cleveland. They were met by a delegation of nearly sixty members of the hooded order, headed by Imperial Wizard Evans. He was flying high just before *Time* magazine put him on the cover, dubbing the Republican national gathering the "Kleveland Konvention." Steve's pick for veep was his loyal supplicant, Senator James Watson of Indiana. But when Jewish, Catholic, and Black delegates got wind of this plan, they threatened to upset the quiet coronation of Coolidge for a second term. The nomination of Sunny Jim was tabled.

Both parties needed the millions of voters who veiled themselves under pointed hoods. But should the Klan's enemies—chief among them, Republican Black voters—peel away, that could upset the electoral balance. Johnson's threat was real. Once again, the head of the NAACP demanded a condemnation of the mass of swollen malignancy that was the Ku Klux Klan of 1924, something Stephenson and Evans would never stand for. The party leaders stood with the hooded order, killing an attempt to pass an anti-Klan plank in the Republican platform before it ever got to a vote. This move, and whispered pledges that Coolidge would not attack the Klan, was assurance enough. Steve sailed back to his yacht's safe harbor in mid-June feeling satisfied, despite his ever-mounting tensions with Evans. They were no longer speaking to each other. Stephenson would try to win every major office in Indiana. Then he would plot his own path around Evans, to the Senate and beyond.

The Democrats were another story. The Klan nearly brought down the national convention, held in the smelly, airless torpor of New York City's Madison Square Garden in early summer. The Invisible Empire arrived with the most powerful single bloc in the party—nearly a third of all delegates. And they were not a confederation of Southerners. The fastest-growing faction, comprising 40 percent of all Klan members, came from just three states—Indiana, Ohio, and Illinois, Stephenson's turf.

In New York, which Evans had called "the most un-American city in the United States," the Imperial Wizard set up shop on the fifteenth floor of the McAlpin Hotel, in a five-room suite. The Klan's preferred Democratic ticket was William McAdoo, the former

Treasury secretary and Woodrow Wilson's son-in-law, paired with Senator Ralston from Indiana. But Ralston, who weighed more than three hundred pounds, was clearly not well. The Klan was united against New York governor Al Smith, a Catholic who fought Prohibition and was favored by many Northern Democrats. Under no circumstances would the Empire allow Smith, "from Jew York City," in the Klan's taunt, to be the nominee.

Before the actual balloting, the Klan had to contend with Senator Oscar Underwood of Alabama, a moderate man of the South whose father had fought for the Union in the Civil War. Underwood put forth a plank in the party platform, similar to the one that never came to a vote in Cleveland, condemning the Klan's philosophy. The language was simple: the Democratic Party would pledge to oppose efforts by any organization to "interfere with the religious liberty or political freedom of any citizen or . . . body of citizens because of religion, birthplace or racial origin." Yet affirming this basic statement of American principles turned the convention upside down.

Nearly all the delegates were white, in keeping with party rules that prohibited Black Democrats from attending the national convention in an official capacity until this year. But there was no brotherhood of race at the 1924 gathering. The anti-Klan faction chanted, "Ku-Ku McAdoo!" Fistfights broke out. Small rockets were lit and aimed at rivals. The cops were called to break up brawls, and firemen rushed inside to keep Madison Square Garden from going up in flames. As a show of support, 20,000 Klansmen in full white regalia marched with torches one night in New Jersey.

They strung up a straw effigy of Al Smith and beat it to a pulp before setting it afire.

For one long day that went into the early dawn hours, Democrats debated the merits of the Klan on the muggy floor of the Garden. William Jennings Bryan, the populist and three-time presidential nominee of the party, spoke out against the resolution. When a vote was finally taken, the Klan prevailed by a single digit, getting 542 against the resolution condemning Klan values to 541 for it. That was a day, said Will Rogers, "when I heard the most religion preached, and the least practiced."

The convention was a broken mess. Nobody could agree on a candidate. Half the delegates loathed the other half. McAdoo led in the early voting, but without the needed majority. Other candidates rose and fell, among them Senator Ralston, the Klan toady. At one point he got 196 votes for the nomination. Some delegates went home, unable to pay their hotel bills. It took 103 ballots and sixteen days—the longest political convention by a major party in American history—to arrive at a candidate. At last, an unassuming former ambassador to the United Kingdom, John W. Davis of West Virginia, was named the standard-bearer. He would be crushed in November. It didn't matter to the Klan. Its members left New York feeling smug and victorious. They were on a roll. They'd shown they could nearly bring down one of the two major political parties.

A few weeks later, Evans embarked on a triumphant tour of new chapters in the West. He was given a police escort to a welcoming at City Hall in Denver, toasted by Scottish Rite Masons in Spokane, honored at the Masonic Temple in Tacoma, and feted at a

Chamber of Commerce luncheon in downtown Seattle. The Klan had staged large rallies in Spokane and outside Seattle over the summer. Evans was awed by the growth in the Rocky Mountains and the West Coast, while lamenting that "some of the Eastern states are lost to true Americanism." Denver had 30,000 Klansmen; Portland at least 15,000.

In early October, more than 5,000 delegates from around the country gathered in Kansas City for the Klan's second national convention. "This Klonvocation, held here in the great Middle West, is assembled on the battlefield of the immediate future," said Evans. "You are of superior blood. You are leaders of the only movement in the world, at present, which exists solely to establish a civilization that will ensure these things."

But the Indiana Grand Dragon was not invited to Kansas City. His fight with Evans had turned to open warfare over money, power, and control. Evans had decided to oust his rival. With little public explanation, he expelled Stephenson from the national Klan. Stephenson was unbowed. Instead of taking his millions and moving on, he announced the formation of his own Northern Klan. He'd built the membership to record heights; now he wanted to formally own it. Steve had been working on expanding the Klan's reach through his own movies and records. He'd recorded discs at Gennett studios and sold them through the *Fiery Cross*. He'd hired several actors and a director to put together Klan motion pictures. Now he summoned the horse thief detectives, the regional Klan captains, the politicians and ministers to assemble at Cadle Tabernacle for his second crowning.

"With ninety-two percent of its citizenship native born and of the best blood and traditions of the nation, Indiana has a contribution of her own to make instead of outside control," Stephenson told the delegates. He named himself Grand Dragon of a new Ku Klux Klan, independent of Atlanta, answering only to him. Dues and membership money would still flow his way. But he'd also expanded his shakedown and graft schemes to such an extent that steady money was coming in from multiple sources—all of it dependent on his clutch over the nation's largest Klan society.

"We're going to Klux Indiana as she's never been Kluxed before!" he shouted. He went on a tirade against Evans, implying that he was controlled by Jews and Catholics—and was a hayseed, to boot. "The present head is an ignorant, uneducated, uncouth individual who picks his nose at the table and eats his peas with his knife."

That fall, the Grand Dragon of newly independent Indiana dispatched thousands of Klansmen to deliver a sample yellow ballot, folded and held together by a clothespin, labeled "The Right Ticket to Vote." The instructions for the November general election were dropped at the doors of voters who'd already been put on notice by regional operatives. At the top of the ticket was Jackson. At the same time, Stephenson's message to the Black community was a threat by masked men with torches into the heart of African American neighborhoods.

Black residents of Indianapolis were outraged. They had stood by the Republican Party since being given the vote. But the GOP of 1924 was not the party of Lincoln. When no help—not even a word—arrived from President Coolidge, the city's Black leaders rebelled. They formed a breakaway political bloc and vowed to vote Democratic for the first time. They staged a massive march of their own down Indiana Avenue, 5,000 strong, with banners blasting the Klan. More than 7,000 people filled Tomlinson Hall for a rally and speeches—going ahead despite threats by the authorities to close the hall and arrest everyone inside. The voices of Black Republicans, whose lives, dignity, and intelligence had been insulted on a daily basis, would be muffled no more.

"The Negro and the Republican Party have come to a parting of the way," announced the local office of the NAACP.

Johnson, the national secretary, had been urging a break for months, after Coolidge's ongoing snub of his request that the president condemn the Klan. Jim Crow was a bipartisan crime. Both political parties were guilty of a "gentleman's agreement," Johnson said, that denied the vote to 4.5 million Black citizens in the South. He noted that the 18th Amendment, outlawing alcohol, was fully enforced with regular raids, while the 15th Amendment, upholding the right to vote regardless of race, was given no protection. "The federal government will use a navy to prevent a man from taking a drink, but will not empower a deputy marshal to protect the Negro's ballot," said Johnson.

Though neither party had taken a stand against the Klan, Republicans in the North had allied themselves with the enemy of every African American. Now it was the "duty" of Black voters everywhere to rise up against them for the first time, Johnson said. But they didn't have to back the Democratic Party, either.

"Keep the politicians guessing," he said.

Inspired by Johnson, George L. Knox, born enslaved twenty years before the Civil War, a business owner, newspaper publisher, and the most respected and powerful African American in the state, roused himself for one last fight. He was eighty-four and ailing.

"The Republican Party as now constituted is the Ku Klux Klan of Indiana," he wrote in his influential paper, the *Indianapolis Freeman*. "The nominees for governor, house, the senate and city offices are all Klansmen." The ballot, he said, "is the only weapon of a civilized people and it is up to the Negro to use that weapon as do other civilized groups."

Stephenson was not impressed. The Black population was too small in number to stop the freight train he was running through the Heartland. But just in case, he bribed a handful of Black community leaders to suppress the vote. And a poison squad plant spread the word that Black federal workers, mainly postmen, would be fired if they didn't back the Klan ticket.

Hoosiers couldn't say they didn't know what they were voting for. Because of Stephenson, they knew *exactly* what they were voting for. Ten days before the election, he had issued a statement to the national press: "The eyes of the Nation are upon Indiana. Klansmen from all over the Nation are watching and wanting Indiana to win." A screaming headline across the front of the *Indianapolis*

Times pleaded with voters to come to their senses: NO SECRET OR-DER SHALL RULE INDIANA! The paper noted that its owner and managers were Protestants, but were appalled at the prospect of state rule by a hate group. The choice was government of the people or government by the Klan.

On the eve of the election, a reporter paid Stephenson a visit. The Grand Dragon was smoking a cigar, feet on his desk, sipping from a flask. He was asked what the outcome for governor would be on Election Day.

"We'll win by about 80,000 votes."

The margin was 82,000. But for the first time, the Black vote went Democratic—by three to one. It was the start of a tectonic political realignment, in Indiana and elsewhere. Johnson had forced a divorce. Never again could Republicans count on a monolithic vote from African Americans.

Elsewhere, the Empire elected not just a governor in Colorado, Clarence Morley, but a United States senator, Rice Means. In Denver, an oath-bound Klansman, Ben Stapleton, survived a recall election in a city where one in seven voters had taken the same vows. "I will work with the Klan and for the Klan," he pledged afterward. "I shall give the Klan the kind of administration it wants." As promised, he named a Klan police chief and filled the prosecutor's office and law enforcement with fellow brothers under the hood. The new governor promptly launched a campaign against Catholic sacramental wine—an attempted ban that would effectively outlaw the Mass in Colorado. In Illinois, the Klan put dozens of legislators into the chamber. "We know we're the balance of power in the state," boasted Illinois Grand Dragon Charles Palmer, an attorney.

In the nation's capital, the Klan purchased a building and staffed it with sixty members.

"We can control the United States Senate," Evans told his associates. And soon, he added, get a Klan-owned president. Forty years of Jim Crow in the South and voter restrictions aimed at immigrants in the North were able to shrink the American electorate as never before: just 48.9 percent of eligible voters cast a ballot in the 1924 presidential election—an all-time low.

In Evansville, the congressman of conscience, William Wilson, lost to a Klansman, Harry Rowbottom—just as he'd predicted to his son a few months earlier. Across the state, every Klan-supported candidate won, from the top of the ticket on down.

The Invisible Empire's success, as Stephenson told an associate, was divinely sanctioned. Feeling the breath of God at his back, Steve opened his mansion to a hundred people one night in the late fall of that year. A string quartet played in the main room and drinks flowed freely. The house was thick with politicians and thick with Klansmen, one and the same. Lucille Fuller, who'd been hired by Steve to work as an actress in one of his Klan films, showed up with a male friend. Steve greeted her at the door with a drunken grasp, too close for comfort, as she recalled. She ran into Earl Klinck, the head of Steve's private police force, who showed off his latest badge—from the Marion County Sheriff's Office.

Fuller's escort was too drunk to drive her home. She asked an acquaintance for a ride and went upstairs to get her coat. As Fuller walked down toward the front door, the host came staggering back into the house, red-faced and agitated. Stephenson seemed to be blotto, but was very forceful. In a fury, he grabbed the actress by the arm and pushed her out a back door. She caught a glimpse of his girlfriend-for-the-night sobbing in the rear of the house. He dragged Fuller along the driveway, passing Klinck and another bodyguard.

Fuller cried for help. She was shoved into the garage and marched upstairs to an apartment. Stephenson locked the door, dropped his pants, and lunged for the woman. Fuller fought back, slapping and poking at him. He lost his balance and fell to the ground. He managed to bound up on his feet, and with a mighty heave threw Fuller to the bed.

Now he tried to rape Fuller, climbing atop her and pinning her. When she wriggled out of his hold, her attacker looked around for his gun.

"I should kill you," he said. He tore her clothes, clawed at her breasts. Growing more frenzied and agitated, he bit her, ripping into her flesh with his teeth. Fuller screamed so loud it seemed to knock him back. From a crouch, dazed and drunk, he looked up at the woman and waved her off.

Like Stephenson's other victims, Fuller feared going to the police. No one would believe her, as he warned her afterward. And even if they did, they wouldn't dare to go after him.

Stephenson now owned a governor—for all the world to see. On January 12, 1925, he stood next to his prized possession in the receiving line of the inaugural ball. At dinner, he was again paired with Jackson, along with Steve's escort, and Senator Watson and his wife. Seated directly across from the Grand Dragon was Madge Oberholtzer. Together with her friend Stanley Hill, who'd worked with the new governor at the secretary of state's office, she'd helped to organize some of the logistics for the biggest political bash of the year, and slipped her name among the honored guests. They dined on a seven-course meal.

After the band played "Back Home Again in Indiana," and then something slower, Stephenson asked Madge to join him on the dance floor. He was nonstop chatter, an open faucet of compliments. When she tried to excuse herself after the number, he insisted on a second go-round, leaving his date at the table to fend for herself.

"I like you," he told her. "I like you very much." A few days later, he gave her a call and asked her to come by his office.

15

Hoosier Hysteria

1925

From miles out, you could see the concrete obelisk, rising 351 feet into the mid-American sky, the largest monument in the world to a republic of slaveholders. A dream of the rebuilt and fortified twentieth-century Ku Klux Klan was to have something grand, imposing, dominant, and everlasting sprouting from the soil that gave birth to Jefferson Davis. It was designed to look exactly like the Washington Monument, the walls of its limestone foundation eight feet thick at the base, tapered into a pyramid at the summit. Davis owned at least seventy human beings when he was sworn in as president of the rebel states in Montgomery, Alabama, on February 18, 1861. Unlike the founding document of the United States, the constitution of his Confederacy specifically enshrined slavery as an irrevocable right, removing all doubt about the reason for that new nation's existence. Davis was vanquished, indicted for treason, and forced into prison. Yet nearly sixty years after he surrendered, he was honored with the Tallest Thing in Kentucky, a state that had never joined his breakaway nation.

This solid symbol of the Lost Cause was the final shrine at the end of a newly designated route through the South that would take people from one sacred site of the Confederacy to the other. It was the pinnacle of the long effort to revise the narrative of the war. Traitors were now heroes, and slaveholders were gentlemen. More than 100,000 people had turned out to see the unveiling of the giant statue of Robert E. Lee on Monument Avenue in Richmond, Virginia—the first of four prominent Confederates to be immortalized barely a hundred miles from the capital they'd plotted to destroy. At the same time, Gutzon Borglum, the Klan insider and eventual sculptor of Mount Rushmore, a man Stephenson had called "my close personal friend," started work on a marble carving of Alexander Stephens, vice president of the slave states. The Confederacy, Stephens had said, was founded "upon the great truth that the Negro is not equal to the white man; that slavery subordination to the superior race is his natural and normal condition." The carving was bound for Statuary Hall in Washington's Capitol Rotunda, home to the most iconic totems in the nation.

Now, after seven years of construction, the Davis monument was finished in the same year of the Klan's greatest electoral victories. To mark the occasion, masked white men burned a fiery cross from the top, to the cheers of those gathered at its base. To this day, the Jefferson Davis Monument is the tallest unreinforced concrete structure and the second-highest obelisk on the planet. It's ninety miles south of where D. C. Stephenson built the first outpost of the Klan of the North.

As the new year dawned, Steve had no time for touring. He was Grand Dragon of the most powerful Klan in history, the only realm that had complete political control of a state. He had legislators to command, many bills to pass, and some not meant to pass at all. Among the 150 members of the General Assembly of 1925, only two were women and four were Catholics; there were no Black or Jewish representatives. It was known as the Klan Legislature, and bipartisan in that regard. Edward B. Bender, a farmer and Democratic legislator from Zionsville, had joined three years earlier as an act of political survival. Now he was all in, and didn't mind taking orders from an outsider in a hood.

Bender's rural Klan den would occasionally "take out" someone—using the Klan euphemism for kidnapping—often a man accused by poison squads of cheating on his wife. As Bender recalled, "They wouldn't whip him or anything. Just warn him and we'd *take him out.*"

The Invisible Empire had an ambitious legislative agenda: A new eugenics law, to replace the one struck down by the courts, to prevent parents with "degenerate hereditary qualities" from having children. Abolishing parochial schools, with jail sentences for those who tried to send their kids to them. Criminal penalties for adultery or sex outside marriage. Prohibiting baseball games from being played on Sunday. State censorship of movies; films labeled "immoral" by a government commission would be banned. Mandatory Bible reading in public schools—but only the King James Version, the scripture favored by Protestants. Putting road-building contracts directly under control of the governor—Stephenson's governor, a way to get his hands on millions. And one very curious proposal: a bill ordering nutrition education in all public schools.

"We grabbed everything there was," said Court Asher. "We cleaned up."

For those who could smell the rancid stench of corruption rising from the statehouse, Steve had reassuring words. "The Republican Party is in the cleanest hands and it is guided by the most lofty motives," he wrote one party official, David Hoover, in Elkhart, Indiana. Hoover replied: "I wish to take this occasion to ask just *who you are*, anyway? You seem to want to be a kind of guardian in general for all of Hoosierdom. I confess that I am not aware of the state of Indiana having created any position of overlord for you."

Indeed, the state had invented no such position. There had been no change in the constitution, nor any law written specifically for the leader of the Ku Klux Klan to run the affairs of three million people. Stephenson's name had never appeared on a ballot. When the legislature was in session, a Klansman sat next to the majority leader—he was known as the fifty-first member of the Senate. But the real action happened in Steve's office.

"They'd go over the bills of the day and Stephenson would say which ones would be passed and which ones would be killed," said Asher. "There was no argument. Just an order."

One measure that was approved with little dissent was the Wright "Bone Dry" Law, a top priority of the Klan and its chief evangelical ally, the Anti-Saloon League. The new law incentivized the authorities to snoop and seize even the tiniest amounts of liquor, awarding prosecutors a bounty of cash for every conviction. It also outlawed medicinal prescription of alcohol, a dagger to a flourishing industry. Under Prohibition, people with a doctor's note could buy a pint for all that ailed them every ten days at a drugstore. This business made a wealthy man out of Charles Walgreen, whose Chicago-based chain of drugstores grew from nine in 1920 to 525 by the end of the decade.

The nutrition act was where Madge Oberholtzer could help. She showed up at Stephenson's office, a little nervous. His Klan had aggressively shamed people Madge knew. The price of doing business with him, at this point, involved a certain amount of looking away, or willful ignorance.

Ushered inside, Madge faced the Grand Dragon in his swivel chair, dressed in his customary serge suit, with that bust of Napoleon on a stand, the eight telephones lining his desk. A large American flag hung on the wall behind him. Steve was fast-talking, full of himself, but also a fount of well-aimed compliments. She made the case for saving her job. He wrote down a few details. Her little department was nothing in the big ship of state government that he controlled. Perhaps he could make some calls, it wouldn't take much. Steve said "he would use his influence to kill the bill," as Madge recalled. *But no guarantee, no promise.*

He liked Madge—that's what he told her for the second time. Had his eye on her from the moment they met at the governor's ball. Perhaps *she* could do something for him. Madge was familiar with the style and format of schoolbooks. What if she ghostwrote a textbook for Steve on proper diet? Once the mandatory nutrition bill passed, every school would need a standard book, in this case one owned by him. It would be another income stream, perennial, for the Grand Dragon.

He had another favor to ask: dinner. When? *Tonight*, at his regular table at the Washington. Steve had just set up a new operation at his favorite hotel, run by the two Earls who never left his side—Klinck and Gentry. They were directing the "vice cleanup" squads of the city police, overseen by the rapist and raging alcoholic D. C. Stephenson. He moved quickly when he wanted something, and Madge was a bit taken aback by the suddenness of things between them. Maybe later, she said. It was a small act of resistance in her moment of need.

Over the first two months of 1925, Madge gave up her hesitation and met Steve on several occasions. She controlled the play: she would go along with his flirting and the flaunting of his power to save her job and then forget this awful man, as he would surely forget her. She'd recently had her long dark hair cut into a short bob—a style of independent women of the twenties, and for Madge another way of saying she could take care of herself.

Stephenson picked her up, curbside, at the family home in his Cadillac one winter evening and drove to the Washington for dinner. After that, he called her repeatedly. He had pushed his nutrition bill close to the finish line and was finalizing plans to write the textbook. But he had yet to deliver on her request to him. Holding out was his leverage.

Madge sensed some menace, something off about Stephenson.

His refinements were showy and forced: the flowers, the parties, the fine clothes, the words pulled from the famous to give him heft. God, he was a twitchy fellow, his hands shaky and the nails bitten. And why were the shades in his office, like those in his home, always tightly drawn? When the big bang of a backfiring car in the streets below reached his office, he would duck on impulse, cowering beneath his statue of Napoleon, as if expecting to be hit by a fusillade of bullets. He frequently fondled his gun. His face had become florid and puffy, and he had bags under his small eyes—deep concern for a man with a hyperinflated sense of vanity. He'd gained a fair amount of weight since arriving in Indianapolis. His hair was starting to thin as well. It was rare for any conversation to pass without Steve's dropping examples of his domination, the snap-into-action at the end of his commands—the mark of an insecure man.

Madge could detect a load of crap when she heard it from men with a surfeit of swagger, especially crap layered with charm. She wasn't sure what to make of *this guy*. Steve's stories always changed slightly in the retelling, in detail and place. Also, he often started drinking early in the day. His top aides were foul-mouthed and rough-edged, and guns were always on display. But after going to one of the parties at his mansion, and taking note of the prominent and prosperous people in attendance, she started to feel more comfortable. It was reassuring to see the best of Indiana paying homage to him. How dangerous could he be with all this high-ranking validation?

Once, he made an explicit reference to greater power soon to come.

"I've just made a governor," he told Madge. "Ralston is going to die, and Jackson will give me the appointment as the next United States Senator from Indiana."

Before he could assume high political office, the Grand Dragon still had a few criminal issues to clean up. He continued to fear that Lucille Fuller, the actress he'd tried to rape in the loft above his garage, would turn on him. On the day after the attack, Stephenson and the armed Earls had shown up at her place with a request. He wanted Fuller to sign an affidavit saying that one of Stephenson's political enemies had attacked her. She refused. Months later, she bumped into him at a small party. He approached Fuller and extended his hand. *Everything good?* She would not shake the hand of the man who'd assaulted her. Face scrunched up in anger, he reminded Fuller that he could destroy her. On top of that, he could buy his way out of anything.

"I've got six hundred grand that I can put my fingers on in a minute," he said. "I've got two airplanes at my disposal. I'm the boss of this state."

In the end, Fuller was sufficiently intimidated to do nothing, and Steve opened his house to ever more bizarre and excessive parties. In March, the Grand Dragon staged a dark ceremony before a small group of invited guests. He was celebrating news that the highway commissioner who stood in the way of Steve's plan to get control of road contracts had stepped down. He crumpled a newspaper clipping of that story into a tin pot and lit it on fire. As if overseeing a pagan ritual, he solemnly offered last rites.

"Oh, Earth, take charge of this maggot of the dung hill, who for a brief space inhabited our sphere of life," he said. "Just as we must kill our prized dog when he goes mad, so must we separate the disloyal from our ranks."

Then a toast: "I am the counterpart of Napoleon!"

At that moment, several naked young women appeared. The room was darkened as tapers of incense were lit. Stephenson assigned the women to individual men and sent them off with his blessing.

Days later, over dinner at the Washington, Steve startled Madge with an off-the-cuff statement.

"I would never hurt you even if you asked me to," he said. *Why would she ever ask him to hurt her?*

And then he said something equally odd a second time. While dropping her off at home, he turned to Madge with a smile.

"Are you afraid of me?" She couldn't tell if he was joking. "You shouldn't be so aloof," he said, as she moved to get out of the car. "I always get what I want."

16

The Last Train to Chicago

1925

He started drinking on Sunday afternoon, March 15, and continued pouring down the whiskey well into the evening. The Earls were with him, Klinck and Gentry, as was his driver, Shorty DeFriese—a nineteen-year-old who'd become one of the Grand Dragon's most dutiful acolytes. The day had been clear and cool, winter hanging around in the morning, spring shoving it aside in the late sunshine of the lengthening days. As dusk fell over Irvington, Stephenson ordered one of his men to call the Oberholtzer home and ask for Madge. Both of her parents were ill, her father bedridden, her mother not much better, with coughs, sore throats, off-and-on fever. When Matilda Oberholtzer roused herself to pick up the phone, she was surprised to hear the emissary of D. C. Stephenson on the line, requesting to speak with her daughter on a Sunday evening. *No, Madge was out.* An hour or so passed and another call came in from the Stephenson compound, more insistent. Mrs. Oberholtzer promised to pass on the message. Then two more calls.

Earlier that day, Madge had picked up Ermina Moore and they went for a spin in the country. The hardwoods had yet to leaf out and the flowering trees were still holding their coiled clusters, but the season of renewal was at the starting gate. It was like old times, Ermina and Madge on the open road again, free of constraints. Madge came home before five, changed, and went on a dinner date with a man she'd been seeing casually. She returned around ten p.m. Her mother came downstairs and told Madge about the phone calls. Mr. Stephenson needed to speak with her tonight. It was urgent—state business. Madge called Irvington 0492.

Six days earlier, the legislature had passed HB 287, requiring public schools to teach a course in diet and nutrition. The new law was very specific in the curriculum outline, tailor-made for the book that Madge would possibly write, Steve would own, and every public school student in Indiana would be required to buy: *One Hundred Years of Health*. Stephenson's stranglehold of the capitol compound had never been tighter. Stepped-up Klan extortion schemes—Jewish, Black, and Catholic merchants paying to avoid boycotts—were a steady source of income. To avoid trouble, one large manufacturing company made membership in the Ku Klux Klan a qualification for employment. Per an unwritten agreement, city streetcars would hire only members of the hooded order. At bus stops near Indiana Avenue, Black passengers were left stranded. When they tried to board at other locations, the doors were slammed in their faces. Drivers were specifically instructed not to pick up

Black bus riders. The Klan was also promoting construction of "Liberty Hall," a community and residential center for exclusive use by white Protestants.

Madge was hesitant. It was late and she had to be at work early the next day. She suggested getting together early in the morning. Steve pressured her to come now. Though his words were somewhat slurred, she understood him to say he wanted to finalize some business before leaving for Chicago. It wouldn't take long. He would send one of his bodyguards, Gentry, down University Avenue to pick up Madge. He hung up before she could object. The bulky bullet catcher arrived and ushered Madge out the door, mumbling a few words. She had no time to change out of the black velvet dress she'd worn on her date. She had barely enough time to grab her coat, and not a spare second to fetch her hat. Madge never left the house without a hat. Her mother went to the window and caught a glimpse in the dark of the man leading her daughter down the street.

At Stephenson's mansion, the thick wooden front door closed quickly behind Madge. It was eerie and quiet inside, and most of the place was dark. She heard men laughing—low, guttural voices. The bodyguard guided Madge into the parlor, where Stephenson sat without his usual jacket and tie. His nose was pink, his hair uncombed, his shirt collar open. He was sharing drinks and obscene stories with Shorty and Klinck. She mentioned something about the "urgent" business that had brought her to his lair on a Sunday night.

"Get a drink," he said, motioning toward the kitchen.

"I don't want a drink."

Steve snapped his fingers at his lieutenants. "Take her to the other room and get her a drink."

Surrounded by four men in various stages of drunkenness, she noticed that the housekeeper, a woman who could usually be seen cleaning up at all hours, was nowhere around. She was trapped. Shorty and Klinck grabbed Madge on either side and guided her into the kitchen. They poured a drink and told her to swallow it. It smelled foul. Again, she said she didn't want a drink. It was late. She was tired, spooked.

"I need to make a phone call." She picked up a receiver and called home—an attempt to alert her mother that she was in danger. Nobody answered. A few minutes later, she tried again. This time, Klinck cut off the call before she could get through.

Stephenson came roaring into the kitchen. He had that glassy-eyed look that she'd seen before at his parties; he was talking loudly and making little sense. He ordered his guards to force the drink on Madge. She swallowed and coughed. He demanded that she drink a second glass, and a third.

"I'm going home," said Madge. Steve grabbed her hands and pulled her in close to him. His grip was so tight it hurt and reddened her wrists.

"You're going to stay with me," he said.

Within a few minutes of swallowing the last drink, Madge felt dizzy and nauseated. She wiggled out of Stephenson's hold and made a run for the toilet, where she vomited. On her way out of the bathroom, she looked around for an escape route. The men grabbed their coats and hats and closed in on Madge.

"We're going to Chicago," said Steve. "I want you to go with me." *Chicago!* He'd dialed up an assistant at the Washington and asked for three tickets on the last overnight train out of Indianapolis to Chicago. It left just after midnight.

"I can't go to Chicago," Madge replied. "I can't. And I won't." She put on her jacket and turned for the door. "I'm going home."

"You can't go home!" He started to laugh. "Oh, yes! You're going with me to Chicago." It was all happening too quickly; she knew then that they intended to kidnap her.

"I love you more than any woman I've ever known," said Stephenson. Madge was startled again. *Love?* Where did this come from? Three men forced Madge upstairs. She resisted, but they dragged her along. Steve opened a dresser drawer that was stuffed with revolvers and told each of his men to grab a gun. He reserved a shiny, pearl-handled pistol for himself. They loaded the guns, flashed them at Madge, and ordered her down the stairs, out the back door toward the garage. They piled into a car, Shorty at the wheel, Madge in the back with Stephenson on one side of her and Earl Gentry on the other. She begged them to stop at her house.

"Just let me get my hat."

The car pulled up in front of the hotel for the tickets. Shorty went inside. They were just across from Monument Circle, the pulsing heart of the city, with its nearly three-hundred-foot tapered obelisk, but few people were out on a Sunday night. Madge could bolt and find help; it would only take a few seconds. But she was immobilized by fear. She was sure they would kill her and dump her body next to the most iconic landmark in Indiana. She begged Steve. When that failed, she tried to reason with him. He'd be ruined by this crime. His dynasty would fall apart. This felony would lock him up for a very long time. He smirked, stifling a laugh at the suggestion of the Grand Dragon getting hauled into a court.

"I'm the law in Indiana," said her kidnapper. It was not the first time she'd heard him make that declaration. But now it applied directly to her. He turned to Gentry, looking for approval.

"I think I'm pretty smart to have gotten her."

They drove from the hotel to Union Station, a short hop. She knew it well, for it was also the place where her father worked as a mail clerk. More than two hundred trains passed through every day, but the station was nearly empty as midnight approached. When they left the car for the train, with a gun pressed into her rib cage, she was told to not say a word. In the darkness, she briefly caught the eyes of one other person, a Black porter, who nodded as they boarded. She was strong-armed down the galley to a private compartment. The door closed and was locked. Gentry climbed on the top berth. Stephenson threw Madge down on the lower berth and started to disrobe.

The Klansman acted quickly as the train pulled out of Indianapolis. In a swift motion, he took hold of the bottom of Madge's black dress and pulled it up over her head. She felt sick, weak, and wanted to vomit again. Stephenson grabbed both her hands and pinned her down. She squirmed and tried to fight back. He was on her, and he was heavy. He ripped away her underclothes. She couldn't move. He tried to penetrate her. Then he went after her with his teeth. He bit her neck, her face, her breasts—a burst of savagery. He chewed at her flesh. Blood flowed out. He chewed her tongue and spit out blood. He chewed her breasts again. He moved onto her legs, her ankles, mutilating her body. The pain was excruciating. All the while, she heard nothing from Gentry on the bunk above them. She passed out.

In the predawn darkness, Madge was snapped into consciousness by a loud knock. The porter walked by and said this was their stop—Hammond, Indiana. *Hammond?* They were 160 miles from Indianapolis. Chicago was just a few minutes away. But Steve had decided not to go on to Chicago. He knew enough not to cross the state line, not to risk a federal offense. That would involve police he had no control over—the Bureau of Investigation, run by J. Edgar Hoover, a hustling young bureaucrat who'd just been named director by President Coolidge. Stephenson dressed, his gun visible at all times. He grabbed the revolver and pointed it at Madge. She was in extreme pain, dazed, woozy and sobbing. The sheet of the lower berth was covered with her blood. Her wounds were fresh and wet. In places, he'd bitten her very deeply and she could see teeth marks.

"Go ahead and shoot me," she said. He pressed the gun against her skin.

"Kill me. I don't care."

Gentry and Stephenson threw clothes and a coat over Madge, and rushed her off the train. It hurt to walk and it was cold outside, near freezing. They went a short distance to the Indiana Hotel in Hammond. It was 6:30 a.m. Gentry checked into one room. The Klansman registered himself and Madge into another, listing them up as a married couple, Mr. and Mrs. W. B. Morgan of Franklin, Indiana. Steve showed no trepidation; he had a smirk on his face as he signed the guest register. Madge might call the police or some other authorities. They might ask a few questions—honest, polite men in badges serving honest, polite citizens, most of whom answered to the Grand Dragon in some fashion. He could tell them who he was, show them his own badge, reassure them that he was the person leading the largest fraternal order in Indiana, representing the highest values.

With the gun still poked in her side, he marshaled Madge into room 416 of the hotel. Gentry was in 417. Madge begged Stephenson to allow her one phone call or a telegram to her mother, to let her know she was alive. She knew her mother had been awake all night, sick with worry, waiting for her return. Steve shook his head. There was no reason for Madge to contact her mother. As Madge wept and recoiled at the pain of her broken and lacerated body, Steve ordered breakfast—grapefruit, sausage, toast, juice, and coffee. He gave the bellboy a $1 tip and devoured the meal while sitting on the bed in his undershirt. She ate nothing. Steve made a few phone calls, ordering Shorty to bring a car up from Indianapolis, and arranged to send a telegram through the front desk. He had changed his mind: Madge could send a note to her mother, but he would dictate. Gentry came into the room and took notation. The message was simple—everything was fine, no cause for concern, they were on their way to Chicago for business.

Gentry got hot towels and tried to clean up Madge's wounds. From her face to her legs, Stephenson had gnawed at her body. Many of the bite marks were open and still oozing blood at a slow trickle. As he watched Gentry tending to Madge, he offered an apology of sorts.

"I'm three degrees less than a brute," he said matter-of-factly.

"You're worse than that," she replied. She would not look at him.

After Gentry left the room, Stephenson fell asleep again. Madge took hold of his gun, the pearl-handled revolver. In a halting fashion, she waved it around, pointing it at him. She wanted to kill him now, to kill him quickly, to show *the bastard* that he could not get away with this. She thought of the shame this would bring her mother, and the web of Stephenson's connections. She thought how hard it would be to get people who answered to the Grand Dragon to believe killing him was an act of self-defense. Still, she wanted him dead. She aimed the pistol at his puffy face and tried to pull the trigger. Her mind was in a cloud. She was badly dehydrated. What she desired most was to still the screaming pain and protect herself from further predations. The quickest way to do that, she now decided in the foggy logic of trauma, was to turn the gun on herself.

She went to the bathroom and stared into the mirror at her misshapen and nearly unrecognizable face. In less than a day's time, she had been transformed from a lively twenty-eight-year-old into a bloodied and bruised mess. Her face was smudged. Her tongue was swollen and still bleeding after Stephenson had chewed it. The mark of his teeth was on her breasts and her hips. She aimed the gun at her temple, to get it right with just one shot. Then she heard the turn of a doorknob. It was Gentry.

Shorty arrived at midmorning. Madge said she needed to get medication, bandages, disinfectant, and a hat. She had no money, no purse. Shorty gave her $15 and took her outside to his car. Madge found a store not far from the hotel and bought a black hat for $12.50. She asked the teenage chauffeur to drive her to a drugstore for makeup to cover her wounds. He reminded her not to try anything. She was too exhausted to think of an escape plan. Her only way forward was a way out—suicide. At the pharmacy, she bought a box of bichloride of mercury tablets, and hid it under her coat. The compound is a highly toxic poison and household disinfectant, extremely corrosive to the body's internal organs, made by the Indianapolis-based company Eli Lilly—where Madge had briefly worked. The pills were the cause of the death of Olive Thomas, a silent film star, by suicide or foul play, in 1920—a case that was widely publicized.

Back in room 416, Madge pleaded with her captor to let her get some rest in the chamber next door. He refused.

"You're going to lie down right here by me."

When Stephenson nodded off again, Madge rose quietly, grabbed the box of pills and crept into the bathroom. She laid out eighteen tablets of the poison. She took three pills and went into a seizure of gagging. She forced herself to take another three. The poison inside her burned like embers of hot coal. It was a torturous way to die. She passed out briefly, snapped back to life, stumbled around in a half-conscious state. Steve rose and left the room without saying anything. Late in the afternoon, when Shorty walked in, he knew something was wrong because Madge had a look of horror and despair, her face pale but for the marks where Stephenson had chewed her. She'd been spitting up a lot of blood into a cuspidor.

"What's wrong?"

"Nothing."

"Where's your pain?"

"Everywhere."

She pointed to the spittoon of blood. "Can you keep a secret?"

"Yes."

"I took poison."

"What kind?"

"Bichloride."

She begged him not to tell his boss. Shorty left the room immediately. A few minutes later, all three men returned. Stephenson was furious. If Madge died, there would be an investigation, an autopsy, multiple levels of law enforcement asking questions and conducting forensic work, perhaps too many people to control the situation.

"What the hell have you done?"

He screamed at her. She responded in a weak voice.

"I asked Shorty not to tell."

"Why'd you take it?"

"I wanted to die."

"You're a fool."

He ordered a quart of milk from room service and told Madge to drink it.

"What are you going to do?" she asked him.

"We're taking you to the hospital. You can register as my wife. Your stomach will have to be pumped out."

He was thinking aloud, sketching a plan on the fly. He said he would tell the hospital that she had meant to take aspirin, but had swallowed poison by mistake. As to registering Madge as his bride—that was an old ploy for Steve, giving him immunity. He'd battered his first two wives and nothing came of it. As his wife, he thought, Madge could never tell the authorities about him. Anyway, who would believe her word against his?

"I'm not going to be your wife," she said, a flicker of her old self. But Stephenson made it clear: the only way Madge could get emergency medical help was if she agreed to be married to the Grand Dragon. In extreme pain, she was defiant.

"I refuse."

Stephenson snapped his fingers, turning to Shorty.

"Let's get out of here."

New plan: he would take her back to Indianapolis. She said she didn't want to move. What strength she had left was ebbing out of her. He pressed on with the only way out that made sense to him.

"We can drive on up to Crown Point and get married," he said suddenly.

"I'll never marry you."

She asked again if she could call her mother. She wanted to say goodbye.

Stephenson looked around for the guns and loose baggage.

"Pack the grips," he said. They left Hammond just before five p.m.

In the car, with Shorty driving, Steve at his side, Gentry guarding Madge in the back seat, the Grand Dragon started to sweat. He knew he needed to keep her alive to avoid a murder charge. He told Shorty to stop the car and remove the license plates. If they were pulled over, he would explain that the plates had been stolen overnight in Hammond. The car had never been in Hammond for the night, but Steve was making it up as he went. He ordered his driver to stop at a store and get milk and ginger ale. Madge couldn't hold it down. She choked and coughed. She vomited all over the back seat, infuriating Steve. He threw the milk bottle out the window.

The car started up again for Indianapolis, following back roads. Steve and Gentry began to drink from one of the whiskey bottles in a side compartment. Twilight settled over the fields surrounding prim little towns, places where the Old Man was revered. They drove south, passing Logansport, where Steve had ordered that flaming cross to frighten into submission the family of his now crushed foe, Patrick O'Donnell. As darkness fell, they passed by Kokomo. The Klan had opened a fifty-bed hospital—the fruition of the funding drive started on the Fourth of July, 1923. Steve could close his eyes and remember that day, the multitudes shouting his name, the pastors blessing him, the men waving from cornfields with their three-fingered Klan salutes, the women blowing him kisses through their hoods, the children feeling the pulse of true power, learning the ways of their parents and grandparents.

Madge's life was slipping away in the back seat. It was unclear if she would live to see Indianapolis. "I need to see a doctor," she said at one point. "Please, take me to a hospital." They drove on, approaching the city, Monument Circle's exclamation point coming into view. Over and over, she begged Steve to get her some help. Her pain was excruciating. She moaned and screamed. Steve told her to *shut up*, that whining was not going to do her any good.

"Just drop me off," she pleaded. "Anywhere on the side of the road. Please! Just drop me off."

In the hours since she'd taken the poison, Madge had come around to a different view—now she wanted to live. The suicide attempt had been a terrible mistake. She felt deep regret at an impulsive act. Her hope was that someone would pick her up on the roadside; it was a chance, perhaps the only one, to fend off death. He promised to stop at the next little town before Indianapolis. But as lights came into view, he told Shorty to step on it. He was only toying with her.

"Drive fast," he said, "but don't get pinched." He drifted into his own thoughts, then said, loud enough for everyone to hear, "I've been in a worse mess than this before and got out of it."

In Irvington, an hour before midnight, the car pulled up at the Stephenson compound and parked at the big garage. The dogs in the kennel, his many German shepherds, started barking loudly, prompting a neighbor to turn on a light. As they drove up, Steve had spotted two people at the front door of his house; he ordered

Shorty to investigate. When his young underling came back, he had some unsettling news: it was Madge's mother and another woman at the door, distraught, demanding answers, looking for the missing girl. Shorty sent them away, told them he didn't know *nothing about anything*. He said the master of the house was gone. Out of town. *You're trespassing.*

But this news sent another jolt of fear into Stephenson. Once again, he went to his backup plan, and directed his words at Madge.

"You will stay right here until you marry me."

He'd kidnapped her, raped her, ripped her body with his teeth. Now he asked her again to pay an ultimate price: marry him or die. She refused.

The men dragged Madge up to the loft above the garage, the place where Stephenson had attacked Lucille Fuller. He turned to go. In his parting shot, he told Madge that she had been in an auto accident—that was the story, and she damn well better stick with it.

"You must forget this," he said. "What's done has been done. I am the law and the power."

She passed out again. In the middle of the night, a neighbor heard blood-curdling screams coming from the Stephenson compound. The prisoner of the Grand Dragon's garage was awake. On Tuesday, March 17, Klinck came into the room and told her it was time to leave. To move was to activate a thousand points of pain. Klinck shoved her into the back seat of a Cadillac and drove the few blocks to Madge's house. One of the boarders, Eunice Shultz, was making lunch when the door opened. Without saying a word, Klinck carried Madge upstairs and dumped her. As he rushed out, he said his name was Johnson from Kokomo, in response to a question. He mumbled something about a car accident and left. The boarder went upstairs to the bedroom and knocked on the door. She gasped at the sight inside: a young woman she knew well but now barely recognized, filthy, her clothes ripped, soiled, and bloodied, her hair matted and greased. Madge's face was bruised and purpled, with indented circle marks on one cheek. She moaned and cried.

"I'm dying, Mrs. Shultz."

17

A Vigil in Irvington

1925

A young attorney, Asa Smith, was getting dressed at home in the bathroom upstairs when his wife summoned him. A Mrs. *Matilda Oberholtzer* was on the line, sounding panicky and desperate. Smith remembered the name. He'd helped her on a property matter a few years earlier. He knew Madge as well, from their mutual friend Ermina Moore. Matilda told him the story of Sunday night, the four calls from Stephenson, the strange man who came to the house late and fetched Madge, the empty bed in the morning. She spoke in a whisper, from a cloakroom, trying to keep it from her husband, who was ill. He asked her to repeat some of the details, and as she did, she let her suspicions spill out. She had a horrible feeling about all of this. Smith knew a private detective who worked the bootleg racket and had an office downtown. He'd pay him a visit.

Smith had his own thoughts about D. C. Stephenson. He hated the Klan, hated the way they waved the flag while hiding their faces, hated that a secretive order had taken over the Republican Party, and now controlled Indiana from the Grand Dragon's office just off Monument Circle. While fighting Germans in the Great War, crawling to within six yards of an enemy machine gun nest, Smith had been doused with mustard gas. He was unconscious for three weeks and lost part of his vision. He wasn't a hollowed-out man like so many of the Lost Generation of the 1920s. But when he returned home he was a different man, shell-shocked, not the same in body and soul, prone to bouts of isolation, memory loss, and insecurity.

Smith's family was from Wabash, a short drive up the road from the capital. They were lifelong members of a Methodist church there, one of the many where the minister took a bribe from the Klan. Smith had little tolerance for hypocrisy in high places. Those churchmen speaking the one hundred percent Americanism language—he was disgusted by it. He wrote a letter to his minister and told him to remove his name from the rolls. And it was shameful that Governor Ed Jackson was a sealed-for-eternity Kluxer. Smith thought he was an idiot—"not such a bad guy, just an ignoramus," as he put it. Jackson had asked Smith for his support as one of the few Republicans in the state who had not bowed before the Invisible Empire.

"I can't, Ed," Smith told the governor. "It's on account of the goddamned Ku Klux Klan." Smith's grandfather had been a surgeon in the Union Army, and his father, as a young soldier, had fought against the slaveholders, part of General Sherman's march through Georgia.

Monday afternoon, Smith was at the private dick's office when a second call came from Mrs. Oberholtzer. She'd just received a telegram, sent from a hotel in Hammond. It was a message supposedly from Madge—she was on business, nothing to worry about. "We are driving through to Chicago. We'll be home on the night train." While this news was a relief of sorts—at least she knew her daughter was alive—it made no sense. Madge had not packed a bag or told her parents of travel. It wasn't like her to take off somewhere overnight without planning, without notification. She was due at work. Smith picked up Ermina Moore and Mrs. Oberholtzer and went to Union Station. They walked the platform, checking with clerks and travelers, questioning strangers while showing a photo. *Nothing. Nothing.*

Smith drove the women to the Stephenson mansion, just past eleven p.m. on that Monday. Matilda and Ermina knocked on the door. They waited ten minutes. These were the people on the porch whom Steve had seen when he pulled into the garage.

As the sun rose over Indianapolis on Tuesday, the day cold and bright with frost in the air and the previous night's snow still on the ground, Madge's mother went back to Union Station, this time with her husband. Weakened by flu, George could barely stand. They searched all morning, poking around the grand station with its stained-glass rose window and 185-foot clock tower. The wind was starting to gallop. At the lunch hour, Mrs. Oberholtzer called her residence to see if there was any news. Eunice Shultz picked up. The boarder was breathless: *Madge was home!* Upstairs in her bedroom. Shultz had summoned a physician, Dr. John K. Kingsbury, a family friend who lived just a few doors away in Irvington.

Kingsbury got to the Oberholtzer home before the parents. By then, Madge had been cleaned up some, but still looked battered and disheveled, dried blood on her clothes and in her hair, fresh blood on the pillowcase and sheets. Her black dress was slightly open at the front. The doctor took her hand, checked her pulse. She was cold to the touch and her heart was racing. She was very pale. He noted pockmarks, which looked fresh, on either cheek, in a field of bruises. One of the indented marks was the size of an egg. There was a deep laceration on one of her breasts, and a fist-sized bruise on the other. Other cuts and odd-shaped incisions were visible on her legs, around her groin. One contusion was nearly a foot long and six inches wide. She'd been spitting up blood into a pan.

The doctor felt along her arms, her rib cage, along her legs, below her knee, looking for signs of broken bones.

"How did you get hurt?"

She looked at him blankly, her face chalk-white. In his opinion, she was in a state of profound shock. She shook her head slowly, closed her eyes.

"When I'm better I will tell you the whole story."

The doctor prodded her gently. He wasn't sure how long she would live. Tell him now, if she could. She gave him a rough outline of what had happened. He asked if she'd been offered any medical help. No, Stephenson had refused. She was his prisoner. The doctor posed a few follow-up questions about the wounds, particularly the open cuts on her breasts and cheeks. How did he do this?

"With his teeth," she said.

"His teeth?"

"I'm going to die," she told the doctor. "I'm . . . going . . . to . . . die." He did not try to convince her otherwise.

Madge's mother arrived. George was feeling feverish again, and his wife did not want him looking in on his daughter, not just yet—fearing exposure of his illness. When Mrs. Oberholtzer walked into Madge's bedroom, she was staggered by the stricken look on the face of the boarder, Mrs. Shultz, and the first glance at her daughter. A mother can be instinctively strong when a child is in serious peril, but this mother could not hold up. She broke down in tears and fell to the floor. When Mrs. Oberholtzer recovered, she moved to the bedside, stroked her daughter, and ran a cloth over her wounds.

Ermina Moore arrived with Asa Smith. Madge's best friend took one look at the woman in bed and fainted.

Dr. Kingsbury called a nurse, asking her to bring equipment from his office. He put a heating pad against Madge's skin and heavy blankets over her to try to bring her body temperature up. He forced her to drink warm liquid. He cleaned the wounds with soap and water and rubbed antiseptic over them. Between heavy sobs, she wailed in deep pain. When Ermina was on her feet again, Madge summoned her old road mate to her bedside and spoke in a bare whisper.

"Oh, honey . . ."

That same Tuesday, Stephenson's ex-wife Nettie touched down in Indianapolis. It was pure coincidence. She had not seen him since he deserted her, leaving her with a newborn girl and no means of support in a small Oklahoma town. Ignoring his warning to never track him down, Nettie had spent a decade looking for him. Finally, with all the national press over his role in the recent election, she had traced him to Indianapolis. When Steve abandoned her, he was adrift and penniless, in debt to people he'd stiffed in towns all over the Southern Plains. Now he was lord of an empire, controlled a state, was extravagantly wealthy, and issued grand pronunciations as a venerated and mysterious presence—the Old Man. When she filed for divorce in 1917, he didn't contest it, or make his presence known in any way. She had remarried, becoming Nettie Stephenson Brehm, and settled in Poteau, Oklahoma. Her daughter with Steve, Florence Catherine, was about to turn nine. Steve had never contributed a penny to her well-being. Nettie had come to town now to file suit in Marion County Superior Court, asking for $16,795 in child support. In her pleading, Nettie could not supply even the most basic background material on her former husband. She had no idea where he had come from, who his parents were, or whether D. C. Stephenson was even his real name.

George was allowed into his daughter's room on Wednesday. It made him sick and bollixed up with rage to see the person he still called "my baby girl" in such a sorry state. He paced the room. She shivered, her face swollen. She lifted a hand and patted the blanket.

"Daddy, sit down on the edge of the bed with me."

He sat and stared into her reddened eyes, wiping some tears.

"Would you stroke my hair?"

He ran his rough hands through her fresh-washed hair, the short bob. She said how good that made her feel. He asked her to tell him what happened. With some hesitancy she told her father the story, sometimes pointing to the individual wounds as she recalled the attack on the last train to Chicago. Even worse was the following day in Stephenson's car.

"Oh, Daddy, that was the longest ride from Hammond to Indianapolis."

At times, she closed her eyes and gasped for breath. She knew she was dying, she said again—nothing could save her. He tried to encourage her. She had to be strong. They talked about going to the police. Madge was still concerned about the publicity and disgrace it would bring her family. And she feared Stephenson's control of the levers of power.

The attorney Asa Smith arrived, after promising to come by every day. He also wondered if they shouldn't go directly to the authorities. The family resisted. As Madge feared, the shame would fall as much on them as Stephenson—likely even more. And what chance did a family headed by a postal clerk have against the Grand Dragon? Madge continued to push back as well.

"Don't do anything," she said in a tiny voice that faded with each word. "He'll crush you. He'll crush you. He'll crush you."

Later that day, the family agreed on some quiet initial legal steps. Smith went to Stephenson's office in the Kresge Building, joined by an older lawyer and friend, Griffith Dean. Steve met them at the door, out of breath. He'd just returned from a business trip to New

York, he said, and had heard that *something terrible* had happened to Madge Oberholtzer. Poor Madge. Wonderful gal. He'd been trying to *help* her keep her job with the state.

"The whole thing has struck me like a thunderbolt," he said. The attorneys didn't budge; they said they were planning to sue Steve for what he'd done. He acted surprised. *He had done nothing.* But he couldn't hold the pose for long. Now he was enraged.

"I'm a scrapper!" he said. "I've stood more than any other human being, I suspect, but I can stand more!"

Smith replied that Miss Oberholtzer had endured more pain in the last three days than Steve had taken in a lifetime. This seemed to snap him into a more calculated tone. He said he would send his personal attorney to meet with them later in the afternoon. It was best to look at this entire episode, he said, as a professional problem—not a personal matter.

Later that day, Steve's lawyer Robert Marsh showed up at Smith's office with startling news. What D. C. Stephenson had said earlier, about being "struck like a thunderbolt," was not true. The new story was this: Steve knew Madge had been attacked, and he knew the man who had done it. She was mauled by a drunken guest during a party at his house. And because it happened at his home, under his watch, by one of his guests, he assumed some liability. He wanted to take a small bit of responsibility for the actions of a violent acquaintance. In his benevolence, he was willing to pay several thousand dollars in compensation to the family. How much, exactly? He would pay $5,000, no more. The attorneys told Steve's man they didn't believe his story and thought his offer was preposterous. After Marsh took the news to his client, the Grand Dragon dialed Asa Smith, brimming with fury. They were done—he would have nothing more to say about the case of Madge Oberholtzer.

"I've been blackmailed before by experts," said Steve. "Amateurs can't get away with it."

Her kidneys were failing. She'd lost a tremendous amount of blood. Results from the lab showed a large quantity of albumen in her urine, evidence of severe inflammation. Should her kidneys cease to excrete urine, Madge would die of toxic nephritis. Dr. Kingsbury knew the odds of her living were not good; the longest anyone had stayed alive after taking a similar dose of the same poison was twenty-five days, according to the medical literature he'd consulted. Bichloride of mercury does not just attack the kidneys, but has a corrosive effect on other organs. The pain is ceaseless and widespread, with burning in the mouth, throat, lungs, abdomen. Gums bleed. Reflexes are delayed. Sleep is difficult. Tremors are frequent. Still, people did survive smaller doses. In the best light, Madge had a fighting chance against the toxicity of the poison.

But at the same time, she was burning up. Several times a day, the sheets had to be changed. The heat was from inflammation in the places where Madge had been bitten, Dr. Kingsbury believed. He rubbed her open wounds with a topical compound and tried to drain the abscess, but the infections only worsened, the red areas expanding. In the time before antibiotics were discovered by a London doctor in 1928, an infection, even one that started as a simple cut, could kill a person. Madge's body was a furnace.

Every day, Ermina sat by the bedside of her beloved friend, usually joined by the attorney Smith, and one of the parents. Madge didn't talk much during these visits. She went days without speaking at all, and days when she lapsed into long periods of unconsciousness. Her small bed, with metal bars as a headboard, was tucked in a corner of a second-floor bedroom. Her mother would press her hand over the hot forehead. Her fever rarely dropped below 103.

Around town, rumors had spread about a sordid story involving the most powerful man in Indiana and a likable young woman of Irvington. Her absence at work was unexplained, prompting a wave of gossip. It was a small world, the Hoosier statehouse. Stories, particularly ones with a hint of scandal, spread quickly. People knew she'd been involved in some legislative business with Steve. And now, word got out that she was dying after a night out with him. Among those in Madge's circle, the people who loved her most, a decision was made at last to bring in the law. They would risk the shame, risk Stephenson's fist and his exhaustive network. With every passing day of pain, the cruelty of what he had done became more of a focus. He must be brought to justice. But how? Madge was the principal witness, and she was fading fast. Without her testimony, without her voice in court, the case would be nearly impossible to prove. The Grand Dragon's wall could never be breached.

Hiram Wesley Evans, Imperial Wizard of the Ku Klux Klan, marching in Washington, DC, on September 13, 1926. Under Evans, the Klan grew to nearly six million members. They practiced vigilante violence and politics in equal measure. *(Courtesy of the Library of Congress, LC-DIG-npcc-16221)*

William J. Simmons, the founder of the twentieth-century Klan, before a House Committee investigation of the terror group in 1922. This itinerant minister brought the Klan back to life in 1915, only to lose control to Evans. *(Courtesy of the Library of Congress, LC-USZ62-104018)*

The Klan parade in Washington, DC, September 13, 1926. With numerous senators and congressmen under its control, the Klan proudly strutted through the capital. *(Courtesy of the Library of Congress, LC-USZ62-93080)*

James Weldon Johnson, the literary polymath and leader of the NAACP from 1920 to 1930. When he urged Black voters to abandon the Republican ticket in 1924 because the party refused to denounce the Klan, he sparked an epic political realignment. *(Portrait by Carl Van Vechten, Courtesy of the Library of Congress, LC-USZ62-42498)*

Portrait of Madge Oberholtzer. A woman of her age—smart, independent, daring. *(Courtesy of the Indiana State Library)*

D. C. Stephenson's mansion in Irvington, Indiana. The Grand Dragon's home, and a house of horror. *(Courtesy of the Irvington Historical Society)*

Mourners gather outside the home of Madge Oberholtzer, April 1925. *(Courtesy of the Irvington Historical Society)*

Protestant church, circa early 1920s, Knox, Indiana. Klansmen regularly paid off ministers to preach a gospel of hate. *(Courtesy of the Indiana State Library)*

The June 6, 1923, front page of *Tolerance*, an anti-Klan paper in Indiana, unmasking thousands of Klansmen, among them many prominent members of the community. *(Courtesy of the Indiana State Library)*

D. C. Stephenson, an undated portrait from the 1920s.

D. C. Stephenson, Grand Dragon of the Indiana Ku Klux Klan. This is the only known photo of him in Klan regalia.

Night rally of the Ku Klux Klan in 1925 in Denver, where the Klan had political control. *(Courtesy of the Denver Public Library, Western History Collection, Call # X-21546)*

Klansmen and Klanswomen parading through Muncie, Indiana, on June 2, 1923. The Klan had control of the town. *(Courtesy of Ball State University Libraries' Archives and Special Collections)*

The Ku Klux Kiddies, masked in a parade in New Castle, Indiana, August 1, 1923. *(Courtesy of Ball State University Libraries' Archives and Special Collections)*

Two thousand people take the Klan oath in an initiation ritual in Marion, Indiana, 1922. Eight years later, two young Black men were lynched in this town. *(Courtesy of Ball State University Libraries' Archives and Special Collections)*

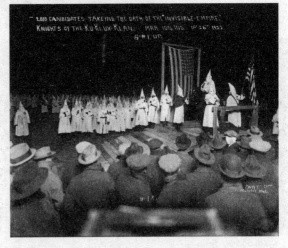

Crusading Muncie newspaper editor George Dale, during one of his stints in the Delaware County, Indiana, jail. *(Courtesy of Ball State University Libraries' Archives and Special Collections)*

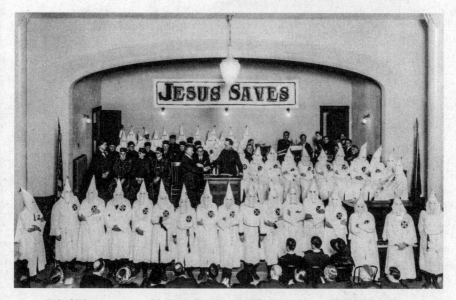

Robed Klansmen meet with Protestant clerics in Portland, Oregon, in 1922. The Klan and white Protestants were closely allied in Oregon, where the Klan controlled the governor's mansion at one point. *(Courtesy of the Oregon Historical Society)*

CHIEF KLUXERS TELL LAW ENFORCEMENT OFFICERS JUST WHAT MYSTIC ORGANIZATION PROPOSES TO DO IN CITY OF PORTLAND

MORAL and political clean-up will be the object of Ku Klux Klan's first campaign, the King Kleagle, ranking officer for Oregon, told a group of citizens at a meeting yesterday to which his guests were summoned by mysterious telephone messages. The King Kleagle is the sheeted figure in the center. The one at the extreme right is the Cyclops of Portland Klan No. 1. The civilians, from left, are: H. P. Coffin, of the National Safety council; John T. Moore, senior captain of police; L. V. Jenkins, chief of police; Walter H. Evans, district attorney; Lester W. Humphreys, United States district attorney; T. M. Hurlburt, sheriff; Russell Bryon, special agent of the United States department of justice; George L. Baker, mayor; P. S. Malcolm, sovereign grand inspector general in Oregon for the Scottish Rite Masonic lodge.

Civic leaders, including the mayor and chief of police, pose with hooded Klansmen in the pages of the *Portland Telegram*, August 2, 1921. Civic leaders in Portland embraced the Klan. *(Courtesy of the Oregon Historical Society)*

The two lead attorneys in the trial of D. C. Stephenson. On the left is Ephraim Inman, lead counsel for the defense. Next to him is the prosecutor, William Remy.

Smith had a possible solution: a "dying declaration," made by a witness in advance of certain death. There was one major challenge. Under the confrontation clause of the Sixth Amendment to the Constitution, every criminal defendant has a right to confront the witness against him or her. A dying declaration violates that right; the words of the witness are hearsay. Still, these words could be used in court if recorded properly and approved by a judge. Getting her statement down was the best, perhaps the only, chance of bringing Stephenson to justice. Smith had been taking notes, as had Ermina Moore, on the story Madge had told of the thirty-eight hours she spent as a captive. They drew up a 3,000-word document, outlining how Madge had met Steve, what happened on Sunday night, the train ride, the continued abuse in the hotel in Hammond, the medical neglect on the drive back to Indianapolis, stuffing her in a garage. It was in her voice, in the first person as she had told the story.

They presented the statement to Madge on Saturday night, March 28—not quite two weeks after the attack. On the same day, Dr. Kingsbury had told the family that she had no chance of recovery. He'd just gotten back the results from the latest blood tests, and they were grim. He presented his conclusion to Madge that night, though he hedged somewhat, holding out a small possibility of a miracle.

"That's all right, Doctor," she said with a serenity that prompted tears from others at her bedside. "I am ready to die. I understand you, Doctor. I believe you and I'm ready to die."

Smith read the statement to Madge, with Ermina Moore, Madge's mother, and the doctor all seated around her. It took him some time, going over every paragraph, every sentence, every quote, very slowly. Madge corrected him in numerous places, and added key details. She showed flashes of surprising strength and resolve. She remembered the room numbers in the hotel in Hammond. She recalled Stephenson's statement that he was "three degrees less than a brute," and that he felt clever for being able to get Madge alone in a Pullman car. She was sure he had claimed that as the Grand Dragon of the Ku Klux Klan he was the law in Indiana, and was invincible.

Madge signed her name to the statement, witnessed by a notary who'd been brought into the room. Everyone else was sobbing. Ermina was losing a soul mate. The Oberholtzers were watching their only daughter slip away forever. Smith saw the beastly mark of the Klan in the face of the dying woman.

The attorney went home, exhausted. Later that night, he got a phone call from the Marion County prosecutor, Will Remy. Someone close to the family had been relaying events to him. Remy and Smith were both war veterans and Phi Delta Theta fraternity brothers. Remy was a short man with a face so smooth it looked as if it was years from meeting its first razor blade. He could pass for a boy of seventeen—with prominent ears and slicked-back hair.

"Is there not something I better see you about?"

Not long after the 1924 general election, Remy had been at an opulent dinner inside the Severin Hotel—a ritual of Stephenson to consolidate his power. It was all men, all white, all in bow ties and tuxes, all officeholders who'd just won. In Marion County, every major elected official but two was a Klansman. The Grand Dragon sat at the head of a long, U-shaped table with the politicians circled around him. At the end of the repast, Steve clinked his glass, rose, and congratulated his supplicants on their victories.

Then the sheriff of Marion County, Omer Hawkins, stood.

"Well, I guess we all know why we're here," he said. "I'll start it off. I realize I owe my nomination and my election to the Old Man. I now pledge that I will make no official appointment, nor do any official act, which does not meet with the approval of D. C. Stephenson."

One after another, the public officials rose and recited this pledge to the head of a private political order. But when it was Will Remy's turn to speak, the mood changed suddenly. He'd been silent through most of the meal, visibly uncomfortable. The young prosecutor, a Republican like everyone else in the room, had barely won his election. After rebuffing the demand of Stephenson's emissary to name Klansmen to the prosecutor's office, he got no support from the Machine. They made plans to neutralize him.

"I've had a good meal," said the Marion County prosecutor, "and I want to thank you for it."

With that, Remy dropped his napkin on the table, turned, and walked out of the Severin Hotel, leaving Steve steaming.

When Remy met the Oberholtzer attorney on Sunday, Smith shared the dying declaration with him. Smith had his doubts about his friend the prosecutor taking on such a mighty foe. Remy assured him he had convicted men worse than D. C. Stephenson. When he was in pursuit, he gave up his weekends and nights, to the chagrin of his wife. Remy thought there was a strong case against the Grand Dragon. But everything would rest on Madge's statement. If the declaration were ruled inadmissible, they would be left with very little. Plus, the system was loaded against them.

In the first week of April, Remy presented an outline of the crimes to a grand jury. He had affidavits from family members and some witnesses. A formal complaint, alleging multiple felonies, was signed by George Oberholtzer. Armed with a warrant, Remy ordered Stephenson's arrest. Initially, he was stymied by the top tier of the Indianapolis Police Department. "I could find no police officer to make the arrest," Remy wrote in his diary notes. "The chief of police was a member of the Klan." A veteran detective, Jesse L. McMurtry, volunteered to pinch him. When he knocked on the door, a man answered and refused to give his name. He said Steve was not in; he was away on business. But McMurtry heard something inside and pointed to another man, well dressed, in a hurry, a suitcase at his side. He was minutes from fleeing Indianapolis.

"I'm Mr. Stephenson," the man said. "What's your racket?" McMurtry said he had a warrant for his arrest.

"Read it."

The detective informed him that he was being arrested on suspicion of assault with intent to kill, assault with intent to rape, kidnapping, malicious mayhem, and conspiracy to kidnap. After a few minutes, Steve took a different tack.

"I'm armed," he said. "I'm an officer of the law and I have a right to carry this gun." He lifted a .45 caliber revolver from his traveling bag and placed it on the table. Well, what kind of officer? Steve whipped out his badge from inside his vest, showing him to be one of about 30,000 members of the Horse Thief Detective Association—not just the Klan's private militia, but an Indiana lawman's best friend.

The Irish cop didn't blink. He escorted Steve downstairs to a waiting police car on the street. At the Marion County jail, Stephenson was greeted by Sheriff Omer Hawkins, the first man to rise at that dinner at the Severin Hotel. They shook hands and both men smiled. Within a short time of being booked, Steve posted a $10,000 bail bond. He walked out, striding confidently back his to his headquarters in the Kresge Building. John Niblack, the reporter from the *Indianapolis Times* who had interviewed Steve in Kokomo, asked him for comment. Steve waved his hand and said it was a trivial matter, trumped up by a vindictive prosecutor and a rival faction of the Klan.

"Nothing to it," he said with a smile. "Nothing to it. I'll never be indicted."

A day after his arrest, Stephenson was indicted on five felony charges, along with his two lieutenants, Gentry and Klinck. At the time, Klinck had a job with the department charged with holding him in jail. The two Earls were missing on the day of the indictment— one said to be fishing, the other out on official police business. Sheriff Hawkins claimed his force was too busy to look for them.

They'd come in eventually, he said with a shrug. Stephenson posted a fresh $25,000 bond. He was seen "laughing and joking" during his brief stay in the Marion County hoosegow. As usual, he was dressed like a million bucks, with a showboat hat, three-piece suit, and a shine to his shoes.

"It's a frame-up," he said, "a smear supreme."

18

The Witness

1925

Madge would not die, not as everyone thought, not on schedule. One night as Dr. Kingsbury was leaving for the evening, Madge said goodbye. The next day, when the doctor arrived, she said she was surprised to be alive. "When I said goodbye to you last night, I thought it was *goodbye*." As she went in and out of consciousness, tests continued to show that her kidneys were no longer functioning. Her fever did not abate. Her older brother Marshall came home and volunteered a pint of his blood—a trickle of hope. "Her color is better and the pulse is somewhat stronger," Dr. Kingsbury told the press. The improvement was cosmetic. Kingsbury began giving his patient regular doses of morphine. Beyond that, he felt helpless.

Her room filled with flowers and cakes and tributes written on cards, but she could not smell the floral well-wishes or read the expressions of love. In the week after the arrest of D. C. Stephenson,

Madge fell into a coma. Her condition was updated every day on the front pages of Indiana's papers, a vigil followed throughout the state. She was "the most popular girl in Irvington," reporters wrote, but her doctor had started to speak of her in the past tense. The medical history was against her, as was the medical present. Lab results told of a body shutting down. "With each day, we have less to work with," said Dr. Kingsbury. Immediate attention might have saved her, he said. But going twenty-seven hours without help, from the time she took the poison in Hammond to her captivity in Stephenson's garage, had allowed the bichloride of mercury to make a toxic tour through her internal organs.

Just outside her window, it was incongruously beautiful, the first flowering trees at full bud, the daffodils showing their color. Sunlight streamed through the big windows fronting University Avenue, giving a shine to the dark wainscoting of the living room of the Oberholtzer home. Four blocks away, the Stephenson mansion had become such a curiosity site that police were posted to keep people back. One of the papers ran a large photo of the four-car garage, under the headline WHERE GIRL SAYS SHE WAS TRAPPED.

Beyond the rubbernecking and sympathy, many questions lingered. A Klansman, Stephenson's subordinate, was a favorite to win the mayor's race in Indianapolis. Did he condemn the man who'd been arrested for this monstrous crime? He was silent. The Republican chairman of the state's most populous county, who'd worked with the Klan to run the electoral table six months earlier—did he disassociate himself from the person George Oberholtzer called "this beast"? He was silent as well. Only the national Klan—aligned with Steve's enemy, Imperial Wizard Evans—took a public stand. Joe Huffington, who had recruited Steve to join the hooded order in Evansville four years earlier, issued a statement saying Stephenson was now banished from the national order, "for conduct unbecoming a Klansman."

In Washington, DC, the national Klan burnished its pose as a lobby for morality, meeting with loyal senators and members of Congress on a new agenda of social issues. But elsewhere, terror was still part of the tool kit. In that spring of 1925, a posse of hooded Klansmen on horseback rode up to the house of Earl Little in Omaha, Nebraska. He was a Baptist preacher who led the local chapter of Marcus Garvey's Universal Negro Improvement Association. The Nebraska Klan had swelled to an all-time high, 45,000 members, with a women's brigade and a Ku Klux Kiddies as well. The marauders waved torches and smashed windows at the house. They demanded that the preacher come out and face the mob. His pregnant wife, Louise, with three small children at her side, said her husband was not home. Had he been in the house, he might have faced a lynching. The Klansmen told her that "good Christian white people" would not tolerate a troublemaker stirring things up among "the good negroes." They smashed every window in the house before galloping off into the night. A few days later, the preacher's wife gave birth to a son—the boy who would become Malcolm X.

On Monday night, April 13, Madge's fever rose to nearly 107 degrees. She died the next morning, with her family by her bedside. She had clung to life for twenty-nine days. The *Indianapolis Times* carried the news with an eight-column banner across the top fold of the front page: DEATH TAKES MADGE OBERHOLTZER. The next day, a coroner's inquest was convened, hearing testimony from Madge's doctor and her father, while awaiting results of an autopsy. Funeral services were held on Thursday, at the family home on University Avenue. Her body was covered with a dark dress, on which was pinned a pearl Pi Beta Phi arrow. Eight of her sorority sisters served as honorary pallbearers. Madge's father was catatonic with grief. Already, he'd buried his first wife, who died on his twenty-second birthday, and his first son, who died when the boy was seven, after a freak accident. The third family tragedy was almost too much.

The preacher said Madge's spirit belonged to Irvington, and Irvington must be there for her memory: "Let us not forget that in coming here today we have not fulfilled our obligations of friendship," he said. In the days, weeks, and years ahead, the family "will need us as never before."

On the same day, Stephenson pleaded not guilty at a formal arraignment, along with Klinck and Gentry—the two men in custody after three days of dodging the law. He entered his plea before Marion County judge James A. Collins, who'd been identified two years earlier in the pages of O'Donnell's *Tolerance* as a sworn member of the Klan.

For so brief an appearance, the courtroom was crowded. People wanted to see, in person, this presence they'd known as the Old Man. There was little evidence that his domination was diminished. One of Stephenson's most prominent Klansmen, John L.

Duvall, had welcomed the backing of the Machine in the mayor's race. The primary was just a few weeks away. A Klan slate, pledging to prevent Black residents from moving into white neighborhoods or attend most public schools, was running for city council. A decision had already been made to build a separate high school for Black youths, a way to keep African Americans out of the city's three other high schools. The capital, along with most other urban areas of the state, was becoming more segregated than any time since before the Civil War. Stephenson, Duvall, and the Republican County chairman had huddled at the Washington Hotel in February to plot a takeover of municipal government—a scheme that was not revealed until well after the indictment. Also kept secret was a contract that Duvall had signed with the Grand Dragon, ceding control of key positions in the city to the Klansman.

Now, for the second time in less than a year, people had a chance to vote on a Klan referendum. Once again, it was a straight choice: they were with the hooded order or against it. Barely fifteen years earlier, when Indianapolis opened its new city hall, civic leaders cited a Bible verse to characterize the average, high-minded resident: "I am myself a citizen of no mean city." But this mean city had 40,000 Klansmen in 1925—twice as many as Atlanta. One national magazine called it "Klanopolis."

"I want to see the people of Indianapolis rise up and put the stamp of disapproval upon this man Stephenson," said Duvall's chief rival in the Republican primary. "What a great disaster, what a disgrace to the Republican Party it would be, to have a man like that dominating our primaries, our candidates, our legislature."

Two days after Madge was buried, Irvington was rocked by an explosion at 1:30 a.m. Steve's neighbors rushed outside to see flames and smoke rising from his compound on University Avenue. Fire trucks doused the blaze, but not before it blackened the porch with its Ionic columns and all three stories of the front of the house. The cause was no mystery: it was arson, investigators said, after finding empty containers of gasoline and oil nearby. Months earlier, the *Reomar II* had been shattered by an explosion, the exquisite cabinetry and mahogany planks of Steve's yacht reduced to smoking splinters raining down on Lake Erie. Steve announced to the press that Evans was trying to kill him, a claim without evidence. Both the yacht and the mansion were covered by large insurance policies. Curiously, Steve had already moved out of the home, taking up residence at the Washington Hotel. His most valuable furniture, and the Oriental rug upstairs, had been removed just days before the fire.

Madge's death presented the prosecutor with a new case. Will Remy was losing sleep as he assembled the pieces against Steve. A few months earlier, he and his wife had bought a house six miles north of downtown, in part to be away from the industrial smoke that hung over much of the city. But the new home was no refuge from Klan enforcers. People called in the middle of the night with blood-curdling threats to kill Remy and his wife. Because he didn't trust the Indianapolis Police Department to protect him, he enlisted Detective McMurtry, who'd arrested Steve, to be his bodyguard.

He felt the weight of the entire Indiana establishment against him. "Threatening letters poured in on me by the sackful," he wrote. "My telephone was tapped. I was charged with framing an innocent man and even some of my best friends doubted my sanity."

Remy went back to the grand jury and once again outlined what had happened, but with death as an outcome of the crimes. The panel returned with a fresh indictment against Stephenson and the Earls: murder in the second degree, carrying a penalty of up to life in prison. They were arrested and held without bail.

Now, for the first time, the fortress protecting D. C. Stephenson started to crumble. Women called the prosecutor's office with stories they'd been afraid to go public with until the murder indictment. A beautician described showing up at Steve's house one night with a male friend, for what was supposed to be a big party. The house was dark. They pushed the door open and walked in. Just then, a naked girl stumbled down the stairs. She looked underage, a child of fifteen or so, and drugged or drunk. The beautician called a cab and said the girl must be taken home.

"Sit there and keep your mouth shut," Stephenson told his teenage captive. When the taxi arrived, he ordered everyone to keep quiet while he sent away the cab. The girl staggered upstairs. She crawled out the window, down the side of the house, and fled. A statement from the taxi company backed the story. Other women came forth and told of similar nights locked in Stephenson's house or a hotel with him. A member of a sorority at Indiana University said he took her to Chicago, raped her, and then said they were going to get married—his old ruse.

Two weeks after Madge died, five hundred women rallied outside the Marion County Courthouse, demanding that Stephenson not be released on bail. "We would remind fathers and mothers of daughters that they have something at stake in this trial," said one speaker. Stephenson's legal team had insinuated through their press contacts that Madge was no paragon of virtue. She was twenty-eight years old and still unmarried, almost an *old maid*. She'd had a boyfriend or two or three, they whispered. Who knows what really happened in that rail car? But the women of Butler College would have none of it. Female faculty members met in the campus chapel and pledged justice for their former student. God was on Madge's side—not with the Klan. In her three years at the school, and ten years as a resident of Irvington, Madge was "highly esteemed and beloved," the women wrote in a resolution.

Stephenson wasn't worried. He'd assembled the best-connected legal talent in the state, led by Ephraim Inman, a man who knew the world of Indianapolis jurisprudence like the inside of his home. It was all just furniture to be rearranged. The coroner's report concluded Madge had died of "mercuric poisoning, self-administered." As Inman saw it, the case was simple: Madge Oberholtzer had killed herself. You couldn't charge a man with murder if the victim had died of suicide. *Well, yes you could*, Will Remy countered—if the poison was taken under duress. The Klan judge took under consideration Inman's motion to quash the indictment.

On Election Day, May 5, police were called to break up roving mobs of Stephenson supporters among the Horse Thief Detective Association. They were out in force on the streets of Indianapolis, distributing circulars urging a vote for the Klan's mayoral candidate, Duvall. The "Official Protestant Ticket," as the sample ballot put it, won easily in the primary—evidence, for Stephenson, that people were willing to overlook or outright deny the charges against him. The Grand Dragon may have been under guard at the county jail, but his reach went well beyond the bars of his cell: Duvall won the primary by 7,000 votes. In Evansville, where the Indiana Klan got its start, Herbert Males took the mayor's race. A year later, Males was called before a United States Senate committee investigating Klan corruption in local governments.

"Are you a Klansman?" Senator James Reed asked the mayor.

"Yes," he replied. His admission was a surprise only to those who were unwilling to read the true mood in the Heartland of the 1920s. As D. C. Stephenson had learned from his early days building the Invisible Empire along the banks of the Ohio, being a Klansman was no encumbrance in the great American midsection. When hate was on the ballot, especially in the guise of virtue, a majority of voters knew exactly what to do.

PART THREE

RECKONING

19

Big Man in a Small Town

In the folds of forested land that hold the meander of the White River sat an ideal-looking small town, with a snuggle of Victorian Gothic buildings on its main street, covered bridges over the waterway, a Jeffersonian courthouse in the square, and a ring of steeple-topped churches spreading out to cornfields at the edge. With 5,000 people, Noblesville had none of the commotion of Indianapolis, just to the south. By design and dedication, the town's metabolism was set to a clock from another era. But change came in a hurry in the 1920s with the arrival of that secretive order of men calling themselves knights. In January 1923, Reverend Aubrey H. Moore took to the pulpit of his First Christian Church to answer the question from the title of a much-publicized sermon: "Is the Ku Klux Klan a Menace to America?" He was Noblesville's most popular preacher, and this was the largest gathering in a house of worship in some years, the local paper reported—no small feat in a place known for its devotion to pew and prayer. The pastor rose now to praise the Klan. The menace was its enemies. He warned against the mingling of races, saying, "Every colored person should keep his place." He inveighed against "the poison of the melting pot." He attacked Jews as "untrustworthy," and for not accepting Jesus Christ as their savior.

In closing, Reverend Moore asked God to "bless every Ku Kluxer who may be under the sound of my voice." The congregation said *Amen* to that and rose with their hands in the air. "I would rather wear a white sheet in the dark," said the preacher, "than see my country in a shroud."

With this kind of benediction, it did not take long for the Klan to become the dominant organization in Noblesville. By the summer of that year, a Klan rally drew 12,000 people—more than twice the population of Noblesville and the largest gathering in the town's history. They burned a cross atop the dome of the stone courthouse, waved signs proclaiming "White Supremacy," and initiated 250 new Klansmen in a ceremony at the fairgrounds. None of this was considered un-American or cruel by most people in town.

One of the few who stood out and stood up was the Civil War veteran William Stern. He was outraged at this variant of Christianity that urged people to loathe their fellow man. His faith taught him that all God's children were equal in the eyes of the Creator. "Now, if the Negro is human," he argued in the *Noblesville Ledger*, "he is just as much human as any white man or woman who ever lived." The Klan-sympathetic daily seemed to doubt even that,

running a headline about the living curiosity who THINKS COL-
ORED RACE SHOULD BE RECOGNIZED SAME AS WHITES. At eighty-
two, the aging warrior in Lincoln's Union Army was still a prominent
presence around Noblesville, with a paintbrush of a white mustache
that covered his upper lip. When the anniversary of the Battle of
Shiloh rolled around, he was available to recount two nights in the
mud from the spring of 1862, a Union victory that cost 24,000
casualties—the most of any war on the continent to that date. The
only time he'd ever left Hamilton County was the three years when
he fought against the slaveholders. And those three years had
shaped a country boy into the man who would never forget what
the war was about.

Years before, Stern had moved from his family farm into town,
prospering as a merchant and a realtor. He knew everybody, knew
their birthdays and the names of their grandkids and their favorite
kind of ice cream on their pie. Now, the city attorney, four members of the town council, the chief of the fire department, and the
school superintendent were all Klan. The Exalted Cyclops, as the
leader of the local den of sheets was called, ran a clothing store.
The treasurer was a former schoolteacher. By 1925, about 35 percent of Hamilton County's native-born white males had taken
the Klan oath—the second-highest percentage of any in the state.
Noblesville's daily paper ran a regular front-page feature, "Klan
Komment," a helpful-hints column, to publicize the virtues of the
hooded order.

Where did all of this come from? What had calloused the character of so many of Stern's neighbors? What did they want? As

W. E. B. Du Bois had written, behind "the yelling, cruel-eyed demons who break, destroy, maim, lynch, and burn at the stake is a knot, large or small, of normal human beings, and these human beings at heart are desperately afraid of something." Noblesville had just a few dozen Black residents, a mere ninety-four Catholics, and no Jews or recent immigrants so far as anyone could tell. Well, there was a Greek household, the Kostos family, who ran a confectioner's store and tried to keep a low profile after someone dropped a dead raccoon at the front door. The menace, as the preacher said, was just beyond the reassuring predictability of the town, somewhere in the urban churn and moral flexibility of the Jazz Age. And those alien forces were closing in on the Noblesvilles of America.

The biggest jolt in Noblesville's history arrived in the form of a court order: on May 23, 1925, the trial of D. C. Stephenson and his two lieutenants was moved from Indianapolis to Noblesville. All of Indiana's attention would be drawn to a bucolic town along the White River. The fate of the Grand Dragon would be determined by a jury from a county whose leading preacher was the Klan chaplain, a community with ten companies of horse thief detectives. It was a brilliant move by Stephenson's attorneys, but that's what he expected to get for his money. He had hired seven lawyers to defend him.

His lead counsel, Ephraim Inman, tall, bespectacled, silver of tongue and hair, quick on his feet, and ambidextrous in formal legal filings, had pleaded with his friend Judge Collins to move the trial out of Indianapolis. He'd also asked the judge to dismiss the indictment: there was no basis to try his client for homicide, as he'd said earlier. The words and deeds attributed to Stephenson, forming the basis of the charges, were hearsay. Furthermore, there had been too much press, especially in Madge's final days, for his client to get a fair trial in Indianapolis. Inman blamed "the general excitement, bias and prejudice against all the defendants and the odium which attaches to the defense of said defendants." He suggested three towns to host the trial. The Klan-backed judge came through with one big favor: Noblesville was a perfect venue for a Grand Dragon.

The "odium" that Inman spoke of was the rise of protests and denunciations from women. The Irvington Women's Club issued a strong statement, making a religious appeal very different from the one Klan preachers made to the same God on Sundays in Indiana: "Here was a crime that strikes at the very foundations of our life as Christian people. If we permit perpetrators of such acts to go unpunished it will show that our ideals have become obscured and our sense of justice has been blunted."

Upon arrival in Noblesville, Stephenson was greeted by Hamilton County sheriff Charles Gooding, who lived with his wife in the ornate stone-and-brick jailhouse, right next to the courthouse. It was a handsome building, befitting the civic aspirations and general prosperity of Noblesville. Gooding gave each man an airy room to himself, and promised home-cooked meals from the missus. During one of Stephenson's first evenings in Noblesville, a man knocked on the door of the building, holding a basket of jellies, fruits, and cookies.

"Pass this along to Steve," he said.

On June 16, Stephenson and his two strongmen were brought into Hamilton County Court to hear the latest rulings in response to his team's requests. The Oberholtzers—George, Matilda, and their son, Marshall—were there, facing the Grand Dragon for the first time as a family. Reporters who knew him well described Steve as looking "fat and rosy." Holding back sobs, Matilda stared at the defendant, trying to catch his eyes. She wanted him to feel some of what she felt, a hatred so deep she could kill him with her bare hands. After Madge's death, her mother had suffered a nervous breakdown and spent a week in a sanatorium trying to recover.

The new judge, Fred Hines, refused to release the men on bail. This ruling was a disappointment for the defense's legal posse. But they would be given access, now, to Madge's dying declaration. And this was very much a victory for Stephenson. Inman had been trying to get a look at the notarized last words of Madge, the basis of the murder charge. But he didn't want the statement allowed into evidence—a tricky legal juggling act. Should a trial proceed, the major thrust of his strategy was to keep *her* voice out of the courtroom. For now, the defense would get to see a copy of the dying declaration, the judge decided, without ruling on its admissibility.

Steve's lawyers took one look at the statement and all but danced a jig. They were elated, Inman said, because it showed that Madge took the poison at ten a.m., and didn't tell anyone until four p.m. How could his client be guilty of lethal negligence, let alone murder, when he was in the dark as Madge was in the throes of killing herself? Ira Holmes, another of Steve's attorneys, the man who led the legal effort of white homeowners to keep a Black dentist from residing in the house he'd purchased, gave a statement to the press.

"No matter what medical attention would have been given her after that lapse, it would have made absolutely no difference," he said. "That knocks the murder charge in the head. The statement also shows that Stephenson wanted to marry the girl. So where's their case?"

What Stephenson's attorneys had not anticipated was the impact of the news coverage that came roaring out of the release of Madge's last words. In the statement, she quoted him as saying he could get away with this monstrous crime because "I am the law in Indiana." That was the headline, in one form or another, that screamed from papers throughout the state. The Old Man was king beyond his Klan realm. Two years earlier, O'Donnell's *Tolerance* had said as much, as had Remy, George Dale in Muncie, Rabbi Feuerlicht, the local NAACP, and political opponents. But they were dismissed as enemies of the Klan. A more reliable source was the murdered woman from Irvington. Coming from her, the words finally carried their full weight. Several hundred thousand Hoosiers had pledged fealty to and were effectively governed by a rapist, a murderer, a drunk, and a dictator. He was not a man of God, but a fraud. He was no protector of women's virtue, but a violent predator. If he embodied the highest character traits of one hundred percent Americanism, what did that say about them? As usual, Dale did not hold back in his Muncie *Post-Democrat*.

"Stephenson is the ruler of a mob of four-hundred thousand temporarily insane men and women of the Hoosier state," he wrote. It was well past time for Indiana to look in the mirror and face this ugly reality: Stephenson's boast was true. The Klan *had* been running its own shadow government. For those now paying attention for the first time, Dale told his readers that Stephenson had put Jackson in the governor's mansion, that Senator Watson was "groveling at his feet," and that "a whole flock of legislators refused to budge an inch without the dictum of the Grand Dragon."

But three years after he'd written that "strange things are happening in Muncie," Dale also sensed a slight change of the Hoosier heart—all of it because of Madge. The Klan had been exposed. The trial was a chance for everyone else in Indiana to see what the unbowed editor of a small-town weekly paper had long seen.

The uprising of women in Irvington, and the reaction to "I am the law," was a start of something, perhaps a step out of the darkness. In June, a Klan convention in Muncie drew "a rather inferior-looking crowd of hicks," Dale reported. The Klan had taken over Muncie before it conquered much of the Midwest and West. Now, in the initial decline of Muncie's Klan, Dale saw a harbinger for his home state. "In some communities, the Klan foolishness is still at fever heat," Dale wrote. "But it's like typhoid fever; it has run its course."

This sentiment, even though it came from a battle-scarred soldier against the hooded order, was precisely the kind of thing that put the Imperial Wizard in a cold sweat. Hiram Evans was scrambling to contain the flames from the immolation of the man he had anointed in Kokomo two years earlier. Stephenson's indictment for murder, the sordid story of rape, kidnapping, and assault with his teeth, not to mention tales of the Grand Dragon's regular dissipation, was not going over well in the Heartland, or any of the other fast-growing realms of the Klan. Evans had spent much of the previous year trying to explain away news accounts about the Klan's national chaplain, Caleb Ridley. He was well known on the virtue circuit, barnstorming around the country spreading racial and religious bias while hailing the principles of the Invisible Empire. But Ridley, like Simmons and Stephenson and Clarke and Daisy Barr, had a strong taste for the things he condemned. He was arrested in Georgia for driving while drunk. Police found two bottles of whiskey in the preacher's car.

Now the Klan was getting more publicity than ever—all bad. Evans had broken with Stephenson more than a year earlier. They had fought in court, and they had fought in print. But the struggle was over power, position, and disposition of the millions that had made these two men wealthy. Steve's violent sex crimes, his ties to bribery and bootlegging, and his control of a knot of criminals—all of that had been largely kept out of the press. If he was to save the Empire at the height of its influence, Evans had to sever any and all links between D. C. Stephenson and the Ku Klux Klan.

Under Evans, the order that had been outlawed a half century earlier had become a major force in the nation's capital. The Imperial Wizard oversaw a factory of fear in a building just a mile from the White House; his Klansmen, as he boasted, were thick among members of the House and the Senate. They worked at multiple levels of government by day, and attended regular Klan monthly meetings by night. To the major victories of outlawing alcohol, disenfranchising Black voters, and closing the door on most new immigrants, the Klan now hoped to set up a parallel government in the capital, just as it had done in Indiana.

The other goal was to prohibit teaching of evolution. The Klan backed a new law in Tennessee that made it a crime for a public school teacher to explain "any theory that denies the story of Divine Creation of man as taught in the Bible." The fear was that if evolution were accepted, it would imply that all people had a common origin. For the Klan, that meant there was "no fundamental difference between themselves and the race they pretend to despise," as the *Defender*, a Black newspaper in Chicago, put it. A part-time science teacher and high school football coach, John T. Scopes, challenged the new law. William Jennings Bryan, the aging populist and former Democratic presidential nominee, was enlisted to take up the creationist cause in what became known as the Scopes Monkey Trial. Bryan withered in the summer heat of the outdoor courtroom in 1925, and melted under questioning about biblical literalism from his opponent, Clarence Darrow. The trial ended with a $100 fine of the high school science teacher. Bryan died five days later.

"We will take up the torch as it fell from the hand of William Jennings Bryan," the Klan declared, as it burned crosses throughout the land in his memory. "America cannot remain half-Christian and half-agnostic." Thereafter, the Klan lobbied for teaching the biblical story of seven days of creation in public school science classes—a core demand of any politician who expected to get support from the Empire. Acceptance of evolution by young minds, the Klan preached, was part of a Jewish plot.

As the Scopes Monkey Trial was wrapping up, Evans decided to stage a mass rally, summoning members from all parts of the country to Washington, DC. The plan was to march right down the heart of the nation's capital to show the world, the president, the Congress, and the newsreels the everyday Klan. He sent out a call to the knights and the women of the Empire. He set a date of August 8, the same time that the trial of D. C. Stephenson was supposed to open. Two Americas would converge—the Ku Klux Klan at the peak of popular support, and the inexorable workings of the rule of law. On August 9, Evans had scheduled a trip to Noblesville. It was Klan Day at the local Chautauqua, a time for sessions on moral uplift, history, and eugenics. The Imperial Wizard was the featured speaker.

20.

One Nation under a Shroud

They marched down Pennsylvania Avenue in lines twenty-five abreast, from the Capitol to the Treasury Building, wave after wave of white, sheets on but masks up. Here was the Invisible Empire unveiled, not afraid of daylight or the mass of policemen posted along the parade route. The press had predicted that only 5,000 would attend. But there were up to 50,000 in the parade, cheered by spectators ten deep, roughly 200,000 people on the sidelines. Some of the marchers formed a human letter K or a cross as they paused. The *Washington Post* called it "one of the greatest demonstrations this city has ever known." A headline in the *New York Times*, taking up much of the front page as the lead story in the world that day, was: SIGHT ASTONISHES CAPITAL. The largely uncritical story noted the "absence of drunkenness" and said marchers were "warmly received" by crowds along the streets. No mention was made of Stephenson, except one reference to the "troubles" of the Indiana Klan. "As far as the eye could see, Pennsylvania Avenue looked like a gigantic snowbank."

They had come by chartered trains, "Klansmen Specials," from Toledo, Cleveland, Columbus, Pittsburgh, Detroit, Chicago, Indianapolis, Rochester. Klansmen and Klanswomen and Klanschildren scurried around town flashing the three-fingered sign. Wealthy members and Grand Dragons stayed at the Willard Hotel, a long block from the White House. Others put up tents at a "one hundred percent American" campsite on a corner lot at 13th and H Street. The papers had warned that Black residents, who made up a third of the capital's population, should stay home and out of sight. Few were seen anywhere in the heart of the city on Saturday, August 8, 1925, a day when the center of American democracy belonged to the Ku Klux Klan.

At the head of the parade was Hiram Evans, in a purple robe of satin with gold trimmings, a sash, a red cross on his heart, complying with a local ordinance that prohibited marching with face covered. For nearly three hours, the Imperial Wizard beamed at the crowd, waving and seeming to bless the spectators.

Nearly 90 percent of the marching delegations hailed from Northern states. Georgia, South Carolina, Alabama, Mississippi—the core of the old Confederacy, as well as Tennessee, the cradle of the original Klan—were barely represented in the parade. The largest delegations came from the vibrant center of the twentieth-century Klan—Pennsylvania, Indiana, Ohio, Michigan—which surprised many reporters. That summer, W. E. B. Du Bois had been similarly startled at what he found in the Heartland. He was giving a lecture in Ohio, in "one of those states upon whose essential Americanism and devotion to the finer ideals of democracy I have long banked," he recalled. And yet there in Akron, "I found the Klan calmly and openly in the saddle. The leader of the local Klan was president of the Board of Education and had just been tremendously busied driving a Jew out of the public schools. The Mayor, the secretary of the Y.M.C.A., prominent men in many walks of life, were either open Klansmen or secret sympathizers. I was too astonished to talk."

That was the face of the Klan on parade in the nation's capital. But for all the band-playing of patriotic classics, all the red-white-and-blue bunting, and the unfurling of a pair of forty-by-seventy-five-foot flags, the Klan also worked to get out its dirtier message on the side. Thousands of leaflets, warning that white Protestant rule still faced many foes, were distributed among the crowd.

"Americans be on guard," was the message in one handbill. "The Jews control the moving pictures, jewelry and clothing industries and own us financially. The Greeks control the restaurant and confectionary business, the Italians the fruit and produce business." Another read: "The Irish Catholics control us politically and are trying to control us religiously. The public press is controlled by Irish Catholics and Jews."

The Klan had asked President Coolidge to review today's parade. It had been a mere fifty years since another president, Ulysses Grant, had waged war on this very organization, imprisoning its leaders and forcing the Klan to go into hiding.

Opponents urged Coolidge simply to condemn it. He remained

silent, choosing to escape the August heat for the summer White House in Swampscott, Massachusetts. Coolidge worked a bare four and a half hours a day, but had neither the energy nor the stomach to take a stand. Throughout his public life, he seemed to pride himself on never saying much of anything, even when laboring through multiple sentences on momentous occasions. In Washington, people shared the story of a woman who once sat next to Coolidge at a dinner. She told him she'd bet a friend that she could get him to speak three words that evening. "You lose," said Coolidge.

As the heavy hand of humidity bore down on the parade, and skies started to thicken and darken, many people fell victim to the 90 degree heat. The march had started at three p.m. By 6:30, the tail end had pulled up in front of the Washington Monument, just south of the White House, for the grand finale. The plan was to finish with a flourish—a speech by the Imperial Wizard and the lighting of a sixty-foot cross. A minister, the chaplain of the DC Klan, assured the crowd that God was on their side of the weather. "It will not rain," he said through a loudspeaker. "Never yet has God poured rain on a Klan assembly." But within minutes, a heavy downpour fell from the skies. "Don't leave," the preacher pleaded. "God . . . won't . . . let . . . it rain!"

It rained heavily, forcing people to scatter and take cover—an abrupt end to a day showing off the Klan's might. For Evans, the march was a tremendous success. People in power took notice. H. L. Mencken, the premier pundit of his day, seemed to like what he saw. "The Klan put it all over its enemies," he wrote. "The parade was grander and gaudier, by far, than anything the wizards had prophesied. It was longer, it was thicker, it was higher in tone." The *New York Times* called it "the greatest demonstration ever staged by the Ku Klux Klan." The rally in Kokomo two years earlier had attracted more people "but that occasion was not a parade," as the paper parsed the difference between the two largest demonstrations of the Klan in America. "Except in wartime, few men have led such a host as marched behind the Dallas dentist today."

The tooth-puller from Texas did indeed feel exalted. The bleeding from Indiana had been replaced by a storyline more along the Klan's mythologizing. In place of headlines about a cannibalistic Grand Dragon were feel-good stories about average white Americans. If the goal was "impressing the government and the American people," as the *Times* wrote, the hooded order had succeeded. Now it was on to Noblesville, the next day, there to finish the task of rescuing the Klan at its moment of maximum peril. Evans got on a train to Indiana just after the rain began to fall.

In the Hamilton County jail, Stephenson had more material comforts than any prisoner could expect. Cigars, good liquor, and treats did not have to be smuggled into his cell; they were delivered by the sheriff. Steve dined on fried chicken and corn on the cob, or fat pork chops and fresh-baked bread from the home kitchen of the sheriff's wife. His alcohol came from a cache of good whiskey that had been stored in the basement of the federal building in Indianapolis. Ever since his days in Evansville, Steve had curried favor with Prohibition agents. It was the best way to assure that only the finest of the forbidden drinks of Indiana were at his disposal. Gifts arrived daily—money, baked goods, books, a typewriter, more liquor—accompanied at times by handwritten notes from a senator, a congressman, and many state politicians, or a flirty solicitation from a woman. The big suppers were starting to show. In the few months since being transferred from Indianapolis to Noblesville, Steve had gained a noticeable amount of weight. He snarled at one reporter, threatening to punch him, after he'd described Steve as "a plump, balding man." To ensure that the press coverage would be favorable, Steve spread money around the pool of reporters at the courthouse. John Niblack, now a star reporter at the feisty *Indianapolis Times*, was slipped a $100 bill by another hack.

"Here's a little present from Steve for you," he said.

"What's this for?" asked Niblack. He'd met Steve at the Kresge Building, was thrown out of that interview in Kokomo two years earlier, and was now banging out multiple daily takes on the biggest story in decades. His coverage was sharp and aggressive, but every now and then he wrote something that pleased the Klansman.

"It's for the good story you had in the *Times* yesterday. Keep it up!" Niblack took the bill, equal to a month's salary, and put it in his wallet. It was tempting. He had been working long days while going to law school at night—and trying to live on his miserly salary. He often bought a pint of baked beans for a dime and made it last for two nights' dinner. Later the same day he returned the defendant's money.

On Sunday, August 9, Steve noticed a clot of Klansmen milling in the courthouse square, just below his jailhouse window. They taunted him. They were part of Evans's team, in town to separate the image of the Klan associated with the man on trial for murder from the Klan that had paraded through the capital one day earlier. Though Stephenson felt threatened, he could feel assured—by the flow of gifts and the hundreds of letters—that the locals were still on his side. In Noblesville, it was more dangerous *not* to be a Klansman, as the hooded order showed with a farmer who'd refused to join. They paid one visit that was neighborly in tone. A second visit was less so. The third time, the man was warned that "funny things happen to farmers who don't join. Their cattle die of a mysterious illness called bullet in the head." The farmer ponied up his $10 and took the oath. Of late, the *Noblesville Ledger*'s Klan Komments could have been penned by the Old Man himself.

The look in the mirror, as Dale had urged Hoosiers to do, did not prompt a reexamination—at least not in this town. To the contrary, the paper sought to rally its considerable community of Klansmen—*they* had nothing to be ashamed of. The Klan could not possibly be a lawless organization because a lawless organization could never be chartered by the state, the paper pointed out. "All such charges against the Klan are false, unwarranted and unbelievable," the paper wrote of the run of bad publicity. "It is strictly a white man's organization—not to foster racial hatred or harm the Negro; but to preserve the purity of the white Caucasian blood, oppose the inter-marriage of races and maintain forever the doctrine of white supremacy."

Evans drew a large crowd at the Noblesville Chautauqua on Klan Day, the women fanning themselves in the summer heat, the men eager for ideological reinforcement at this moment of confusion. Chautauqua assemblies were adult education courses under open skies, often coupled with song, musicians, sometimes a play or a reading from a political speech. The idea was to freshen the mind, sharpen perspective, punch up lazy thinking. Noblesville was thrilled to have a man of the Imperial Wizard's standing in its little town. Though tired after the long, overnight train ride from Washington, Evans still radiated a shine from the big parade. He avoided most questions about the Grand Dragon in the jailhouse, except to remind people that Stephenson was no longer a member in good standing.

"The principles of the Klan are plain home doctrines of common honesty, decency, law and order," Evans told the Chautauqua gathering. He ticked off the Klan's extraordinary political accomplishments over the past year, and looked ahead to new goals. "We've passed this immigration bill and built a stone wall around the nation so tall, so deep, so strong, that the scum and riff-raff of the old world cannot get into our gates," he said. Criminalizing alcohol "has resulted in a higher plane of living for all." The attendees responded with many a nodding head and frequent applause. The Imperial Wizard had one more point to make before intellectually curious citizens of Noblesville retired to their homes and he got back on the train to Washington. He was responding to an earlier question about the Invisible Empire's recent troubles. Some had even predicted the demise of the order. He had not answered it then. But he did now.

"If the Klan is dead," he said, "then America is dead."

When court was called to order the following day, Judge Fred Hines had two surprising announcements. One, he would be stepping down. This was just what Steve wanted. Hines, the second judge in the case, had refused to free the three murder defendants on bail, and he'd turned down their request to throw out the indictment. The fate of Madge's dying declaration was yet to be decided, though it was not looking good for the defense team. A few weeks earlier, Inman had tried to prove that Madge was not of sound mind when she signed off on her final words. They were not even her words, he said, but those of the attorney Asa Smith—*hearsay!* But after a series of medical experts testified that Madge was mentally competent when the declaration was notarized, the judge indicated he was likely to admit the document. Stephenson's half-dozen-plus-one attorneys were angered enough by early skirmishing before the trial that they had petitioned for a change of judges. A new judge, the third one to hear the case, William Sparks from Rushville, would oversee the trial in Noblesville.

The other bit of news was a gut punch to Steve, who'd expected to be out and about well before summer's end. The case would not be dismissed. Judge Hines said court would be adjourned for the duration of the hot-weather months. Steve's trial for murder would open in October.

21.

To Slay a Dragon

As he prepared for the biggest trial of his life, Will Remy appeared to be wasting away, his nervous energy and the external threats to his life sapping him of sustenance. He had few pounds to spare. Remy was a year older than Stephenson, but looked at least a decade younger. With his stick-out ears, suits that draped over him like hand-me-downs on a scarecrow, and slicked-back hair parted down the middle, he was known among the press pool as "the boy prosecutor." As a war veteran from the lung-choking trenches of France, he thought he knew how to control his trepidations. But he went from 156 pounds when Madge died in April to 129 pounds at the start of the trial in October. And he was sleep-deprived.

Having initially faced Stephenson as the only officeholder to refuse a pledge of obedience to the Grand Dragon after the 1924 election, Remy certainly knew what he was up against. He was "surrounded by enemies," he wrote in his unpublished memoir. He hired one other Irish cop to join the detective, McMurtry, to protect him at all hours. He trusted no one else on the Klan-thick Indianapolis Police Department. After the snub at the Severin Hotel, Stephenson had gone to see the county commissioners in the Klan's stable. They agreed to cut funds to the prosecutor's office. Remy was forced to reach into his own pocket to buy law books, office supplies, and stenographic material, and to arrange for transport of witnesses.

He told himself the case against Stephenson was just another criminal trial. He outlined the two sides in a black leather-bound notebook. Under "The Evidence," he listed the dying declaration, testimony from the train porter, workers at the hotel in Hammond, the doctors and expert medical witnesses, the infected bites on Madge's breasts. In the category of "Defense," he wrote "suicide" and "escapade," meaning that Madge went for a thrill ride without coercion. The prosecutorial act was one part mechanical, in the evidence and witness presentation, and one part personal, trying to humanize the victim while demonizing the defendant. As always, the most important thing was shaping a narrative—a story the jury would believe, or want to believe, by unanimous consent.

But Remy had a larger goal: to break the Ku Klux Klan in Indiana. He knew—and took seriously—that Stephenson wanted to be president of the United States, and would employ the same ruthless mix of power, threat, and fear that had allowed him to take over a state in less than four years. If he could convict Stephenson, he might also be able to drag the hooded order down with him.

Stephenson's fate would be determined by a jury drawn from a pool filled with the waters of the Indiana Klan. Remy couldn't put the evil of the Empire on trial, for that would put these citizens on trial. What did it say about *them* if they had pledged obedience to an order led by a colossus of corruption? Paradoxically, the way to destroy the Klan was to separate the man from the Klan. And for this task, up against the best legal talent in the state and the dean of criminal lawyers, Remy needed help. He brought in Charles E. Cox, a former Indiana Supreme Court judge, who agreed to work for free. Born one year before the Civil War, Cox grew up in Noblesville, a descendant of Quaker abolitionists and revolutionaries who'd fought the British in the War of Independence. He'd been married for forty years, and projected a balanced sense of moral vigor, aided by a gravity-defying shock of biblical white hair. He was the gravitas that Remy lacked. At the same time, he could slip into neighborly talk to the locals when addressing his peers—fellow Hamilton County folks.

Jury selection was not easy. By custom, though not law, only men, and only white men, were given a chance to sit on the panel. Women were considered fragile, emotional, impractical, and unable to sustain hard thinking. When voir dire started on October 12, a steady parade of citizens was brought forth and dismissed, as each side tried to find a persuadable fit. The men were asked if they knew Stephenson or Madge, and if they had an opinion about rape and violent crime and the death penalty. They were quizzed on their religious background, their reading habits, on how much they knew about the case. Remy questioned only a few about the Klan, and that was done cryptically, asking about membership in fraternal orders. After thirteen days had passed, and 260 potential jurors had been interviewed, the judge finally lost patience and brought the voir dire to a close. Twelve middle-aged white men were impaneled—Cash, Sam, Leotis, Ben, Clyde, Ralph, Harley, Larry, Bob, a pair of Wills, and a Zeno. All but two were farmers. One was a truck driver. The other managed a small gas company. After the jury had been sworn in, Cox tapped into his local connections to see what his team was up against. An insider told him that three members of the jury likely belonged to the Invisible Empire.

Could this panel ever convict a Klansman? That question drove William Stern, the local Civil War veteran, to fits of rage as he made his daily walks around the courthouse square. Since his boyhood in the 1840s, he'd trod over nearly every inch of ground in this county, his beloved piece of Indiana. The change of seasons, a new pet, a shopkeeper's joke—these small pleasures still made him smile and gave him a reason to get out of bed. He'd just been feted in the *Ledger* for his sixtieth wedding anniversary—dating to an evening in 1865 when he and Mary Ellen Bush started a life together. It would be easier for Stern if he merely played the role of grand old man of Noblesville, a benign gray presence whose life marks were noted in the pages of the town daily along with stories of guests coming to town for Thanksgiving or "a resident with a severe cold." But the weight of his years had only increased the weight of his sense of duty—as a lifelong Republican, he was obligated, he said, to sustain Abe Lincoln's legacy. What he'd heard from the local Klan of the last four years—"these so-called one-hundred percent Americans," in his words—made his blood boil. He urged fellow Republicans in Noblesville to imagine what Lincoln would think "if he stood here upon this earth with the remnants of the mighty army who yet survive" and heard the sordid tale playing out inside their own courthouse. Lincoln would find a state given over to "hypocrites and traitors." As to the remnants of that force, Stern was the last surviving member of Company E, in the Indiana 39th.

Under the protection of Sheriff Gooding, Stephenson and his two underlings walked the few steps from the jailhouse to the three-story brick courthouse on the opening day of the trial. It was a small-town set piece of a building, with its tapered clock tower, pilasters of Indiana limestone, just a short stroll from the lazy crawl of the White River. It had snowed the day before, and a few inches were still on the ground. That night, the temperature had plunged to 22 degrees—tying a record low for October. The Klansman lit a cigar at the start of this stroll, and waved to people along the way. Up the marble steps they went, to the second floor, into a chamber of high ceilings, varnished oak window trim, matching wood wainscoting, and an antique grandfather clock on the wall. It was packed well before Judge Sparks brought the trial to order on the morning of October 29. The judge was known as a straight-shooter, without political ties to either side. The courtroom could hold 176 people, not counting scores of reporters gathered from across the nation. A veil of tobacco haze soon settled overhead, as people smoked their cigars, pipes, and cigarettes in the courtroom. Members of Madge's

Pi Beta Phi pledge class were also there, joining other women who would form a cohort of conscience on behalf of the dead woman from Irvington. As farmers, most of the jurors likely had dirt under their fingernails. But with the eyes of the nation on them, they were all clean-shaven and dressed in their formal best, in ties and matching wool pants and jackets.

Stephenson, in a beige tailored suit, was behind his phalanx of attorneys. Matilda Oberholtzer found a seat on the side that gave her an unobstructed angle on the man accused of murdering her daughter. Dressed in mourner's black, she locked eyes on the Grand Dragon and never let go. In the days leading up to the trial, her family had received death threats, not unlike the chilling calls lobbed into Remy's home. Klansmen in cars would drive slowly by the Oberholtzer house in Irvington, occasionally flashing their lights into the house.

Judge Cox, as the court addressed the aging anchor of the prosecutorial team, was the first to face the jury. After outlining the charges and assuring the panel that the state would prove the case against the three men, he summoned the deceased from the grave. The dying declaration had yet to be admitted, but the prosecution assumed it would after Steve's team had failed to knock it out during the summer skirmishes. From the opening words of Cox, it was clear that Remy was going to bet the house on the words of a ghost.

"The principal witness for the state will be Madge Oberholtzer, the dead victim of the foulest murder that stains the history of our state. Under exception to the rule which generally excludes hearsay testimony, Madge Oberholtzer, clean of soul, but with her bruised, mangled, poisoned and ravished body, standing by her grave's edge, will tell you, so far as possible in the circumstances, the story of her entrapment, of being drugged and kidnapped, assaulted, beaten, lacerated with beastly fangs, ravished and finally . . . finally . . . forced by the loss of all a good woman holds dear to take the deadly poison which contributed to her untimely and cruel death."

Cox pointed to Earl Gentry, the meat-faced bodyguard, his 230-pound bulk testing the seams of his suit. "She will tell you that this man, Gentry, remained in that compartment all the time until Hammond was reached. She will tell you that they threw her in the lower berth and undressed her. She will tell you of the horrors of the night drive in an automobile from Hammond." Cox paused to run a hand through his unruly thicket of white hair, moving slowly toward the jury and then back. "She will tell you of help refused her, of her imprisonment, not in Stephenson's palatial home, but a garage."

Next, he played the Hoosier card, to ensure that the jurors knew the victim was one of them.

"The evidence will show that Madge Oberholtzer sprang from the soil of Indiana. Here, she first saw the light of day. Here, her childhood was passed, and here she grew to womanhood. Here, she lived an ambitious life, a useful and a chaste life. None knew her but to love her. None named her but to praise her."

The descriptor of "chaste" was no sly hint at her character. The prosecution knew that the defense team planned to tear Madge down, to show that "the loss of all a good woman holds dear" had not happened for the first time in the rail car to Chicago.

On the other side was this invasive weed of a man, D. C. Stephenson, no Hoosier at all, a thug in a fancy suit. "He was born in the state of *Texas*," said Cox, letting the word linger like gas passed in a church. "He had drifted to many parts of the country and undergone many and varied experiences. He had drifted into Indiana four years ago and took up his abode in Evansville. He quickly rose to a position of great affluence and social and political power. The evidence will show that he had a double personality; that on one side of him was the magnetic, sympathetic, cultured, attractive man of the world; that he was an impassioned orator; that there was something about him that enabled him to attract and dominate better men and good women.

"The evidence will show that there was another side of him, and that side showed him a violator of the law: to be a drunkard and a persistent seducer and destroyer of women's chastity." His residence, "the palatial mansion in Irvington," in Cox's words, also had a dual personality. "It was not a home, it had a double character like its master. There on occasions were gathered as his guests people of character and high repute, and all was propriety and decorum. But on other occasions were drinking and lascivious debauch . . . virgin girls and good women were lured to be entrapped and debauched."

Cox tried to link the outcome of the trial to the protection of all women. "This is not an ordinary murder case. Usually murder is a deed of hate, of revenge, a deed committed with a gun, a knife or a bludgeon. This was murder committed by a man, aided by his two satellites, a man who, the evidence will show, said, 'I am the law in

Indiana.' This case is to determine whether we are to protect the sanctity of the honor and chastity of womanhood." Much of Cox's story had elicited gasps from the spectators, prompting a warning from the judge.

Cox finished after an hour and fifteen minutes, and never mentioned the Klan.

Now it was the turn of Stephenson's team to shape the narrative. Inman rose, fidgeted with his short tie, looked at the judge and scanned the jury. Then, to everyone's surprise, he chose to say nothing: the defense would not offer an opening statement. While it was baffling that Inman would cede the first-impression battle to the maiden in the grave, he had larger legal goals, as well as strategy questions he'd yet to resolve. The quickest way to acquittal was to get the judge to dismiss the charges after the prosecution had presented its case. This was a common thing for defense lawyers to do in trials where there was some doubt, when it was obvious that the case had not been proved. As he'd claimed on numerous occasions, this was not a homicide case, but a suicide, with Stephenson having no hand in the poison Madge had taken. All Inman needed to show, he believed, was that bichloride of mercury was the cause of death, by self-ingestion—case over. The bite marks on her body were something else, but not evidence of a fatal attack. As for the kidnapping, who could say that Madge didn't go willingly with Steve on the last train to Chicago, acting on her free will and her fascination with this magnetic man? They'd been seeing each other. They'd gone out to dinner at least twice. The train ride was simply an extension of their social entanglement. Perhaps a lovers' spat.

Outside the courtroom, the defense attorneys promised that a "startling revelation" would be forthcoming.

One big question was whether Inman would allow Stephenson to testify or speak to the jury at trial's end. Steve wanted to take the stand and to make a closing argument. Forceful flimflam had never failed him. As the world's "foremost mass psychologist," as he'd called himself, he could move any audience to see his way. He was a spellbinder. People who'd packed into auditoriums, grange halls, barns, and churches were held in his hands, rapt guests to a maestro of words. By trade, he was a salesman; selling himself to save himself was the ultimate test of his only real skills. But Inman knew that if he took the witness stand, he would be fair game for questions about his unsavory character. The prosecution could destroy Stephenson—showing him to be a liar, drunk, rapist, con artist, blackmailer. For years, he'd been telling war stories about Belleau Wood, a fabrication that incensed two genuine war heroes, Remy and Asa Smith, one of whom had been gassed at Belleau Wood. Since Stephenson's lockup in Noblesville, more women had come forth to give Remy detailed accounts about the Old Man—a pattern of drunken sexual assaults that made the attack on the train look anything but anomalous. If Steve opened the door to his character, these women would be called to step through it.

Finally, Inman was counting on the worldview of the jurors. "Say, dear readers, which crowd are you in?" the *Noblesville Ledger* had asked just before the trial started. "The one described as qualified for membership in the Klan, or the measly, motley mob of miserable misfits listed under our enemies?"

Like the prosecution, Steve's attorney didn't have to bring up the Klan; it was there in the jury box. If they were not all Klansmen, surely they sympathized with the Klan. Their neighbors were Klan. Their kin were Klan. Their ministers were Klan. They attended churches where Klan values were preached and Klan members blessed. They shopped in stores with "TWK" stickers. They subscribed to the *Fiery Cross*. They voted the straight Klan ticket, following the guidance on clothespin-clipped ballots sent out by the man on trial for murder. They boycotted Catholics, berated Jews, shunned Blacks, feared immigrants. For several years, their lives had been influenced by the words of the Old Man well before they looked out at one David C. Stephenson in the docket. The Klan must protect its own. Inman could hope that the oath would hold, even under this trying circumstance. *I swear that I will most zealously and valiantly shield and preserve by any and all justifiable means and methods White Supremacy. I will seal with my blood by Thou my witness, Almighty God.*

The first person to testify, Matilda Oberholtzer, was dressed in black, as before. She looked worn-out, eyes red, with bags of grief underneath. Remy walked her through Sunday night, March 15, when her daughter was led away sometime after ten p.m.

"When she left the house did she have a hat on?"

"No, just the coat." Madge had left quickly. "I heard the voice at the front door. It was a man's voice. I heard the door close, and she left. I went to the window and looked out, and saw her and a large man cross the street to the other sidewalk."

"When did you next see her?"

At this, Madge's mother began to weep. She tried several times to regain her composure, but the sobs came in fresh waves as she dabbed at her tears.

"I saw her on Tuesday afternoon."

"Just what was your daughter's condition?"

She bowed her head in tears. After several minutes, she drew a word picture. "Oh, she was torn and bruised. She was bruised, and an open wound on her left breast . . . Round bruises on her cheeks and both sides of her face . . . Her breasts had open wounds all over."

Remy asked her about the phone number left that Sunday night. There had been four messages, all from the same source. She remembered Irvington 0492.

On cross-examination, Inman asked routine details about Madge's life. As soon as the questions turned personal, the judge ruled them out of order.

Next up was Eunice Shultz, who lived at the Oberholtzer residence with her son, a teacher at Butler. She recalled Tuesday, preparing lunch. "I heard a terrible groaning at the front door . . . I dried my hands and went in and saw Madge being carried upstairs." The man quickly hurried down the stairs, facing Shultz.

"I asked the man, 'Is Madge hurt?' The man said, 'She's been in an automobile accident.'"

"I said, 'Bad?'"

"He said, 'I don't think any bones broke.'" She asked the big stranger his name. "He said, 'Johnson from Kokomo.'" With that, he dashed out the door. Asked if she got a good look at this face, she said she did. Then she pointed to a row behind the defense attorneys. "I see him. Behind Mr. Stephenson. That's him, the man with the dark hair." This Johnson from Kokomo was Earl Klinck.

Mrs. Shultz was the first to see the victim after Klinck had dumped her upstairs.

"Describe her condition."

"Very deplorable."

When Remy asked if Madge had said anything, the defense objected. The lawyers huddled with the judge. After a few minutes he waved them off and the witness was allowed to continue.

"She said, 'I'm dying, Mrs. Shultz.'"

Steve never flinched during the testimony. He seemed to wear a different suit to court every day, and flashed the diamond in his Shriner's pin. When the trial opened, he appeared nonchalant, whispering back and forth with his attorneys—"not a care in the world," as one reporter noted. But he looked away when the first two witnesses took the stand, furiously scribbling notes on a pad. "Stephenson sat at the defense table with his chubby fists poked into his face and a trace of worry visible on his countenance," Niblack wrote, ignoring the earlier threat after he'd described him as "pudgy."

In the courtroom this week was a white-haired little man, the seat of his pants worn to a sheen, dandruff on the shoulders of his suit jacket, a chomped-on cigar sticking out of one pocket—George Dale. The editor was broke from the constant pressure of the Klan judicial and police authorities in Muncie—so much so that he'd taken to begging people to help him keep going "on behalf of free speech." But he was not broken. Women of the Klan still spit on him in the street. Still, as he'd written earlier in the year, he sensed that Indiana's time in the farthest reaches of Hell was about to end. Now, he scribbled a note, tore out the page, and handed it to a bailiff, asking him to pass it to the defendant. The Grand Dragon appeared startled when he read the contents:

Though the mills of the gods grind slowly, yet they grind.

Steve looked back, searching the crowd, and there he met George Dale's gaze.

Later that afternoon, Dr. Kingsbury took the stand. He relayed the whole story as Madge had told him on the day she was returned home. The Sunday-night forced drinks. The kidnapping, guns in her rib cage. The rape and ride to Chicago. The unbearable pain of her wounds. The decision to take poison. The even greater pain caused by the bichloride of mercury eating away at her insides. The long auto ride back to Indianapolis, and Stephenson's refusal to get her any aid or even allow her to seek help on her own. Her captivity in the garage. All of this took some time, and Remy walked the doctor through it with careful deliberation. At the end of the story, Dr. Kingsbury answered a series of medical questions.

"From the appearances of the bruises and lacerations would you say they might have been inflicted by human teeth?

"In my opinion, yes."

Remy asked him to elaborate.

"He bit her, he chewed her, he pummeled her."

Remy asked, where, specifically, she had been bitten.

"The lacerations on the left breast and the right cheek." These wounds became badly infected, he testified, swelling and oozing pus, eventually leading to blood poisoning.

"Was the infection one that might have resulted from a bite?" For the prosecution, this was a crucial distinction—teeth were the murder weapons. Remy framed the question several ways. One of the defense attorneys, Floyd Christian, was quick to object.

"The death was not the proximate result of any act of the defendant," said the attorney. The lawyers huddled again. The judge allowed a narrow answer, without a definitive conclusion.

"It most certainly hastened her death," said Kingsbury.

The doctor had held up well. But Remy was less confident of his next witness, the family attorney Asa Smith. During the summer bail hearings, Inman had rattled him; he appeared so confused that the court took a long recess to give him time to recover. He lost his temper as well, snapping at Inman. The Great War had nearly destroyed Smith. The constant bombardment and machine gun fire at Belleau Wood, where the marines held off one of the last offensive drives of the German army in 1918, had left 9,777 American casualties—the biggest battle of U.S. forces since the Civil War. The mustard gas, the sickness and infections, the weeks of convalescence around dying men with missing limbs and melted faces, had shattered the young Hoosier. Now, Inman intended to gut him.

On Friday morning, Smith was the first witness to take the stand. He outlined his role as family attorney, sitting at Madge's bedside every day, preparing a final document of her words, serving as liaison first to Stephenson and then to the prosecution. Worried that Smith would unravel under defense questioning, Remy asked the veteran to tell the jury about his war experience. Then he moved on to his role in preparing the dying declaration. Remy had to dance around the actual statement, not mentioning any of Madge's words, because it had not been admitted.

"I wrote down the substance myself, from memory, of her entire story as she told it to me at different times." He then took the pages to Madge. "I read it very slowly and distinctly. Every word. Every sentence. Every paragraph. And every page, slowly and distinctly. Every sentence I stopped and asked her if it were true. She interrupted me several times in the midst of sentences to say, 'Yes, that's right.'"

"Did she request any corrections?"

"Yes, three or four times."

When it was Inman's turn, he tore into Smith and the document. These were not the dying words of a lovely woman, but the skilled hearsay of a conniving lawyer. He implied that her signature was a forgery.

"*You* wrote the first draft of this statement," he said.

"No, sir."

"*You* dictated the statement . . ."

"No, sir, that's not right."

Inman quickly jumped into another controversy, hoping to catch Smith off guard. He wanted to show that it was money—a shakedown attempt—not loyalty to Madge or the cause of justice that motivated this lawyer.

"I ask you, Mr. Smith, if you didn't go to Mr. Stephenson's office to extract money from him?" Spectators murmured and reporters scribbled.

"No."

Inman asked him his role—bagman, or legal go-between?

"Mr. Oberholtzer employed me to sue, or do anything I thought proper."

"Did you go to the office of D. C. Stephenson and demand $100,000?"

"No, sir, I did not."

"Then you went back and asked $50,000, then $25,000 and finally got down to $10,000, did you not?"

"I did not," said Smith. He had been calm but was starting to fidget, crossing his legs several times and wiping his brow.

"You didn't collect anything, though, did you?"

"No, sir."

Inman returned to the dying declaration. He was nearly eight hours into his interrogation. The witness looked exhausted.

"Now, Mr. Smith, are you sure, sir, that Madge Oberholtzer wrote that name [on the affidavit]?" Again, Inman insinuated forgery.

"Yes, sir, she did."

With no further questions, Smith was done. But Inman had planted two seeds of doubt. The jury was excused and the lawyers argued one last time on the admissibility of the core evidence in the case against Stephenson. Judge Sparks said that he would rule in the morning.

It was dark outside as the courthouse emptied, daylight now

slipping away well before five p.m. Dark and cold. Tomorrow was Halloween. The jack-o'-lanterns were out on the porches of Noblesville, and windows outfitted with ghosts and goblins. The displays of the holiday of the dead were even more pronounced in Irvington, named as it was for the author of "The Legend of Sleepy Hollow." Remy went home and tried to close his eyes for the night. The wind blew cold, kicking up some of the snow still on the ground. He had done well, in the estimation of the press, but it had been a rough day for the prosecution. Inman had painted Madge's lawyer—and by extension, her family—as money-driven schemers, trying to blackmail the Old Man. Indeed, the banner headline in even the most anti-Klan of the Indianapolis papers implied something nefarious: OBERHOLTZER LAWYER DENIES BRIBE.

At a morning session on Saturday, the last day of October, Judge Sparks called the attorneys into court without the jury. Remy had not slept, and appeared uncertain of himself, more frail than usual. Inman towered a full head over him. The judge ruled that the dying declaration could be admitted, a decision that merited headlines around the country, including one in the Sunday *New York Times*. "There is no doubt but that the dying declaration should go in," the judge said. Further, he would allow the entirety of Madge's story to be read to the jury except for a few paragraphs about her first reaction to Stephenson, after they'd danced at the governor's inaugural.

It was a blow for the defense, which wanted to show that Madge was enthralled with Steve and that they had a romantic relationship. But removing the part about Steve's ability to save Madge's job took away the reason she would spend any time with this repulsive man, a small advantage for Stephenson's team.

It was now up to Remy to bring her back to life. An Irish American barrister, a tireless Muncie editor, the leading Black publisher, and the outgoing mayor of Indianapolis had all taken big swings at Stephenson and the Ku Klux Klan. None of the blows had landed. It fell to Madge Oberholtzer—in spirit, in words that might outlive her—to slay the Grand Dragon.

22.

She Said

In court on Saturday morning, Remy read Madge's dying declaration to the jury. It was the biggest day of the trial, and the prosecutor knew he could not fail his star witness. That same day, the Klan scheduled a get-out-the-vote rally at Cadle Tabernacle in Indianapolis. Once again, election season was in full swing, competing now with the trial in Noblesville of the man who would have led that rally had he not been in jail. At first, Remy was visibly nervous, clutching the sheaf of papers that held her words, the indictment of the Klansman told in two days of terror. His cadence was deliberate, without special emphasis.

"I, Madge Oberholtzer, being in full possession of my mental faculties and conscious that I am about to die, make as my dying declaration the following statements:"

The basic story of the crime was familiar by now, if not to every member of the jury, then to most who packed the courtroom, a standing-room-only crowd. She told how she met Stephenson, her job at the state, his insistence that she shouldn't resist him. He seemed a decent enough man except in those times when something strange and vaguely threatening would come out of his mouth. And he certainly could charm, telling Madge how much he liked her and wanted to be with her. As well, she'd attended a party at his house "with several prominent people, both gentlemen and ladies." She went through a tick-tock of Sunday night, March 15, starting when Gentry took her from home to Steve's compound.

"Soon as I got inside the house I was very much afraid, as I first learned then that there was no other woman about, and that Stephenson's housekeeper was away or at least not in evidence."

As Remy read, he appeared to gain confidence, moving along with the momentum of the story, the forced drinks, the kidnapping. She described being shoved into a car, guns poked into her sides, the drive to the hotel to get the tickets, then to Union Station.

"I did not know what to do. Stephenson would not let me get out of the car and I was afraid he would kill me. He said he was the law in Indiana . . . I cannot remember clearly everything that happened after that. I know Gentry got into the top berth of the compartment. Stephenson took hold of the bottom of my dress and pulled it up over my head. I tried to fight but I was weak and unsteady. Stephenson took hold of my two hands and held them. I had not the strength to move. What I had drunk was affecting me. Stephenson took all my clothes off and pushed me into the lower berth. After the train had started, Stephenson got in with me and attacked me. He held me so I could not move. I did not know and do not remember all that happened. He

chewed me all over my body, bit my neck and face, chewing my tongue, chewed my breasts until they bled, my back and legs, my ankles and mutilated me all over my body."

The sadism did not need amplification from Remy. People in the courtroom were trapped inside that train car. Madge said she passed out, was jolted awake at Hammond, Stephenson jabbing his gun at her battered side. She remembered being dragged into the hotel, pleading with her captor to send a telegram to her mother. In room 416, she watched Stephenson stuff himself with a large breakfast. She begged him to let her go into the next room to get some rest. *"You are not going there,"* he told her, *"you are going to lie right down here by me."* She described going to a drugstore under armed escort, getting the poison, then going back to the room.

"I laid out eighteen of the bichloride of mercury tablets and at once took six of them. I only took six because they burnt me so. This was about 10 A.M. Monday, I think. Earlier in the morning I had taken Stephenson's revolver, and while Gentry was out sending the telegram, I wanted to kill myself then in Stephenson's presence. This was while he was fast asleep. Then I decided to try to get poison and take it in order to save my mother from disgrace."

Most of what happened afterward was a daze—blacking out from the poison, spitting up blood, the heat of the mercury burning her insides.

"Stephenson did not try to make me comfortable in any way. He said he thought I was dying, and at one time said to Gentry, 'This takes guts to do this, Gentry. She's dying.' I heard him say also that he'd been in a worse mess than this before and got out of it."

As Remy read, the courtroom was still, people hanging on her words—quiet but for the sobbing of Madge's mother. The prosecutor ended as he had begun, an even-paced tone.

"I, Madge Oberholtzer, am in full possession of all my mental faculties and understand what I am saying. The foregoing statements have been read to me and I have made them as my statements and they are all true. I am sure that I will not recover from this illness, and I believe that death is very near to me, and I have made all of the foregoing statements as my dying declaration and they are true."

The defense could not cross-examine or note inconsistencies in Madge's words, this testimony from the departed. But they could continue to muddy the case, which they did with witnesses who followed on that Saturday, as Remy continued his presentation. A clerk at the Indiana Hotel in Hammond testified that Stephenson registered himself and Madge as a married couple under the name Mr. and Mrs. W. B. Morgan, while Gentry filed under his own name. A maid and a bellboy corroborated Madge's story—an overturned room, blood on the bed and in a cuspidor, guns and half-empty whiskey bottles. Inman presented his own drawing of the adjoining hotel rooms, and walked the witnesses through the movements of people in 416 and 417.

"Are there phones in those rooms?" he asked a night clerk.

"Yes."

"And those phones have connection to the police, mayor and fire department?"

"They have."

The last witness of the day was Levi Thomas, described in the *Indianapolis Star* as "a Negro Pullman porter" on the midnight train to Chicago. While he was making up the beds, he had heard a woman vomiting in a toilet. He recalled at least one sentence from her, later on.

"She said, 'Oh, dear, put the gun up, I am afraid of it.'"

Inman jumped on this. Not the gun. But the way she addressed Stephenson.

"She said, 'Oh, dear'?"

The porter said those were the words he heard.

"Did she call him anything else?"

To Inman, and by insinuation to the jury, what the porter heard was something less than threatening. Maybe Steve and Madge just liked to play rough. Though Inman didn't say that, it was implied in his next question.

"Did you hear her call him, 'daddy'?"

"I never heard her say, 'daddy.'"

With his points scored, Inman was done for the day. Remy had one last request. He asked the porter if he could identify Stephenson in the courtroom. The witness nodded in one direction.

"That fellow sitting in the corner."

Levi Thomas was asked to point him out. He got out of the witness chair, strolled slowly over to Stephenson and placed both hands on the shoulders of the Grand Dragon.

"This man," he said.

A Black man of little standing had walked across the biggest stage in Indiana and reached for the Klansman. This indictment by touch set off a spontaneous ripple of applause in the courtroom, prompting Judge Sparks to bang his gavel. For Remy, it was a good sign.

That night, about 7,000 people packed the Klan rally at Cadle Tabernacle, singing, cheering, and passing around sample ballots for Tuesday's general election. Victory seemed assured in Indianapolis. But Steve was taking nothing for granted, and already plotting his next move, counting on a loyal Klansman in city hall once he'd extracted himself from his current mess. He called up Duvall's opponent, Democrat Walter D. Meyers, with a "proposition," as he put it from a jailhouse phone.

"I'm a little worried about the election," he told Meyers, who had never met Stephenson. "I'll put ten-thousand-dollars in any bank in town for you." All he had to do was withdraw from the race.

"You're talking to the wrong guy," said Meyers, and hung up on him.

The next day, Noblesville Klansmen filled the pews of Sunday services at First Christian Church. The sermon, as usual, was given by Reverend Aubrey Moore, the Klan preacher who had warned against race-mixing and Jewish financial influence, and had asked God to "bless every Ku Kluxer who may be under the sound of my voice." That voice could certainly reach the jailhouse.

23

Inside and Outside

I n politics, the Old Man always said, the only sure way to win an election was with suitcases of "cold, hard cash," as he'd shown with his bribe attempt in the mayor's race. He'd spent a quarter of a million dollars getting Jackson the governor's seat. The same held true in a criminal trial. Throughout October and into November, Stephenson was moving money around the jailhouse. He bribed Sheriff Gooding, giving him enough to pay off the mortgage on his Noblesville house. To show his gratitude, the county's top cop not only kept the good food coming to the man on trial for murder but also allowed anyone inside his prisoner wanted to see. Women spent the night with him, sharing his fine liquor and home-cooked suppers. While Niblack of the *Times* had refused the Grand Dragon's hundred-dollar bill, Stephenson managed to pay off other reporters. It showed in coverage that highlighted the doubts his legal team had raised thus far. But more needed to be done. He had to bring down the sainted Madge. Stephenson planted stories of her personal life, hoping one would be messy enough to send her voice back to the grave. He told people she was part of a plot by his Klan rival, Evans. She was a flapper, a party girl, a lush, begging for Steve's affections. The poisoning was a clumsy attempt to give herself an abortion. The defendant just went along for the ride. Much of this made its way into the papers in some form.

Still, spreading cash and lies with the press was speculative. He wanted a guaranteed outcome. One of his Klan enforcers, a state police operative named Carl Losey, was enlisted to corral a list of witnesses to dirty Madge's image. He rounded up dozens of people who had been on the Klan payroll or done its work. With freedom of the Grand Dragon on the line, it was their duty to save him. Losey presented this as an imperative, backed by the force of the Indiana State Police. These witnesses were given stories and drilled on the details. They would tell these stories under oath. Madge would be presented as a slut on the make against a great man. Stephenson assured this loyalty from his Klan brothers by purchasing witnesses in myriad ways, from blackmail to direct payments.

But even with this elaborate scheme, the only sure way to acquittal was to bribe a few of the jurors. Niblack and Harold Feightner, reporting at another paper, were tracking leads that Stephenson was working to pay off men on the judgment panel. As most of them were farmers, they were probably just scraping by after the rural recession of the early 1920s. It wouldn't take much to get a few jurors to see things Steve's way.

The twelve citizens holding the fate of D. C. Stephenson in their hands were hard to read. Yes, there had been noticeable grimacing, headshaking, and brow furrowing as Remy brought Madge's words to life. The biting of a young woman, murder by an enraged man in a cannibalistic sex act, was a hard thing to hear. But the doubt planted by Inman during his cross-examinations also showed in other facial reactions; jurors seemed to be with the defense when they questioned Madge's story.

Outside the courtroom, Imperial Wizard Evans was still dashing around the country trying to counter the terrible image coming from the dateline of Noblesville, Indiana. He was getting hit from the inside and the outside. A disgusted Klansman in Muncie wrote Evans to say Stephenson had pressured him into joining two years earlier, under false pretenses that it was a fraternal bond of men of high character. "I found your man was a man in disrepute," he wrote, "and drunkards were common in your official family." He sent copies of his letter, as he'd promised, "to every paper in America." Many printed it. In the Klan-cozy heart of Missouri, a local paper urged men in sheets to reconsider their loyalty oaths. No doubt, many had joined because they thought the Klan "stood for high American ideals," wrote the *Star Journal* of Warrensburg. But now, clearly, "it's the greatest source of blight socially, commercially, educationally and religiously upon every community into which it has gone."

During a meeting of Grand Dragons from throughout the Midwest at Buckeye Lake, Evans said it was imperative for these state leaders to return home with a message that the Klan was now resuming "its rightful place in the social life of the nation as a dignified, dependable agency for the achievement of civic righteousness." He also rushed out a pamphlet—"The Klan: Defender of Americanism"—restating the guiding principles of this far-reaching brotherhood of hate. "We believe that the pioneers who built America bequeathed to their own children a priority right to it, the control of it and its future," he wrote. "Also, we believe that races of men are as distinct as breeds of animals; that any mixture between races of any great divergence is evil; that the American stock, which was bred under highly selective surroundings, has proved its value and should not be mongrelized."

But headlines of horror kept rolling out of Noblesville. After nearly six months in jail, Stephenson could no longer give a damn what happened to the secretive fraternity he had once hailed as "the greatest organization ever created under God." His only concern was saving his own skin. His fallback plan could be found in his mailbag, which had plenty of good tidings among the nasty missives. Klansmen wrote him to say they were with him all the way. Ministers offered their blessings and their prayers. Curious readers from throughout the country suggested legal advice. There was no end to the fascination some people had with a beast. But his most reassuring material was the correspondence he kept with a tight circle of well-paid loyalists who knew where his secrets were buried. In nearly four years as a dominating force in Indiana, Stephenson had bought and sold many a Hoosier in high places, from Daisy Barr to Governor Jackson. And he'd kept the receipts—his currency of coercion—in canisters in the ground.

"Mildred, Darling," he wrote one of his facilitators in Indianapolis,

"You hold, absolutely, my liberty and you will be approached by many people who will ask you for those papers . . . Do not give anything to anyone until I tell you in person to release them." He did not say what "those papers" were, or mention Mildred's last name, but both sender and recipient knew. "I wanted to see you tonight, but something happened that no one would be admitted. The sheriff was wonderful and will continue to be tomorrow . . . My love—wholly and completely, my gratitude completely, my devotion always goes out to you."

One night, Court Asher arrived at the prisoner's cell with a suitcase full of cash. He'd made the rounds to those who owed the Old Man a favor, or who feared disclosure from what he knew. The community of the compromised was vast. But when Steve opened the suitcase, he flew into a rage. It was $17,000, no small amount by the standards of the day. He was in a cash crunch, and had expected much more. When the Klan membership spigot was open at full blast, he spent the big bills as quickly as they flowed in. Now he was facing legal fees greater than the cost of the mansion in Irvington. He'd been unable to collect insurance money from the recent fire because of arson suspicion. He needed help to keep The Bank full. All these people—*they owed him!* Steve clutched a fistful of cash and threw it back in Asher's face. *Get more*, he told him.

On Tuesday, November 3, Remy brought his medical experts in to testify. First up was Dr. J. A. MacDonald, who made a couple of crucial points for the prosecution. Most people who suffer the harsh effects of bichloride of mercury seldom have a high fever, he said on the stand. Madge's temperature topped 106 degrees in the days just before she died. MacDonald also said the poison usually killed people within twelve days. Madge had held on for twenty-nine. She died of toxic nephritis (inflammation of the kidneys), "with a terminal infection," he said. In other words—the poison alone was not enough to kill her. Stephenson's teeth were fatal.

Dr. Virgil Moon, who conducted an autopsy on her body, made the same point. The cause of death was infection from her wounds, which was carried by her bloodstream to her lungs and kidneys. On cross-examination, Inman was unable to shake Moon's conclusion.

Inman did better the next day with Dr. J. H. Warvel, who treated Madge with a blood transfusion on April 8. He said she seemed "much improved" afterward. This was very curious, Inman said. He reminded the jury that Madge had signed her dying declaration on March 28, when her doctors had told her she had no chance to live. And yet there she was, ten days later, perking up. Why the rush to sign a murder indictment when death was not imminent?

This testimony seemed to please Stephenson, perhaps nearly as much as the results of Tuesday's election. While waiting in the hallway for the jury to return from lunch on Wednesday, he was observed going over the election returns in the papers. In Indianapolis, it was a clean sweep for the Ku Klux Klan. Duvall won the mayor's race by 9,000 votes. The slate that promised to keep Black children out of most public schools, and to formally segregate city neighborhoods, scored a complete victory. Mayor-elect Duvall promised to stuff city hall with members of the hooded order—from the parks department to the police rolls. In hundreds of small ways these loyalists could make things worse for those who were not white Protestants. In where you could live and where you could send your kids to school, in enforcement of the law, in deciding who would be hired and who would be shunned, in garbage pickup and parade permits and health department inspection of restaurants—all of this would have to go through Klan filters. On January 1, "city hall will be turned over to the Ku Klux Klan," wrote the *Indianapolis Times*. But one promise would be difficult to fulfill, at least under the present circumstances. The new mayor had vowed to make Earl Klinck, now on trial with Stephenson, the city's chief of police. That appointment would have to wait.

24.

He Said

Remy rested his case on Wednesday. On Thursday morning, the defense opened with a medical expert of its own, a doctor who'd studied death by poisoning. Again, the Klansmen's team opted to waive an opening statement and go straight at the evidence. From the beginning, they thought the state's case was thin; the trial had backed up their hunch. Their aim now was to prove the point they'd been trying to drive home: that Madge alone was responsible for her own death. There was nothing Stephenson could have done to save her. And by giving Madge milk, the defendant had actually tried to keep her from dying. As had Gentry, offering her a concoction of witch hazel as she was vomiting in Hammond.

"Now, Doctor," said Inman to his first witness, Orville Smiley, "after concealment of the fact that she had taken poison for six hours or more, in your judgment would medical aid have saved her life?"

"The patient would have been beyond the aid of medical science."

"Is milk a recognized antidote for bichloride of mercury?"

"Yes."

"Is pouring a quantity of milk into the stomach the proper thing to do?"

"Yes."

"But after six hours had elapsed, could even that have saved her life?"

"No, sir."

Inman had made his initial point. Now, to another one.

"If the poison solution came in contact with the tongue, would it affect it?"

"Yes."

"The throat?"

"Yes." He added further what Inman had been leading him up to: that the infections on Madge's breasts, cheek, and lower body might have been caused by her vomiting the mercury—it was toxic to the touch. Or perhaps she had used it as a prophylactic in her vaginal area and it had spread, and this would explain the inflammation in her lower body.

On cross, Remy let his older colleague, Cox, make a run at the doctor.

"Do you know any of the defendants?" he asked Smiley.

"I've seen Stephenson a few times."

"Have you ever been in his house?"

"Why, yes."

Cox let that sink in. The Irvington mansion, as Cox had said in his opening statement, had a dual character, just like the man on trial.

"How many times did you treat him for delirium tremens or alcoholism?"

Stephenson's lawyers objected, which was sustained. Cox rephrased his question, asking him yes or no: did he treat Steve for delirium tremens? Smiley answered no.

"Did you ever treat him or prescribe for him for alcoholism?"

"Not alcoholism alone, no."

"For alcoholism, in part?"

"Yes, one time he was a little nervous and had been losing a lot of sleep. He might have had a little alcohol. I don't know. I didn't see him take any."

Cox then went after Smiley's credentials.

"How long have you practiced medicine?"

"I was graduated in 1908."

"Did you ever attend a veterinary school?"

The witness said he was a teacher at Indiana Veterinary College.

"Do you have some veterinary remedies?"

"No, sir. I am not altogether a 'hoss' doctor."

Amid a smattering of laughter, Cox introduced an advertisement for veterinary products—Smiley's own products. He sold remedies for animal illnesses and for humans as well. Cox read the ad:

"'A tonic, a reconstructive for all the rundown conditions, especially following distemper, influenza and lung fever, causes new hair to grow with beautiful luster. It aids digestion, restores vigor, works for skin infections, chronic diarrhea and chronic coughing. One dollar with the offer.'"

The quack admitted peddling the miracle cure for all ailments.

Inman followed with a line of questioning showing the real reason for Smiley's testimony and the second major thrust of the strategy to free Stephenson. He asked if he'd seen a woman with Steve while treating him.

"Yes, sir."

"Describe the woman that was with him."

He outlined the hair color, body weight, and height of a woman matching the description of Madge Oberholtzer.

"What was she doing there on that occasion?"

"She was very affectionate with Mr. Stephenson. She put her arms around him and tried to quiet him. She seemed to be the only one there who could get him to stop talking."

Stephenson was happy with these opening salvos of his legal team. He appeared "pleasant and affable," and spent most of his time eating mints, as the *Ledger* of Noblesville wrote. But he grew noticeably uncomfortable as the day progressed. He shook his head several times and wrote furiously on a notepad. When court was adjourned for the day, he snapped at Niblack after the reporter pressed him about his alcoholism.

"We have nothing to give out to your paper," he said. He was angered because Niblack had described him, in the prior day's *Times*, as "haggard, for a well-fed fat man." Stephenson lunged at Niblack, trying to slap him in the face.

Klinck immediately jumped in. "Let me hit him, Steve," he said.

"I hate him worse than you do, and I can hit him lots harder." The guards broke up the fight.

On Friday, a woman in her early forties was called by the defense. Cora Householder had been married for nearly twenty years to a fireman, Charles. Remy had seen the name on the witness list but had no idea why she might be connected to the case. The Householders lived in Irvington and knew Madge. Now they were separated and living apart, she said with a degree of sincerity. She had seen her husband with Madge on several occasions.

Remy knew where this was going, and he tried to stop it in its tracks. When he objected that the woman had no relevance to the trial, Stephenson's attorney Ira Holmes said he was trying to establish character—Madge's character. The judge allowed a narrower line of questioning.

"Tell the jury whether your husband, at any time, lived at the Oberholtzer home."

"He did."

"How long did your husband live at the Oberholtzer home?"

After another objection from the prosecution, the judge removed the jury from the courtroom and heard from the attorneys. Cora Householder planned to testify that her estranged husband had had an affair with Madge. This was the "startling revelation" that Stephenson's team had teased at the beginning of the trial. The victim wouldn't be so ashamed about allegedly losing her "virtue" on a train, the defense argued, if she was someone who slept with other women's husbands, a *home-wrecker*. This infuriated Remy. The only thing on trial was D. C. Stephenson and his two henchmen. If the judge were to allow this line of questioning, Remy said, he would bring in a dozen women who would testify about Stephenson's sexual assaults and the depravity at his parties.

At the close of the day, Judge Sparks ruled that there would be no character attack on the dead. Nor could Remy call witnesses to testify on the violent and sordid past of the Grand Dragon. But the damage had been done to Madge. And outside the courtroom, Householder elaborated on the story that had been cut short inside. She told the press that her husband had known Madge since she was a little girl. Over the last year or so, the relationship became sexual. She couldn't prove this. She had no evidence to back this. But she suspected it. Surely, this would find its way back to the jury. Just as Stephenson had planned. Madge Oberholtzer, the woman who "lived an ambitious life, a useful and a chaste life," as prosecutor Cox had described her in his opening statement, was no saint. "None knew her but to love her," Cox had said. Certainly, Cora Householder knew her and didn't love her.

During the half-day court session on Saturday, Stephenson's team continued to chip away at Madge the innocent, trying to destroy her without violating the judge's order. They brought forth the witnesses rounded up by the enforcer. A dentist from south of Indianapolis, Dr. Vallery Ailstock, and a chiropractor from the same area testified about a night the previous December when they saw Steve and Madge together in a car in their town of Columbus, Indiana.

"Stephenson passed us by, rolled down his window and said, 'Hello, docs,'" said Ailstock. He was then introduced to Madge, sitting in the front seat with the Grand Dragon, he said.

"And what else did you hear?" asked Holmes.

"They were talking about liquor. I heard Oberholtzer say, 'You ought to have some intoxicating liquor. It makes good gin.'" He was referring to the medicinal alcohol widely available by prescription. Ailstock testified that he'd also seen Madge sitting comfortably in Steve's office in Indiana.

The prosecution believed that the story about the late-night car in Columbus was a complete fabrication. On cross-examination, Ralph Kane, an ex-congressman recently added to Remy's team, asked for specifics. Like Cox, he'd agreed to come aboard without charging a fee. Why should Stephenson, who had connections with the major bootleggers in Indiana, need medicinal booze? And what were these two men doing on the street at that hour? For that matter, why was Stephenson, with Madge next to him, trolling around a nothing-burger town in rural Indiana on a late winter night? Ailstock was fuzzy on details. He couldn't even offer a specific date. Kane then asked Ailstock if he was a Ku Klux Klan organizer.

Yes, he was. The dentist had partnered with Stephenson in seeking to expand the Empire throughout Hoosierland.

And recently, Kane asked the witness, hadn't he been kicked out of the national Klan for drinking and cheating on his wife?

At the last question, a group of women who had been following the trial every day burst out into applause. Women outnumbered men in the courtroom and formed a kind of Greek chorus on behalf of Madge's departed soul. The judge gaveled them into silence.

The second friend of Stephenson, Chester Clawson, tried to stick to the same story Ailstock had told.

"What did Madge say to you?" Holmes asked.

"She wanted to know if Columbus was a town where you could have a good time."

"What else?"

"She asked about getting something good to drink. I told her there might be some bootleggers about the city."

When it was Remy's turn, he opened with a thread of rapid-fire questions about the time and place of this encounter. Clawson appeared confused, just like his friend, eventually saying he couldn't remember what day it was when Steve and this girl had magically appeared in his little town.

"The fact of the matter is you have a moonshine memory," said Remy.

Then, a different line of questioning: "Were you around the Legislature any?"

"Some."

"Were you a member of the Stephenson branch of the Klan?"

A defense objection prevented Clawson from answering. But Remy had established that the chiropractor was a brother under the sheets, and that he depended on the Old Man to move legislation through the assembly—in his case, bills that were financially favorable to fellow chiropractors.

Next up, an apple orchardist, Ed Schultze, and his wife—

described only as "a pretty housewife" by the Indianapolis papers—
testified about a visit to their home by Stephenson and Madge in
November. The timing was critical: a full two months before Madge
said she had met the Grand Dragon at the governor's ball. If she was
lying about such a vital date, what else might she be lying about?

"She called him 'dear' and 'Stevie' and said, 'Hadn't we be going,
dear,'" said the missus. She also said the two were affectionate with
each other.

Remy, appearing somewhat shaken, had only a few questions for
Mrs. Schultze.

"What was the occasion of their visit?"

"I don't know. They just came."

These orchardists, as the prosecutor then established, were deep
into the Indiana realm of the Ku Klux Klan, and had done numerous favors for their overlord. The Klan would assemble under the
Schultze family apple trees to enact certain rituals, including initiation rites, pledges to white supremacy, and cross burnings. Klan
members had each other's backs. The question was: Would the
jurors care? Stephenson's team had reversed the prosecutorial momentum. What about those images of Steve and Madge—not vil-
lain and victim, but boyfriend and girlfriend, she with her hands all
over "Stevie" and looking for a good time? A flapper, fast and loose.
Everybody knew the type. The depictions troubled Remy and delighted Inman. He told reporters he "felt certain" that the defense
had nullified the prosecution's evidence. But just in case, Inman
called the assistant manager at the Washington Hotel. This man
testified that he saw Madge—alone—in the waiting car on the

Sunday night before they boarded the train. In her dying declaration, she'd said that she was forced to stay in the car with a gun at her side. Remy was frustrated. He couldn't refute what the hotel employee said, but he could impugn the man's motives. Hadn't he been recently promoted because of Stephenson, who may have had financial stake in the place that he considered a second home? It was possible. And why had this key detail about Madge come out just today?

"You never went to the police with this?"

"No."

"You never said a word of this to a living soul until this morning?"

"No."

Over the weekend, Remy worried about how much damage had been done to his case. He'd felt confident a few days earlier. But now, more doubts were creeping in about the jury. On his daily drive up to Noblesville, Remy passed signs with enormous painted letters reading "AYAK," followed by "KIGY." This was Klan nomenclature, used in ritualistic exchanges of strangers, one meaning "Are You a Klansman?" The other was "Klansman I Greet You."

Stephenson seemed content to pop mints in his mouth, flashing that diamond, or manicuring his fingernails as the story against him unfolded. He had support in the courtroom and beyond. Grim-faced men often appeared in the back, eyeballing spectators. A reporter recognized one of these roving men as a high school friend. When the scribe asked the man for a cigarette, he caught a glimpse of a .45 caliber revolver in a shoulder holster.

"We're going to see that Steve gets a fair trial," said the gunman.

Stephenson's ace in the hole was the politicians in high places. Even if convicted, he could expect a pardon—so long as he had enough to bring down the firmament of state politics. In his cell with one of his lawyers one night, he briskly went through a stack of pledges to him by the men who governed Indiana. He was furious that Mayor-elect Duvall had not named Klinck, his codefendant in the trial, as a police captain. In Steve's world, Duvall had to come through with his part of the deal, no matter how preposterous it would look to appoint a man awaiting his fate in a murder trial to a top post in law enforcement.

When court resumed on Monday, Inman called another of Stephenson's longtime allies, Ralph Rigdon, a high-ranking Republican Party operative and sworn Klansman. He testified that he had taken his oath and had been given his robe and hood with Stephenson present at the Schultze orchard. He also testified that he saw Steve and Madge together—alone—in the Grand Dragon's suite at the Washington Hotel. They were drinking gin one afternoon when Rigdon walked in.

On the prosecution side, it was Ralph Kane's turn to throw some punches. He waved away some of the tobacco smoke thick in the courtroom, coughed a bit, then went right to the gut.

"Don't you know there isn't a word of truth in what you just said—"

"—no, no . . ."

"You did not see that girl in the hotel room at all, did you?"

Rigdon stood by his story.

"That statement—that gin was drunk at that time, is a plain lie!"

Kane was shouting. "And you came here, for the express purpose of committing a perjury, and every word you just said on this subject is a lie!"

Rigdon rose from his chair, his face raspberried with rage. "You are not big enough to tell me that on the street!"

The judge pounded his gavel. "Answer the question and then you can do what you want on the street." Rigdon shook his head, flustered. But Kane wasn't through with him. He asked Rigdon what he was doing with Stephenson every day while the legislature was in session.

"We had mutual interests."

"What were your mutual interests?"

"Politics."

"What were you trying to do: what were your political schemes?"

"Trying to elect our friends."

"Who were your friends?"

"Most everyone that was elected."

Having established for the Indiana political press that a knot of Klansmen had run the last session of the assembly, Kane asked for a few specifics. Rigdon, his pride hurt in the earlier questioning, seemed more relaxed in describing the spectacle of an entire elected body under the control of an outside master. Rigdon said the purpose of Stephenson's operation was "manipulating the legislature."

Kane repeated the words, slowly. *Manipulating. The. Legislature.*

Rigdon was incapable of hiding his awe of the Klansman's power. "I was there," he said, "for the fascination of seeing the manipulation."

———

Inman's remaining witnesses all made some variation of the point that Steve and Madge were intimate with each other. An eighteen-year-old stenographer from Stephenson's office told of seeing the couple leaving the office together at the close of a day. The prosecutors felt like they were up against a wall of perjury. But if they couldn't get these witnesses to break from their assigned stories, they could try to get the jury to see what was going on behind the scenes. Remy kept bringing up the name of Carl Losey, the Klan fixer who'd been placed in a high-ranking position in the state police by Stephenson. It was Losey, as Remy got several witnesses to admit, who'd sent out the dragnet that brought these defenders of the big man on trial into the courtroom. Also, as a public service, Remy wanted to remind people how tight the Klan's control over Indiana had been.

"How many legislators did you see in Stephenson's office?" Kane asked the stenographer.

"Well, most of them."

But demonstrating Stephenson's reach could also backfire. What if it frightened the jury into exonerating him?

Near the end of the court session on Tuesday, November 10, the defense rested. Remy was thrown by the sudden curtain call. Were they that confident of acquittal?

"It's such a surprise to the state, Your Honor," said Remy.

And he was perplexed by one large mystery: Where was Shorty DeFriese? Steve's teenage chauffeur, having been so instrumental in all of the crimes—the forced drinking at Steve's mansion, the armed escort of Madge to the drugstore, the back-and-forth with the poison at the hotel, the brutal drive from Hammond to Indianapolis, stuffing the wailing Madge in the garage loft while her mother begged for answers on the porch—could have been a crucial witness for Stephenson. By lying for Steve, he could have countered eyewitness testimony that placed the Grand Dragon at all stages of the kidnapping, rape, and murder. Remy was waiting. He had enough witnesses to counter the diminutive driver should he take the stand to save his boss. But Shorty was missing. He had fled months ago and could not be found. That was the story. He later surfaced in a small town in Ohio, where he'd kept his identity secret.

Remy wanted to present dozens of new witnesses to testify on Madge's character and virtue. The defense had skirted around the judicial warning not to attack the victim; the bulk of their testimony had made her out to be a Stephenson party girl—"community property" for men, as an insider on his team had put it.

"Your Honor," Remy pleaded, "they have brought witnesses here who have testified that Madge Oberholtzer was addicted to intoxicating liquor and that she ran around with questionable people. By innuendo, if by no other way, the defense has said many damaging things about the character of this girl." The judge was having none of it. He would allow just a few more witnesses—among them, Stanley Hill, Madge's friend, who testified that he was certain she had not met Stephenson until the inaugural ball.

On the way out of the courtroom, Stephenson made it a point to

walk in front of reporters and spectators to a little Red Cross donation booth that had been set up in the hallway. He dropped in a few
dollar bills and was given a pin in return. "In his usual pleasant and
diplomatic way," wrote the *Ledger*, "he thanked the lady for the
button and went over to the jail."

25.

The Closers

I am the law."

A cold rain swept in from the north on Wednesday night and fell throughout the next day. The storm lashed against the high windows of the courthouse, an aural beat for the closing act of the trial of the century in Indiana, making it impossible to see anything in the outside world. Not that anyone would want to look away. Closing arguments had begun on Thursday morning, November 12. Every seat was filled, and the judge allowed some spectators to stand in the back, packing the room beyond its capacity. A line snaked outside, people hoping to get a chance to witness history. Many came to hear Inman, who could make an order of a hot dog at a ballgame sound grandiloquent.

By contrast, Remy was an ordinary man with an ordinary voice. His small stature seemed to highlight his shortcomings. He often stumbled or paused when addressing a jury. Judges frequently asked him to speak up. What the boy prosecutor had going for him was drive. This case had been burning inside him since the early spring, before it was a murder indictment. And he'd been seething about the Grand Dragon's control of his beloved state since last November, when he walked out of the loyalty pledge dinner. All these elected officials kissing the ring of a Klansman. His older colleagues had urged him to conceal his rage at the infestation of the Empire in every part of Indiana, sticking with the strategy he'd adopted at the start of the trial. *Just do the job.* He had been methodical, even plodding. Details, details, details, following the outline in his notebook.

He came today with a plan for his closing argument: the way to counter Inman's eloquence was to hit the jury with the blunt force of Stephenson's own words.

"I am the law," he said again, quoting the man who had yet to speak. If these were the only words the jury associated with Stephenson, perhaps Remy had a chance to put him away. The defense had never denied that the Grand Dragon said such a thing or assumed that kind of control. They'd let the impact settle in, by neglect or design, almost as if it were stipulated. *So, maybe he was the law.* He was still not guilty of homicide.

Remy was the first lawyer to take to the floor, striding with papers in hand toward the twelve men who controlled Stephenson's fate. He asked: Why did the defense make no opening statement? *Because they had nothing.* Consider their witnesses:

"Their own private little coterie of men who frequented Stephenson's home and who received their appointments at Stephenson's hand—those were the men they put on the stand. Because they could find no others." By contrast, the prosecution's proofs had held. "He bit her. He attacked her. And it isn't denied by any evidence in this case," he said. "The statement of this girl is completely corroborated, unless you want to take the word of men like Rigdon and the old strong-armed gang Stephenson relied on when he said, 'I am the law.'"

There it was again—the story of D. C. Stephenson and the Ku Klux Klan in Indiana in four words, a boast that might be able to bring down his confederation of the North.

"He said he was the law in Indiana, and gentlemen, I sometimes think he was not far from being the law in Indiana—that is, in some places. His word may be the law in Marion County. Thank God he can't say he is the law here in Hamilton County." This was a direct challenge to the jury and their regional pride. Could Noblesville actually show the guts to buck the Old Man that the rest of the state had not?

He brought up the Klansman's throwaway line in the car while Madge was gagging from poison—"I've been in a worse mess than this before and got out of it." He tossed it back at the jury, another challenge. "I suppose he got to feeling pretty big after he'd been drinking, with this girl writhing on the cushions beside him. No medical aid except the tender services of Gentry and his bottle of witch hazel and Stephenson with this bottle of milk. A pair of fine medics these two are."

The women in the courtroom who'd sat through the trial laughed at that.

"Wouldn't it be interesting to hear about some of those 'worse messes' he'd been in?"

He took the jury inside the inner circle. "There was Ralph Rigdon, loafing around the Legislature, in Stephenson's office every day. Interested, he said, in watching them 'manipulate the Legislature.' There he was in Stephenson's office with Klinck, the deputy sheriff of Marion County paid by the people. Yeah. *I am the law.* No wonder he said it."

As Remy spoke, Stephenson wrote furiously on a notepad balanced on his knees. He sneered frequently at the prosecutor's characterizations of him. He despised Remy and wanted him dead. In jail, Stephenson had met a man on trial for murder. He offered him $3,000 if he would put a bullet in Remy's head. Stephenson would arrange for his escape to do the killing. The plan was aborted after a snitch got wind of it and relayed it to the prosecutor.

"Where is Shorty DeFriese?" said Remy, raising his voice enough to be heard throughout the courtroom. "Where is Shorty DeFriese? He would make the greatest witness in the world for the defense if this story wasn't true."

And another rhetorical question: "If Madge Oberholtzer went on that trip to Hammond on her own free will, why did Gentry go along?"

He expounded on each of the inconsistencies. Taking a trip without packing a bag or grabbing her hat. Returning from an overnight "date" with Stephenson so battered and bitten that her wounds would kill her. And why was she locked up in the garage without medical help, the life oozing out of her, if she had gone willingly?

After speaking for two hours, Remy asked for a recess. Court adjourned for an early lunch. The rain had not let up, forcing people to eat sandwiches in the hallways, sitting on the wide marble steps that rose from the first floor. The courthouse was abuzz with chatter. Reporters filed early takes for their afternoon editions and readers across the country who'd been kept abreast by the large contingent of the national press.

When the trial resumed, Remy still had the floor. He said nothing as he walked slowly up to face the jury. He looked each of the men in the eye, and only then spoke directly to them, not reading from notes.

"Gentlemen of the jury: Madge . . . Oberholtzer . . . is . . . dead. She would be alive today if it was not for the unlawful acts of David C. Stephenson, Earl Klinck and Earl Gentry. They destroyed her body. They tried to destroy her soul. In the past few days, they have attempted to dishonor her character. It's easy to understand that any man who had stooped to the crimes charged against the defendants would not hesitate to assassinate a character. It was the last resort. And yet . . . Madge Oberholtzer's story still stands. Untarnished."

He went back to the table and retrieved the dying declaration. Slowly, he started to read it again, to bring back the ghost of Irvington one last time. He paused between paragraphs to elaborate.

"Madge Oberholtzer was looking into the face of eternity when she made her statement. All the means that were employed by the defense couldn't bring her down. And so they tried to make you think that Madge Oberholtzer was a *bad girl*!" He shouted the last two words. It was loud enough, as Niblack noted in his story, "to make the rafters ring."

He moved on to lethal negligence—this trio of Klansmen denying Madge medical help after she refused to become the Grand Dragon's wife. "This girl's life might have been saved," even after she had been mangled by "the fangs of D.C. Stephenson."

He ended with that image hanging in the smoky blue air of the courtroom, and a quiet challenge to the Noblesville twelve: "We are going to see if any man is above answering to the law." He'd spoken for three hours.

Ira Holmes was first up for the defense. He'd made his name representing white homeowners who tried to keep Black families from their neighborhoods, supporting the right to fence in Dr. Meriwether. Enforcing the tenets of the Ku Klux Klan was a crucial part of his law practice. For a racist in need of muscle—especially an institutional racist such as a bank or a homeowners association—Holmes was the guy. Today, he would leave the lofty language to Inman. His job was to cut and slash. He moved quickly, without making an effort to ingratiate himself with the jury.

"Suicide is not a crime in Indiana," said Holmes dismissively. "Therefore, to be an accessory before or after the fact would be no crime in Indiana."

On to "the alleged dying declaration," as Holmes put it. "I'm not saying Madge Oberholtzer lied. But this statement did not originate with her. It originated in the mind of Asa Smith, with the aim of making money."

Then, to the doubts raised by his team. "Why didn't she make an outcry when she was taken through Union Station?" And what about her trip outside the hotel in Hammond? "She was allowed to go out and purchase a hat and a little later went to a drug store, unguarded, and bought the poison. Couldn't she have sent another telegram refuting the one 'dictated' by Stephenson?"

And what of Madge the woman? What kind of person was she, *really*? "We have done nothing to blacken her character any more than the evidence of what she did during her life serves to blacken her character."

He ended where he began. "If you find Stephenson guilty of murder you must find he forced her to take poison. And there was no evidence like that."

The rain let up Friday morning. The ground was saturated and many a muddy footprint was left on the staircase leading up to the courtroom. Charles Cox, the former chief justice of the Indiana Supreme Court, was slow to get out of his chair, and had some trouble finding all his notes. He ran his hand through his pelt of white hair and cleared his throat.

"If I had my choice, I would have nothing to do with this case." This admission startled courtroom spectators. "I am too old of a man to carry the heavy burden of a five-weeks trial. I am now closing the last argument before a jury in my life." He had agreed to assist

Remy with his case, he said, "because the law must be reinstated on its throne." He compared Stephenson to a medieval tyrant, ruling at a time "when there was no law but the law of force, and when outrages, the despoiling of women, were the general course of events."

Cox nodded in the direction of Madge's parents. "I told you at the beginning of this case that Madge Oberholtzer would be the principal witness." For a second time, he outlined the story of her life, slowing to draw out an image of a mother dressing her little girl, comparing that with Klinck dressing a battered Madge in the Klansman's garage. "There is a man and a woman in this courtroom now, a broken father and mother who brought Madge Oberholtzer into this world, who rejoiced at her coming, who cared for her in babyhood, in her infancy, in her childhood, their only little girl . . . I ask you, gentlemen of the jury, in the name of the law, in the name of this sorrowing father and mother, in the name of virtuous girls, in the name of daughters of us all, in the name of good women everywhere, in the name of justice, I ask you to write your verdict with a view of stopping the sort of thing that has been going on. Write it so that it will be impossible again for one coming as he did to the state of Indiana and in two or three years boasting that he is the law and the government of Indiana."

The old attorney pointed a gnarled finger at Stephenson.

"Look at him! Look at the sardonic grin on his face! You can't get him." Klinck laughed; Steve's face was somewhat blank. Cox seized on the moment to characterize each of the men.

"Stephenson, the degenerate. Klinck, the gorilla. And Gentry, the iron man." He shook his fist at the trio.

"These men would not have treated one of Stephenson's dogs like they treated Madge Oberholtzer!"

When Floyd Christian rose to take a quick turn for the defense, low hissing filled the courtroom before he uttered his first word. The sentiment of spectators, with women still making up a majority, was clearly against Stephenson now. The defense counsel seemed to relish getting in a few licks of innuendo about Madge.

"This girl wasn't dragged to Stephenson's house," he said. "She went to the home of a bachelor alone at 10 o'clock at night. Isn't that a little strange? Why didn't she take her mother along? Why didn't she have a chaperone?"

He was swift in his dismissal of a few select witnesses for the prosecution—the Black witnesses.

"That coon," he said of Levi Thomas, the railroad porter who had identified the Grand Dragon. "He's no different from those four poor n——s they brought up here to testify."

After the racial smear, the attorney went in another direction, comparing the murder defendant to a divine martyr. Stephenson was a victim of "forces out to get him," persecuted, not unlike Christ or Joan of Arc. He ridiculed the idea that Stephenson bore any responsibility for the desperation that drove Madge to suicide.

"If your father turned you out of your house and you felt so bad you committed suicide, your father would not be a murderer."

Inman was the closer. With his first words, he seemed a much more appealing face to the jury than any of the defense attorneys who went before him. He took his time, smiled, and rubbed his head, a world-weary man who spoke now in the staged role of an avuncular guide.

"There probably has been no case like this in the history of the American union. There has been none in the world, so far as I know . . . I wish that you and I, the thirteen of us, could sit down and talk about this case, that you might ask questions of me, and we could clear this thing up."

He had nothing but the deepest sympathies for the family of the deceased. But a murder case should not be tried on sympathy.

"I'm not here to blacken the character or the name of Madge Oberholtzer. I'm here to be of some service to you, if I can in my own feeble and humble way."

It was Inman's great skill to appear feeble and humble, and in this way, try to move the crown of morality from the victim to the defendants. He asked the jurors to think of how much Steve and his associates had already suffered. "And yet . . . Through the bars of prison, the *best people* in this country have come to grasp their hands. They have come with hearts beating with sympathy."

The last pitch was as close as Stephenson's lawyers came to re-minding the jury of the "greater good" of the Klan community stitched to Indiana and much of the nation in 1925. It was the ap-peal of belonging because the "best people" belonged, as Daisy Barr had said, the appeal that ministers made on Sunday mornings to like-minded congregants, the appeal that Steve's parties were harm-less because such fine folks were in attendance. Inman wanted the twelve men to think not of murder, rape, or kidnapping, not of corruption, blackmail, or a state government under siege of aggressive intolerance, but to consider his image of outreach through the jail bars: *The best people in this country have come to grasp their hands.*

He implied that the rape on the train was consensual sex and wondered if Madge shouldn't share some of the blame for allowing herself to be put in such a situation. Inman paused, forcing a half moment of silence before the last gasp of his appeal to save D. C. Stephenson.

"Maybe someone feels that I say these things because I am engaged in the defense of these men. It is true that I am so engaged. But, after a long service in the great profession of the law—and, I pray, an honorable one—my heart gives utterance to this: that I have not, in all my professional life, defended one for murder where I felt in my soul there was a complete absence of justification for such a charge as there is in this sad case . . .

"Gentlemen, I am done. I give this great issue, the safety of my clients, to you. By the law of reason, by the law of courage, by the law of right, I feel your consciences will not allow any harm to come to these men. They have already suffered much—too much—by far. And I am grateful to heaven in the confidence that they are now approaching the end of it all. I thank each one of you for your patience, your infinite patience. And may there fall upon you the blessings of Almighty God."

It was Ralph Kane's bad luck to follow the blessings of Almighty God from the state's best-known criminal attorney, whose closing had lasted four hours without break. But Kane had until Saturday morning, in the last sliver of time allotted for closing arguments, to prepare his speech.

When Judge Sparks opened the trial on its final day, Kane offered faint praise for Inman's eloquence, mentioning his talent to speak for so long without saying much at all.

"Are you going to let this unparalleled, unequal painter of words take the brass brush of scandal and paint the scarlet letter on Madge Oberholtzer's tomb?

"Are you are so credulous that you will believe their theory that this girl went along on that trip with those men willingly?"

He mocked the defense contention that Stephenson was victim of an intricate plot by his political enemies.

"And as a part of that conspiracy I suppose Madge Oberholtzer was to commit suicide," he said.

"We can't bring Madge Oberholtzer back to life and restore her to her bereaved parents. But we can make an example of *them* for the protection of other daughters . . . You are going to write into your verdict whether your daughter, my daughter, will be protected from the vandals and the criminally inclined. That is the responsibility of you."

He defended the Black witnesses who'd been smeared by the Grand Dragon's lawyer. "Take that colored bellhop in the Hammond Hotel—how are you going to get away from that testimony?"

Without mentioning the Klan by name, Kane put the weight of a nation on the dozen Hoosiers in the Hamilton County jury box. "The eyes not only of Indiana but of the whole country are on you, on this courtroom."

The judge then took forty-five minutes to go over technical issues and instructions. The charges had been bundled into a central question on Madge's death. The jurors were asked to determine whether the defendants had committed murder in the first degree, requiring the death penalty; murder in the second degree, which called for up to life behind bars; or mere manslaughter, which entailed a light prison sentence; or to find them not guilty. A few minutes before noon on Saturday, the case was put into their hands.

26.

Verdict

Deliberation began after lunch. Once they were fed, twelve men started arguing over the fate of the man who'd stared back at them for nearly three weeks, trying to read their intentions. After being silent for the entirety of the trial, now their voices could not be bottled up. Opinions were strong, wafflers few. The big question was murder or suicide, just as Stephenson's legal team had framed it. If it was homicide, then what degree? If suicide, should all three defendants go free? And after hearing so much about the Grand Dragon's power, could a dozen average men really hope to evade the long arm of the man who was *The Law*, should they vote to convict? It would take only a single juror to hold out and force a new trial or dismissal. One of the farmers, W. A. Johnson, was chosen foreman.

Stephenson's extrajudicial squad—the same Klansmen who'd assembled a witness list to tell a dubious story in the trial, and planted

armed supporters around the courtroom—had targeted two jurors for payoffs. Court Asher had raised enough cash to get the job
done, but it was not possible to get behind the security wall and
inside the panel. The courthouse, after the oratorical drama of the
closing arguments, had largely emptied, with several cops guarding
the jury room. A verdict was not expected for days. Remy took up
temporary residence in a little room on the second floor, vowing to
stay as long as was necessary. In midafternoon, he settled into a nap.

Stephenson enjoyed another fine meal from Sheriff Gooding's
wife. He was dressed in civilian clothes, pressed shirt and slacks,
and in good spirits. He'd never been shackled or put in handcuffs.
He always entered the courtroom in a tailored business suit, and
frequently roamed the halls without guard during breaks, cigar in
hand. The sheriff had started to carry some of the Grand Dragon's
grievances. He believed the trial was a hoax and witch hunt. The
only way *they* could bring down this giant of a man was to plant a
floozy on him, to entrap him. When the scheme unraveled, she
killed herself. Surely, the jury could see what the sheriff saw—a
great leader being railroaded.

On the other side of the courtroom, inside a small, windowless
confinement that had once served as a restroom, reporters from
around the nation prepared for a long wait. Niblack usually rode his
1919 Model T, with a hand-cranked starter and no windshield wip-
ers, back and forth from Indianapolis to Noblesville. On Saturday,
he planned to spend the night. It was a slate-gray day, featureless,
drab, and cold. A reporter for the *Indianapolis News* brought in thirteen half-pints of white mule, the corrosive swill procured from

local bootleggers, each wrapped in a paper tote bag. He sold all but three of them to fellow hacks for a dollar a bottle. Within a few hours, two of the reporters were under the table, blind drunk. A newsman from Chicago pressed a stethoscope to pipes leading to the jury room, a journalistic innovation that yielded no scoops. Others tried to follow a college football game on this Saturday afternoon through wire reports, Notre Dame against Carnegie Mellon. Knute Rockne's team had started the year as national champions, after defeating Stanford in the Rose Bowl. They fully embraced the name solidified after students, including their quarterback, had routed Klansmen in South Bend in May 1924—the Fighting Irish.

Darkness fell. Around five p.m. came an electric jolt—the jury had reached a verdict. That was quick, a real surprise, and caused a combustion of movement. Remy snapped to life, smoothed his hair, and fixed his tie. He was nervous. In Stephenson's camp, the fast return had to mean good news. The Grand Dragon lit a fresh cigar as he strolled toward the courtroom. The panel filed in at 5:21, looking grim-faced. They had been out for five hours and thirty-five minutes, and had taken eleven ballots. Judge Sparks asked them a question.

"Gentleman, have you agreed upon a verdict?"

"We have, Your Honor," said Johnson. Stephenson stood up, along with prosecutors and defense lawyers.

"Please hand your verdict to the bailiff." It was passed to the judge, who put on his glasses and read the finding:

D. C. Stephenson, guilty of murder in the second degree.

Earl Klinck, not guilty.

Earl Gentry, not guilty.

Stephenson remained on his feet, stiff and unflinching for a long moment, as if clubbed on the side of the head by a two-by-four and trying to keep his balance. The judge asked defense attorneys if they wished to have the jurors polled. One by one, each of the men repeated their finding. They were then dismissed, free to return to their farms and homes in Indiana with a story to tell for the rest of their lives.

Stephenson shook his head and let out a short, forced laugh, an incongruent response. Guilty had never been in the range of his expectations. He had the best criminal defense team in the state, the government on bended knee, the cops who answered to him. But today, at last, he was not the law. His underlings in the Klan had failed to reach the jurors for a bribe that would have set him free. Instead, the holdouts were four jurors who wanted Stephenson to be executed. They'd insisted on first-degree murder and the electric chair. Everyone agreed that the Grand Dragon was responsible for Madge Oberholtzer's death. The only real argument was whether to put him away for life or kill him.

Women rushed to shake Remy's hand, pat him on the back, and hug him. The Madge chorus was surprised and elated. A lone woman had put this bastard away. The boy prosecutor exhaled. He was spent.

Reporters barked into phones in the impromptu pressroom, dictating stories that would be in the hands of newsboys shouting "Extra!" within an hour or so. In its front-page treatment, the Sunday *New York Times* said Stephenson had owned the state, "with the backing of 400,000 Klansmen," using the high number in the range of Hoosiers in hoods. Stephenson was defiant, the paper reported.

"Surrender?" he said, a few hours after the verdict was read, entertaining reporters in his cell while lying on his back and leafing through a magazine. "I am just beginning to fight. The last chapter has not been written." His lawyers informed the judge they would file an immediate appeal. The two Earls were arrested on charges of arson, which had been delayed pending the outcome of this trial. This would keep them in jail for some time. Along with Stephenson, they were indicted for starting the fire at the mansion in Irvington in April—part of a scheme to get insurance money to help pay for the pricey legal talent.

Remy waved off his two Irish bodyguards and said goodbye, a skip in his step. The threat was over. Stephenson was now a sick-hearted little man in a cell awaiting a sentence. A felon. But that night, as the prosecutor made the drive back to his home in Indianapolis, he noticed a car was shadowing him—a black sedan. When he slowed down, the tail slowed down. When he sped up, the vehicle behind him did the same thing. He pulled over and turned off his motor and lights. The spy car parked not far behind him. Remy waited, nervously watching his rearview mirror. After some time, a police vehicle arrived and parked next to the two. Only then did the shadow leave. The cops escorted Remy back to Indianapolis. When he got home, his wife rushed outside to hug him—happy, she said, to see him alive. She'd received a phone call from a conscience-stricken member of Stephenson's defense team who had overheard the Grand Dragon instruct two men to force Remy off the road to his death.

On Monday, November 16, Stephenson walked into Judge Sparks's courtroom for the final time, still unshackled and dressed for success, looking as if he were a local businessman who'd wandered by accident into a criminal court. The judge asked him if he had anything to say prior to sentencing. The fresh-minted felon stood and walked toward the judge.

"I'm not guilty of murder, or any less degree of murder, or manslaughter," he said without emotion. "No man should be deprived of his liberty without due process of law. It is universal opinion that this procedure was not due process of the law." He called the women in the courtroom who'd hissed at him throughout the proceeding "scum." He then switched into the third person in talking about himself, as if speaking for posterity. "Time will unfold the cold, white light of truth that D.C. Stephenson is not guilty of murder in any degree."

Sparks said he believed Stephenson had been given a fair trial. He proceeded with the sentence. "Under the decision of the jury I find you guilty of second degree murder and sentence you to Indiana State Prison for life."

Life.

Five days later, Stephenson was roused from his cell at four a.m., placed in an open-air car and driven by Sheriff Gooding 155 miles north to the state penitentiary in Michigan City, just off the shore of the big lake. The night before, he'd been given a haircut and shave, and one last lavish meal from the lawman's wife. He also spoke to the press, calling his opponents "zero-intellect individuals who have arrayed themselves against me—some through envy, some through jealousy, some through fear, more through political disappointment."

On the same day, a court hearing was held in the case of his first wife, Nettie Stephenson Brehm, still seeking more than $16,000 in child support from the man who'd deserted her a decade earlier. Stephenson's attorney, Ira Holmes, was fresh off the big trial. He denied that his client had ever been married to Nettie. She would eventually be awarded the full amount, though she'd never collect it.

An hour from Noblesville, the prisoner's escort stopped in Kokomo for a breakfast of ham and eggs, and a look at the place where Stephenson was made a king of the Midwest two years earlier.

Behind the gates of the prison where he was expected to spend the rest of his life, Stephenson exchanged his fine clothes for a blue uniform and was given a new identity: convict No. 11148. His pockets were emptied of a few almonds, a white gold watch chain, cuff links, and $26.87 in cash.

"Will I be permitted to have cigars?" No, he was told—they were forbidden.

A master of self-invention to the very end, he lied to the authorities who checked him in, saying he was thirty, not his actual age of thirty-four, and listing his profession as "lawyer." Before he was locked away, a tape measure was taken of his head for the Bertillon system, which was used to identify criminals by body patterns and skull size. As Stephenson had said in one of his speeches on eugenics, science could explain why people with certain physical characteristics were born into degeneracy.

Putting away the top Klansman for life was Remy's victory, the state's victory, but it was also Madge Oberholtzer's victory. Her voice from the beyond, preserved on paper during one of her last days—*as I am about to die*—was not only in the courtroom, as Remy had intended, but had followed the jurors into their cloister. They'd deliberated as fathers of daughters, and husbands of wives. The Civil War veteran, old Bill Stern, could hope that his neighbors had listened to his pleas to shame the inheritors of the ideas he had fought against. It would make it easier to walk around Noblesville, the air smelling fresh again, the sky scrubbed clean. But would the Klan still burn a cross on the hillside west of town at Christmas? Wishful thinking was medicinal.

It appeared that the message sent by the jury was not intended to be political or a grand coda to a decade of sophisticated domestic terror. Perhaps one of the jurors had an added incentive for putting Stephenson away; it came out later that a lone man on the panel was a Catholic. He'd slipped through the defense team's sieve during voir dire. To their credit, the prosecutors had brilliantly drawn a line, challenging the jurors' sense of pride: Was the Grand Dragon the law in *your* county, as he was throughout the state? Stephenson was an evil man who'd committed a heinous crime, the jurors decided with easy unanimity—nothing more.

And yet it was much more. He had battered, bitten, and raped women without consequence because his power—wrapped in sanctimony from Sunday pulpits in idyllic towns, crowned in the Fourth of July glory of the cornfields of Kokomo, displayed for all to see at the governor's inaugural ball—had insulated him. He might have feared federal investigators or someone from his inner sanctum going over to the other side. But he'd never dreamed that one of the women he'd kicked around could bring him down, especially not a schoolteacher, a postal clerk's kid—*this girl*. Madge was nothing in his mind. But her words had just destroyed the Grand Dragon, and perhaps could do the same for the Klan in Middle America.

27.

Dirt from the Dragon

In prison, he was master of nothing, not his time certainly, and not the dead-eyed convicts who shared tin plates of watery mush at dinner with him. Nor was he well liked. One man pushed him down the stairs, he claimed. Another tried to poison him. If he still thought of himself as the reincarnation of Napoleon, his exile was nothing like the Emperor's life beyond his kingdom. He whined about the food, about the damp floor in his cell, about the chill coming off the lake, about the poor light and his failing eyesight, about being able to bathe only once or twice a week. But Stephenson maintained a tight hold on those outside the penitentiary whose secrets he kept. He still believed the governor was his fastest way to freedom, knowing that he could blackmail Jackson with his cache of secrets. As to his guilt, at the end of 1925, his attorneys filed a motion asking for a new trial, listing 387 reasons why he had been wrongfully convicted.

Just before leaving Noblesville, the prisoner had issued a final statement from the county jail. He was the sole victim of this entire episode, he said. Again, he compared himself to Jesus, martyr of a monumental injustice. The trial was a farce, "the most appalling persecution to which man has been subjected to since the days that civilization abandoned the bludgeon." He hinted at retribution to come. "I will not be the sacrificial lamb that will be offered up as the political scapegoat for the whole state of Indiana."

Indiana got off easy. And in that sense, the Klansman in the cell was on to something. All the wrongs of the last four years could be blamed on D. C. Stephenson, who wasn't even a Hoosier—*not one of us!* Fellow Klansmen, from Imperial Wizard Evans on down, claimed no role in building up this man, in giving him control of the North, in his making of them and their making of him. Evans was in a panic as people now shed their robes and masks by the thousands, many of them choosing to burn them in backyard bonfires. The Klan had reformed itself, Evans wrote in another manifesto hurried into wide circulation. It was "a movement of the plain people." But it was too late to dislodge what everyone had seen of the Klan in the Heartland. It was Evans, after all, who had put a crown on the head of a killer in Kokomo. The Klan still stood for hatred of the *other*, for ranking humans by skin color and faith and place of birth, this elaborate caste system that was no liability in many quarters. But now it also stood for rape, murder, political corruption, for the monster of the Midway and his huddle of gangsters.

Across the country, another prominent Klansman was embroiled in a sordid tale that defied the hooded order's professed values.

Dr. Ellis O. Willson, a dentist who'd been a leader of the large Klan chapter in La Grande, Oregon, was charged with raping his clerical assistant, and then killing her accidentally during a botched abortion. He was found guilty of manslaughter just as Stephenson was sentenced to life. The biggest achievement of the Oregon Klan—the vote by a majority of the people to essentially outlaw Catholic schools in the state—also fell. In 1925, the United States Supreme Court ruled that the measure was unconstitutional. By the end of the year, the Portland chapter of the Klan, which once had 15,000 members as part of a statewide organization that was the largest, per capita, outside Indiana, went out of business.

In Colorado, three Klansmen were charged in separate cases of child molestation and statutory rape. The Grand Dragon, Dr. John Galen Locke, was implicated in the kidnapping of a nineteen-year-old who had refused to marry his pregnant girlfriend—a violation of the Klan's professed values of sexual purity and the sanctity of marriage. These scandals, and infighting among the leaders, contributed to the swift collapse of the Rocky Mountain Klan.

As membership plunged nationwide, the Klan was quick to scrub the Indiana Grand Dragon from institutional memory. In Noblesville, a pair of children found two bags floating down the White River. Inside were tightly bundled records of the Empire. The sacks held letters, membership lists, telegrams, and directives from the Old Man—the written proof of a thriving, secretive, masked political order staffed by the leading citizens of the state. At the same time, the *Fiery Cross* went silent and folded, dragged down by internal strife and a decline in advertising.

At year's end, Kansas became the first state to legally oust the Klan, led by a crusading newspaperman, William Allen White. The state withdrew its charter and outlawed Klan activity. "What was once a thriving and profitable hate factory and bigotorium [is] now laughed into a busted community," wrote White. "The Kluxers in Kansas are as dejected and sad as last year's bird's nest."

In Muncie, another small-town editor felt a measure of vindication. But George Dale also recalled, with considerable bitterness, his own time in captivity. He'd been frog-marched into jail by Klan deputies in the sheriff's office. He'd faced a Klan prosecutor and a Klan judge. Stephenson had used a vast fortune to "employ the best legal talent in Indiana," while Dale could not find a lawyer in Muncie brave enough to take on his defense of free speech.

This was no time for Indiana to congratulate itself. "Weakminded politicians, blowing in the wind, hastened to do homage to this grotesque personage," Dale wrote. "Stephenson still dreams of empire. And at that, he is a remarkable man . . . Stephenson really believed he would gain permanent control of Indiana, then widen his influence until every state of the union recognized him as master, and then—but figure it out yourself."

A few other voices followed Dale's lead. A day after the sentencing, Democrats at their annual state meeting vowed to root out every Klansman from their party. Let the Republicans be the standard-bearers of the hooded order. "It will never do for us Democrats to compromise with this evil, unholy, un-American and un-Christian organization," said a lawyer from the town of Lebanon. "What the Democrats must do is come out boldly and unmask them!" They needed no unmasking, as it were, since the leading officeholders, from governor to mayor of the state's largest city, were all bound to the Invisible Empire.

The *Indianapolis Times* reminded Hoosiers of those inconvenient truths—that they had elected a Klansman for mayor of the capital city well after Stephenson was charged with murder. Had the Grand Dragon *not* been convicted, he would be dictating the affairs of state and running the city while preying on women. "He had just succeeded in placing himself in a position of more influence than any one man ever possessed in the free state of Indiana," the paper wrote. "The most amazing and depressing feature of the whole case was not the trial, just conducted, or the episode that led to it, but the career of the defendant. That he could rise from obscurity to wealth and irresponsible power, shaping legislation and making governors is a blot on the citizenship of Indiana."

This was not something many Hoosiers wanted to hear. In a short time, the paper lost 5,000 subscribers.

From his cell, Stephenson corresponded with several women who appeared to idolize him. "Best wishes to my lonely boy," wrote a stranger from San Francisco who offered to send him a fruit basket every month. A woman from South Bend took pity on Steve—a martyr, as he said—locked up for life because he was trying to fight for white people in a fast-mongrelizing nation. "My mind goes back to our association in working to make America safe for Americans," she wrote just before Christmas. His rape of Madge was excusable, as well. "Of course, you didn't do anything that thousands of men aren't doing every day." He appeared particularly close to a married woman, Martha L. Dickinson, whose husband was a well-known Klansman. She tried to visit him at least once a month, bringing him money and treats.

By the summer of 1926, Steve was getting impatient. He arranged for Court Asher to smuggle out a letter to the press. Since taking up residence behind bars, he'd yet to grant an interview with a reporter, nor had he spoken to any of the authorities gearing up probes of official corruption orchestrated by the Klan. Foremost among those investigators was Will Remy. Stephenson's conviction was not the end of the prosecutor's drive to crush the Empire, but a new beginning. Alas, the letter proved to be little but a headline-grabbing nudge of the governor. Steve remained silent months after the note went out. In the fall, Remy convened a grand jury and ordered him to appear.

While Remy worked the courts, a much-respected newspaper-man from Vincennes, Thomas Adams, assembled a group of fellow Indiana editors to shine a light on what had happened to their state. It was a little late, but welcomed nonetheless by the lonely resisters of the Klan. Adams was invariably described as a rock-ribbed conservative and old-school Hoosier, now in declining health. In September, the press squad dropped its first bomb: a mass of documents proving that the Klan had not only run state government, but was in charge of much of the judicial system as well. O'Donnell and Dale had already reported much the same earlier. But they were dismissed as gadflies. Adams brought institutional heft, and a great many new details, to the design of the Klan's hold on an American state.

Democracy was a fragile thing, stable and steady until it was broken and trampled. A man who didn't care about shattering every convention, and then found new ways to vandalize the contract that allowed free people to govern themselves, could do unthinkable damage. So now all the world knew what Stephenson had masterminded. There were two governments in Indiana: elected officials going through the motions of a representative democracy, and a dictatorship run by the Grand Dragon of the Ku Klux Klan.

"Our investigation has shown that Stephenson forced a super oath" on public officials, said Adams. "This super oath was greater than the oath of constitutional authority."

The Republican Party was outraged—not at the disclosures of Stephenson's web of graft, but at the press for reporting it. This journalism was the work of Jews, party officials implied. Clyde A. Walb, the Republican Party state chairman, said a syndicate of international bankers was trying to bring down the GOP in Indiana. The party's Central Committee disowned Adams, a lifelong Republican.

In October 1926, Remy hauled Stephenson before his grand jury. He sat in the witness chair smoking a cigar, happy to be breathing interior air from somewhere other than his squalid cell, especially air thick with tobacco smoke. But he said nothing. He refused to answer even the most basic questions. He felt that if he sang to the prosecutor, Governor Jackson would be useless to him. Better to tighten the leash. Remy called hundreds of other witnesses, building his case to smash the Klan. By the end of the year, Adams said the Klan was in broad retreat throughout Indiana, reduced to 50,000 members—still enough Klansmen to fill a stadium. Hoosiers of conscience could breathe a sigh of relief, Adams said with no small amount of self-congratulation. "We believe we have ended Klan control in Indiana."

He spoke too soon. That year, the Klan-dominated city council passed a new ordinance taking away the freedom of Black residents to live where they wanted in Indianapolis—formalizing a segregation system that had been building in the twenties. A crowd of more than eight hundred people showed up at city hall to ensure that Black people would never reside in white neighborhoods. "It is neither good for the whites nor the Blacks for the two races to commingle," said the group's leader, a lawyer with the aptonym of Omer Whiteman. The crowd hooted and stomped its feet in approval as the council voted. After Mayor Duvall signed the law, it was a civil crime for Black families to move into a white residential area without the consent of a majority of those who lived there. A few months later, a Black physician, Dr. Guy Grant, purchased a home in a white part of town. The city moved to evict him. He was able to stay in his house after the NAACP filed suit to block the law.

The next year, 1927, Indianapolis played host to the annual meeting of Women of the Ku Klux Klan. It was a woman from Irvington whose voice from beyond the grave had knocked the Klan from the highest perch in its history. But these women from all parts of the country would show that they were not deterred. Thousands of white-robed Klanswomen assembled for two days in

Tomlinson Hall. It was the very place where Patrick O'Donnell had vowed to destroy the hooded order five years earlier.

A lead speaker was the Imperial Commander of the women's Klan, Robbie Gill Comer from Arkansas. She was the author of a book, *The Equality of Women*, and preached that females could be equal to males in defense of white supremacy. In Arkansas, she had been instrumental in persuading the legislature to add a fourth star to its flag, symbolizing the four years the state belonged to a Confederacy of slaveholders. In Indianapolis, Comer tried to calm the furor over corruption. "The Klan is forever out of politics," she said. "In the future, its work will be of an invisible nature."

Those words were contradicted the next day when Imperial Wizard Evans took to the same stage. His speech was one he had given many times, "Rum and Romanism." But in the wake of the scandals and cratering membership, there was added urgency to his voice. The year before, in its second march down the heart of Washington, DC, the Klan had been able to attract only 15,000 people—not even a third of the multitudes who flooded the capital in 1925. The "thinned ranks" of a parade that showed "not much life" was evidence that the Klan was in a downward spiral, wrote the *New York Times*.

Lick Skillet Hollow is a listless valley in the southern part of Indiana, not far from where Stephenson laid the foundation for the Klan's empire of the North. According to local lore, the place got its name from settlers who used to leave their dirty pans on back porches to let the deer lick them clean. On July 27, 1927, John Niblack and another attorney drove the length of the state to meet a mystery man outside a barn in Lick Skillet. After three years of attending law school at night and then passing the state bar, Niblack had traded in his reporter's notebook for subpoena power. He was now a deputy prosecutor, making $200 a month working for one of the few public officials he trusted and admired—Will Remy. Earlier that month, Stephenson had asked Governor Jackson for a ninety-day parole to gather evidence for his appeal. Jackson refused. This betrayal by his old master finally pushed the convict over the line.

Deep into his second year in prison, the Grand Dragon was falling apart. He complained of rheumatism that made it difficult to walk, and about how his thin hair was quickly going gray "due to the fiendish workings of the conspiracy" against him. He never explained with any lucidity who or what made up this network of plotters, or how it would make his hair change color. His view of his victim had gone from casual disregard to open loathing. He described Madge's dying declaration as "a filthy document of perjury and forgery" in one court filing and implied that she may have deserved what she got "after going to the home of an unmarried man at the unconventional hour of 11 P.M." He would shed no tears for the woman from Irvington. "I have not developed elastic sympathy for the dead."

But he was ready to rat out the governor who'd failed to spring him. "I've been double-crossed for the last time," he said. Perhaps by currying favor with the law, he could shorten his stay inside the

barbed-wire enclosure in Michigan City. He gave a remarkably
blunt statement to the press:

"I purchased the Marion County and state officials involved in this
investigation in an open market. I paid an excessive price for them."

He asked Remy to meet a former business partner outside a farm.
There, the prosecutor's team was handed two black metal boxes,
eighteen inches long, eight inches high and wide, that had been
buried beneath the ground of a round barn. The next day, Remy
examined his treasure from Lick Skillet. As if combing through an
archaeological find, the prosecutor spent nine hours excavating the
detritus from Stephenson's hold on the state. Some of the papers
were mildewed, but the evidence was clear. Among gold cuff links
and rings without their precious stones was a cache of canceled
checks and pledges to Steve from top political leaders. If anyone in
Indiana needed further proof of how they had turned their state
over to the Klan, the boxes held many directives from the Grand
Dragon. Duvall had promised that 85 percent of his hires at city
hall would belong to the Klan. Ledgers and notes detailed how the
Empire had used Jackson to try to bribe a former governor into
naming a prosecutor owned by the Klan. He'd also been given
thousands of dollars directly from Stephenson. Asked about the
money, the governor said it was for a horse named Senator that he
had sold to Stephenson. When reporters tried to track down the
prized animal, they were told that the horse had choked to death on
a corncob.

In September 1927, Jackson and the top Republican in Marion
County were indicted on bribery charges. Mayor Duvall and six

city council members were also charged, in separate indictments, with violating the state's corrupt practices law. Duvall was found guilty, ousted from office, and sent to jail. The council members met a similar fate. Jackson refused to step down. He stood trial in February 1928. The star witness was D. C. Stephenson. He reveled in the attention, even as most press accounts described him as haggard, aged, and diminished. Under oath, he was quarrelsome and arrogant. He was asked if his personality was so strong that he could persuade anyone to accept a bribe. He smiled at the backhanded compliment.

"I can't answer that."

"Do you deny that you are an egotist?"

Steve turned to the judge. "Do I have to submit to this sort of insult?"

He was questioned about the parties aboard his yacht.

"While you were on the boat, you had all you wanted to drink, yes?"

"If anyone suffered from drought," he said, "it was his own fault."

Testifying in another case, the Grand Dragon said weapons were passed around among Klansmen as freely as illegal hooch.

"I have never met one who didn't have a gun, a knife or often a blackjack."

"Why?"

"Because their minds uniformly ran to violence."

Under oath, Stephenson claimed to have taken in the modern equivalent of $29 million in initiation fees for the Invisible Empire. He got at least 40 percent of that.

"Isn't it strange that with all our educational advantages," noted the Hoosier writer Meredith Nicholson, so many "Indiana citizens could be induced to pay $10 for the privilege of hating their neighbors and wearing a sheet?" To D. C. Stephenson, it wasn't strange at all. Steve's 1922 epiphany in Evansville—that he could make far more money from the renewable hate of everyday white people than he could ever make as an honest businessman or a member of Congress—was brilliant. And true.

In the end, Stephenson gave several exhaustive accounts of the bribery scheme and how he pulled the levers of power in the state. This evidence, along with testimony of other witnesses and canceled checks, proved beyond a doubt that the Klan's governor had been guilty, as the judge said so himself in a directed verdict. But Jackson got off on a technicality: the statute of limitations had expired. He finished out his term and retired from politics.

As the governor's trial was wrapping up, Klan secrets were spilling out of another court case, this one in Pennsylvania. Imperial Wizard Evans had sued the Pittsburgh Klan, saying it could not break away from the national group without compensating headquarters. It was a disastrous mistake. What should have been a boring back-and-forth on contracts and dues owed, instead became a national forum on Klan atrocities during the 1920s. Klansmen from Oklahoma testified about kidnappings, floggings, and hot-iron brandings. One night, a gang of Sooner State nightriders had grabbed two Jewish businessmen from New York and flogged them until they passed out. From Texas, former Klan members said they had burned a Black man at the stake—under a directive from the

Imperial Wizard. Others said Evans also ordered the riot in Carnegie, hoping to force the immigrants and Catholics of western Pennsylvania into a cowering retreat. The state's Grand Dragon encouraged new assaults, similar to Carnegie, as a recruiting tool. Another witness testified about a night when the Pittsburgh Klan grabbed a Black man, tied him up, and strung him from a tree, leaving him gasping for his life.

For years, politicians, ministers, and apologists in the press had claimed that the Klan that had become such an integral part of American life—with its six million members, its senators, governors, militias, preachers, and police chiefs—was a harmless band of brothers. They were white men in hoods bonding over a shared heritage and desire for a simpler life. That image fell apart in a court of law. At the conclusion of the Pennsylvania trial in 1928, Judge W. H. S. Thompson issued a scathing indictment. He found that the Invisible Empire of the Roaring Twenties, one that would later cast itself as a Mayberry Klan of good fellowship and high Christian values, was "an instrument of terror, oppression, violence and a menace to public peace." He called it an "unlawful organization, so destructive of the rights and liberties of the people." After noting that Imperial Wizard Evans and his lawyers came to the court seeking relief "with filthy hands," he awarded them nothing.

Whether hearts were softened and minds opened was another story. In Noblesville, after the scheduled speaker at a Kiwanis Club luncheon in 1928 canceled, a Catholic priest volunteered as a last-minute fill-in. Just a few years earlier, more than ten thousand masked men had paraded around town on a summer night, denouncing Catholics in the harshest of terms. Over chicken salad sandwiches, Father Mike Holand talked about hate as a dead-end emotion. But love was the greatest and most selfless expression. If people got to know him as a man, and not a crude stereotype, they might find something to like about him, and eventually could come to love him. He was given a standing ovation. Seventeen miles up the road, in Tipton, another Catholic was invited to give the high school commencement speech in a town that had elected an all-Klan slate to public office in 1925, one year earlier. Bishop Edwin Holt denounced the "low, vulgar people" who belittled immigrants and Jews. The foulest words a Hoosier could use, he said, were "Dago and Sheeny." The local paper, never an ardent foe of the Klan, called the speech "one of the best addresses ever delivered in Tipton."

Throughout the country, the Klan could no longer claim owners of banks, editors of newspapers, and judges on state courts as sworn members. Those days were gone—a shameful aberration in the American story, the *Chicago Tribune* wrote in the wake of the crumbling Klan. The paper sketched an outline that sounded like a bad fairy tale. "It came about that American citizens in Indiana were judged by their religion, condemned because of their race, illegally punished because of their opinions, hounded because of their personal conduct, and a state of terror was substituted for a state of law."

But was it really an aberration?

As a mass movement, the Klan was finished—membership down

by 90 percent nationwide in the three years since the words of Madge Oberholtzer put away the Grand Dragon. As a political force in Washington and half a dozen state capitals, it was a pariah. "As the lights were turned on again, few would admit, even sheepishly, they ever had belonged to the Klan," recalled Harold Feightner, the reporter friend of Niblack's. But the dead-end emotion that the priest had spoken of in Noblesville, the fog of hatred that lay over the land long after the lockup of the man who most effectively used it, had yet to lift.

On a sweltering August day in 1930, a mob stormed the Grant County jail in Marion, Indiana, a town of about 30,000 people, forty miles north of Muncie. Using crowbars and hammers, they ripped the iron doors of a cell from its hinges. Inside, three Black teenagers fell to their knees and prayed for their lives. Deputies fired tear gas at the surge of enraged men, but refused to draw their guns. The sheriff was said to be a former Klansman. Earlier that day, the three prisoners had been accused of killing a white man during a roadside robbery, and raping his girlfriend. One of the teens, Abraham Smith, was dragged into the courtyard, beaten, and stabbed, and then lynched by rope tied to the bars of the upstairs jail. A second young man, J. Thomas Shipp, was hauled to a nearby maple tree. A boisterous crowd that included many women and children chanted, "Kill the n——!" A few Klansmen circulated among the mob, veiled under white robes that had been gathering moths for several years. As the vigilantes were stringing him up, Shipp tried to struggle out of the noose. He was lowered, both of his arms were broken, and then he was pulled high above the ground as his neck snapped. Women laughed and clapped while the life was choked out of Shipp. The atmosphere was festive—like a picnic, one witness recalled.

The third prisoner, James Cameron, a sixteen-year-old who had fled the roadside crime scene before the assault began, was thrown to the ground and beaten. A woman jumped from the top of a car onto him, driving spiked heels into his back. Begging for his life, he said he was innocent. Just as a noose was tightened around his neck came the voice of a prominent white athlete: "Take this boy back. He had nothing to do with any raping or shooting of anybody." Cameron's life was spared.

A little while later, Smith's body was relocated to the maple tree in the town's main courtyard and hung next to the other dead man. All night, people posed in front of the victims, pointing and smiling for the cameras at the bloodied corpses. The murder in plain sight was the last known lynching of Black people in Indiana and possibly the last north of the Mason-Dixon Line. After dangling in a summer breeze for eight hours, the bodies were cut down by a deputy at dawn. The woman at the roadside robbery scene later said there had been no rape; she had made the story up. Though the leading citizens of Indiana professed outrage and vowed to bring the vigilante killers to justice, a Grant County grand jury refused to issue any indictments. No one was ever charged with a lawless execution witnessed by thousands of Hoosiers in the public square.

EPILOGUE

In 1998, a plaque was mounted at the entrance to the most famous courtroom in Indiana. Three years earlier, a building contractor had discovered an old steamer trunk in a barn outside Noblesville. Inside were three-by-five membership cards of more than a thousand local Klansmen, and hoods, sashes, robes, and a cross with lightbulbs. The find was an embarrassment that made national news and came as a shock to many in the state. Rather than tarnish the image of Noblesville, the Klan materials should have been burned and the names erased from memory, some of the residents said.

"Well, you can't burn history," the contractor told Allen Safianow, an Indiana historian. "That's what's wrong today." After much wrangling, the evidence of the Klan's hold on the town was turned over to the historical society. For the next twenty-two years the membership list would be kept secret except to scholars who agreed to certain restrictions. The townsfolk had decided it was better to focus on what happened in the courtroom, to let the world know about the momentous turn of events inside a small-town house of justice. The plaque reads:

SITE OF D.C. STEPHENSON TRIAL

A jury of Hamilton County citizens convicted Ku Klux
Klan leader D.C. Stephenson in this building in November,
1925 for the murder of Madge Oberholtzer. The outcome
of the trial resulted in the rapid decline of the theretofore
powerful Klan influence in state government.

The heroes in this telling were those twelve average men. All it took were a few good Hoosiers to put an end to Klan "influence" in Indiana, as it was phrased. The Klan was dissolved in Noblesville a year after Stephenson was locked up, bringing some measure of relief to the town's last surviving Union soldier from the Civil War, Bill Stern. He died in 1933, at the age of ninety-one. By inference, the system worked, good triumphed over evil, and the fever that took hold of a most quintessential American state could be time-capsulized and forgotten. The verdict was a bookend. The hysteria that led to the lynching of the Jewish factory boss Leo Frank "was the spark that ignited" the twentieth-century Klan, as historian Wyn Craig Wade wrote, and the Stephenson case "put out the fire."

But take away the courage of Madge Oberholtzer as she lay dying from poison and the sadism of Stephenson, and there is no extinguisher of the flames that enveloped the nation during the 1920s. Without her, the dark assertion that finally shook Indiana from the grip of the Klan, the words that defined how a citizen-run government could be taken over by a silken-voiced sexual predator—*I am the law*—might never have been widely known. Without her, the true nature of the political puppeteer who directed a majority of

Hoosiers at the polls might have remained concealed. Without her, Stephenson might have been named to that vacant United States Senate seat, and gone ahead with a run at the White House while the Klan was still ascendant. There is always some peril in seeing things in the past from a starting point of the present, as if every molecule of chance was put in place by human design. But at the least, Madge Oberholtzer deserves a plaque of her own.

We should also think about another cause and effect, or lack thereof. Stephenson was a charismatic con man—"the most talented psychopath ever to tread the banks of the Wabash," as one chronicler of the age put it. But what if he'd never drifted north of the Ohio River? Would so many of Indiana's citizens *not* have taken an oath to white supremacy and religious bias? Would Jews *not* have been harassed at their places of business? Would Catholics *not* have been targeted with terror? Would Black citizens *not* have been denied the freedom to choose where to live and eat and go to school, or protection from a mob with a rope? What if the leaders of the 1920s Klan didn't drive public sentiment, *but rode it*? A vein of hatred was always there for the tapping. It's there still, and explains much of the madness threatening American life a hundred years after Stephenson made a mockery of the moral principles of the Heartland. The Grand Dragon was a symptom, not a cause, of an age that has been mischaracterized as one of Gatsby frivolity and the mayhem of modernism. It's entirely possible that the Klan fell apart not just because of scandals and high-level hypocrisy, but also because it had achieved all of its major goals—Prohibition, disenfranchisement of African Americans, slamming the door on immigrants whose religion or skin color didn't match that of the majority. Long after Stephenson was put away, the ideas that his followers promoted while marching in masks behind a flaming cross prevailed as the law of the land.

The Klan-sponsored Immigration Act of 1924, which sharply restricted the number of Jews, Catholics, southern and eastern Europeans, Asians, and Africans who could come to the United States, stayed on the books for forty-one years. During World War II, a limited number of Jewish refugees from Germany who'd been allowed into the country—as an exception to the law—formed an elite American intelligence unit, the Ritchie Boys, and helped to win the war against Hitler. The US Army estimated that nearly 60 percent of the credible intelligence gathered in Europe came from this unit of immigrants.

In the years following World War II, Jim Crow was gradually disassembled. President Harry Truman integrated the military in 1948. The United States Supreme Court ended the doctrine of "separate but equal" with the *Brown v. Board of Education* decision of 1954. Ten years later, President Lyndon Johnson signed the Civil Rights Act, which prohibits discrimination on the basis of race, color, religion, sex, or national origin. The schools of Indianapolis remained segregated until 1971, when a federal court ordered them to integrate.

Indiana had pioneered the world's first compulsory sterilization law. And a new measure that Governor Jackson signed in 1927 was enforced until 1974, allowing the state to deny thousands of Hoosiers the ability to bring children into the world. The same year that the new law went into effect, the United States Supreme Court, in *Buck v. Bell*, upheld the right to sterilize a "feeble-minded" woman in a mental institution. "Three generations of imbeciles are enough," wrote Justice Oliver Wendell Holmes in the majority opinion. In the years that followed, about 70,000 Americans who were deemed a threat to the national gene pool—the deaf, the blind, ethnic minorities, people with epilepsy, homosexuals, poor people, and "promiscuous" women—were sterilized against their will. Nazi Germany defended its own 1936 eugenics law by pointing to the United States as a role model. In 1981, Oregon performed the nation's last legal forced sterilization.

Despite repeated calls to outlaw the Horse Thief Detective Association, the private militias remained a force in Indiana well after the Klan dried up. It wasn't until 1933 that the state legislature ended the reign of vigilantes with arrest powers.

That same year, legal sales of beer, wine, and spirits returned to Indiana, as they did throughout most of the land with ratification of the 21st Amendment. After falling at the end of the decade leading up to Prohibition, per capita consumption of alcohol rose steadily during the years it was outlawed. About 5,000 people in Indiana were indicted on federal liquor charges. In 1933, the state also got rid of the Wright "Bone Dry" Law, which was responsible for the jailing of thousands of people for possession of an empty liquor bottle, medicinal spirits, or hair tonic. In 2021, Hall of Fame quarterback Peyton Manning started selling his own bourbon in

Indiana, pushing his $200-a-bottle Tennessee liquor. The Hoosier state, he said, "has a great bourbon history."

Over two decades, D. C. Stephenson filed more than forty appeals. When he'd exhausted his funds, he wrote many of his own briefs. Though he called himself a political prisoner, he changed his story repeatedly.

No court ever saw things his way, or disagreed with the verdict in Noblesville. The Indiana State Supreme Court found that his rape, assault, and kidnapping of Madge was responsible for her death, even if it was a suicide—a decision that is studied in law schools to this day. "To say that there is no causal connection between the acts of appellant and the death of Madge Oberholtzer, and that the treatment accorded her by appellant had no causal connection with the death of Madge Oberholtzer would be a travesty of justice," the court majority wrote in 1932, upholding the murder conviction.

After serving nearly twenty-five years in prison, Stephenson was released in March 1950. He said he'd lined up a job in Tulsa, where he planned to live with his daughter, Florence Catherine, who was in between marriages after being divorced five times. They'd been corresponding over the years, and she was charmed by the letters from the father she never knew. But just days after moving in with the child he'd abandoned in 1916, Stephenson was kicked out of her house. "He just couldn't adjust to the new way of living," his daughter told reporters. He still acted as if he were the Grand Dragon of 1924.

He resettled in Illinois. Within a few months, he failed to report to his parole officer and disappeared, prompting a manhunt throughout the Midwest. He was found in a little town in Minnesota and returned to prison. After serving six years of a second term, Stephenson was set free a few days before Christmas in 1956. He was ordered to stay out of Indiana. But after a year or so of drifting, he took up residence in a large new house in Seymour, Indiana—the "small town" of John Mellencamp's song and birth. He'd married one of his lovers and post-conviction allies, Martha Dickinson. In prison, Steve had designed a type-cleaning machine. Now the master salesman took to the road to make something off the invention. It didn't take long for him to resume his predatory ways.

While traveling through Missouri in November 1961, he was arrested and charged with attempting to molest a sixteen-year-old girl. He was seventy. He had tried to force the teenager into his car. She screamed, bolted, and went to the police. He was found guilty and given a four-month suspended jail sentence because of his age, on the condition that he never set foot in the state of Missouri. Not long after the conviction, he deserted his wife Martha, the woman who had stood by him through three decades of prison visits. He vanished into the vapor of America much in the same way as he'd first appeared. His wife told friends she never heard from him again and had no idea where he had gone.

Stephenson had moved to Jonesborough, the oldest town in Tennessee, to assume a life of aging anonymity in the Appalachian foothills. There, he married a fourth woman, Martha Murray Sutton, who was nearly twenty years younger. She had been his landlady in a house where he roomed. Technically, the marriage was illegal; Steve had never divorced his third wife. In Jonesborough, he worked as a writer and printer at the *Herald & Tribune.* On June 28, 1966, he suffered a seizure and fell to the ground while walking into the house—dead at the age of seventy-four. He was buried in Johnson City, Tennessee. His tombstone was a lie, claiming him as an officer who served with the infantry in World War I.

But news of his passing did not reach Indiana for many years. After his assault conviction in 1961, he'd managed to live quietly with the latest wife in a little pocket of forgotten America. Historians, journalists, lawyers, and those he'd fleeced tried to track him down, but came up empty. It wasn't until 1978, after a three-month investigation, that reporters at the *Louisville Courier-Journal* solved a sixteen-year mystery dating to the time Steve left Seymour without a trace. They found the grave of the Grand Dragon and the last Mrs. Stephenson in eastern Tennessee. "I knew nothing of his background," his widow told the paper. "He was a very wonderful person."

Late in his prison term, Stephenson was visited by Will Remy. His old adversary asked him if he'd been serious about running for the White House. Steve said the plan was real. "You wouldn't have called it President," he said. "The form of government might have changed. You might have had a dictator."

The Klan never recovered from its collapse at the end of the 1920s, when national membership fell to below 100,000. During the

Depression, Hiram Evans was forced to take a job with a Georgia construction company. He was later charged with fixing asphalt prices. In 1939, he handed over his Imperial Wizard title to Dr. James Colescott, a veterinarian from Terre Haute, Indiana—the first Northerner to wear the crown. He'd been personally trained by Stephenson, his mentor dating to the early 1920s. Colescott tried to revive the order, using some of the tricks he'd learned from the Old Man. But he was met with failure and derision. The Klan was broke, forced to sell its Imperial Palace in Atlanta to the Catholic Church, which used the former headquarters as a rectory for a new cathedral. Many Klan members were attracted to the creed of Aryan purity coming out of Nazi Germany, and left the order to join groups such as the German American Bund. In 1944, under pressure from the Internal Revenue Service, Colescott formally disbanded the second and largest iteration of the Ku Klux Klan, birthed in 1915. Evans died in 1966, the same year Stephenson took his last breath.

Court Asher, Stephenson's bodyguard, pilot, and right-hand man, founded a weekly newspaper, the *X-Ray*, which was notorious for spreading anti-Semitic falsehoods and promoting Nazi Germany, out of his home base in Indiana. He also tried to prove that Jesus was never a Jew. During World War II, Asher was indicted for sedition, though he never stood trial. He died in 1967. One of Stephenson's other top aides, Earl Gentry, who was in the top bunk while the Grand Dragon raped Madge Oberholtzer, was found murdered in a car in Wisconsin in 1938. He'd been shot in the head—a contract killing ordered by an ex-lover.

Stephenson had outlived some of the bravest few who fought him when he was invincible. George Dale died at his typewriter in 1936, from a stroke at the age of sixty-nine. Another newspaperman from the era, Harold Feightner, said in his oral history that "those who passed through that dark decade never realized the full import of what was happening." Dale realized it at the time, and never turned off the siren.

He was able to right the scales of justice in Muncie. Clarence Dearth, the Klan judge who had jailed the editor without trial, ordered forty newsboys off the street, and temporarily shut down Dale's *Post-Democrat*, was impeached and later imprisoned for contempt of court. In 1929, the same year the judge was ousted, Dale ran for mayor of Muncie. He used radio, then in nearly every home, to explain why the Klan was an evil force that had duped many a Hoosier. In print, he could sound strident. On the airwaves of Indiana, he was a folksy, reassuring old man telling tales and making common sense. On election night, Dale pulled off a major upset. A heavy turnout of Catholics, Blacks, and blue-collar workers gave him a thousand-vote margin. He promptly fired all members of the Klan-infested police department. Dale was swept into office with a wave of others who campaigned against Klan corruption, including a new mayor in Evansville. Perhaps, as an optimist in Colorado said after that state's Klan was rejected at the polls as well, "the air of America is too friendly to permit such a disease to last."

Dr. Lucian Meriwether, a Black man who knew something about American air, refused to break under the psychological torture of the times. After winning his case against the white homeowners who built a fence around his home in Indianapolis, he and his wife lived in the house for decades. Years after the all-Klan slate was removed from the governing body, Dr. Meriwether was elected to the city council.

James Cameron, who survived that attempt to lynch him in Marion when he was sixteen years old, spent the rest of his long life speaking out against racial hatred. He founded three chapters of the NAACP in Indiana, and America's Black Holocaust Museum in Milwaukee. "I had done nothing that could really be called bad," he wrote in his memoir. "The trouble was, this was Marion, Indiana, where there was very little room for foolish black boys." In 2006, Marion awarded him the key to the city. Cameron died the same year, at the age of ninety-two. In 2022, Congress finally passed, and President Joe Biden signed, a bill making lynching a federal crime—122 years after the first such legislation was introduced. According to the NAACP, nearly 5,000 lynchings took place between 1882 and 1968.

Working closely with his friend W. E. B. Du Bois, James Weldon Johnson served for ten years as secretary of the NAACP, from 1920 to 1930. At the same time, he published hundreds of stories and poems, including the first anthology of Black verse, *The Book of American Negro Poetry*, and *The Book of American Negro Spirituals*, plus his most famous work, *God's Trombones: Seven Negro Sermons in Verse*. All three broke new literary ground and sold well. He also cowrote "Lift Every Voice and Sing," the official anthem of the NAACP. At his urging, Black voters began to break with the Republican Party in 1924. By the 1932 election, the Democratic nominee, Franklin D. Roosevelt, won 71 percent of the Black vote. The trend continues to this day. Johnson died in a car accident in 1938, at the age of sixty-seven.

The boy prosecutor, Will Remy, became an elder statesman with a lived-in face and a mop of silver hair. He died in 1968 at the age of seventy-five.

At Remy's funeral, one of his pallbearers was John Niblack, the Hoosier farm kid who went from reporter facing down the fresh-crowned Grand Dragon in Kokomo, to deputy prosecutor helping to lock up Stephenson's political allies, to state senator, to many years as a circuit and superior court judge. The *Indianapolis Times*, the paper that hired him out of college and broke most of the stories on Klan corruption, won the Pulitzer Prize for meritorious public service in 1928 for its coverage of the hooded order.

Niblack died in 1986 at the age of eighty-eight. Indiana, he wrote in his memoir, is "the greatest, the most American state in the union."

ACKNOWLEDGMENTS

Time traveling, the great passion of historians, can be restorative on those dark days of our present. But spending the past three years in the America of the 1920s was anything but therapeutic for this author. We know this era for its cultural exuberance—flappers and jazz and swanky new buildings reaching into the sky. But it was also a time when millions of people took an oath to hate their fellow citizens. Given that, I felt compelled to follow the words of my fellow Irishman Oscar Wilde. "The one duty we owe to history," he said, "is to rewrite it."

I'm grateful to the scholars, authors, and researchers who have gone down this path before me and tried to do much of the necessary rewriting of that age. M. William Lutholtz, James M. Madison, Allen Safianow, and Irving Leibowitz, all bighearted Hoosiers from multiple generations, have done considerable pioneering work on the most haunting era of their state. May their words find a lasting audience. No author has done more to bring Madge Oberholtzer to life than Charlotte Halsema Ottinger. Looking at the big picture, Kathleen M. Blee, Linda Gordon, and Leonard J. Moore are among the historians who've helped to clarify what happened to the United States a century ago.

My thanks to the institutional keepers of the state's story—the Indiana Historical Society, the Indiana State Library, and archivists at the University of Notre Dame and Ball State University's Bracken Library—for opening their vaults to me, especially during the trying times of the pandemic. For anyone interested in a firsthand account of a state completely taken over by the Ku Klux Klan, the oral histories, photographs, diaries, and newspaper clippings assembled in those places are well preserved for the truth-telling they provide.

Good readers, like good editors, see things that the author cannot. For insight into the state's remarkable jazz history, and a good read of my manuscript, thanks to Indiana producer and film director Todd Gould. A big thank-you to the early appraisers of this work: Knute Berger, Sam Howe Verhovek, Tim Golden; my wife, Joni Balter, and daughter, Sophie; my longtime agent and collaborator in this trade, Carol Mann; and Jada Lightning. At Viking, I benefited more than ever from the exceptional judgment of Andrea Schulz, who has carried more than her share of my work over the finish line. Also at Viking, thanks to Nidhi Pugalia, Carolyn Coleburn, and Tricia Conley; and to the copy editor, Mike McConnell.

NOTES

Introduction: The Quintessential Americans

Inaugural, "Governor Jackson Pledges Fearless Discharge of Duty," *Indianapolis Star*, Jan. 13, 1925, and Harold C. Feightner, his oral history, Feb. 1968, Indiana State Library, Rare Books and Manuscripts Collection, hereafter ISL.

Stephenson wealth, yacht, private plane, dogs, "Stephenson's Life Told in Press," *Indianapolis Star*, Aug. 13, 1924.

Stephenson's office description, "Indiana Klansmen Try to Dominate Politics," *South Bend Tribune*, Aug. 23, 1924.

"I am the law," Irving Leibowitz, *My Indiana* (Englewood Cliffs, NJ: Prentice Hall, 1964), 189.

Six million Klansmen nationwide, a middle estimate, "The Ku Klux Klan in the 1920s," *American Experience*, PBS, https://www.pbs.org/wgbh/americanexperience /features/flood-klan/, and Leibowitz, *My Indiana*, 215.

There is little dispute that Indiana had the highest number of Klansmen of any state. Leonard Moore, *Citizen Klansmen* (Chapel Hill: University of North Carolina Press, 1991), 47, put it at 278,000. M. William Lutholtz, in *Grand Dragon* (West Lafayette, IN: Purdue University Press, 1991), 1, arrived at a similar number. The Klan newspaper claimed 400,000 members, "200,000 Klansmen Meet," *Fiery Cross*, July 13, 1923, the same as *New York Times*, "Indiana Political Volcano Shows Signs of Eruption," Oct. 2, 1927.

"monarch of all he surveyed," ibid., *New York Times*, Oct. 2, 1927.

Klan oath, a membership form and Klan constitution, on file at ISL.

Cross burnings across Indiana, James L. Madison, *The Ku Klux Klan in the Heartland* (Bloomington: Indiana University Press, 2020), 9.

Cross burnings on lawns of Black families, John L. Niblack, *The Life and Times of a Hoosier Judge* (Carmel, IN: Hawthorne, 1973), 194.

Klan controls entire state, "Court Asher Tells How Stephenson Rules State," *Richmond Palladium*, Oct. 8, 1926.

Steve's vigilantes, the Horse Thief Detective Association, had more than 30,000 deputies in Indiana, Linda Gordon, *The Second Coming of the KKK* (New York: Liveright, 2017), 104.

Over half the members of Indiana Assembly Klan, Wyn Craig Wade, *The Fiery Cross: The Ku Klux Klan in America* (New York: Simon & Schuster, 1987), 215, and https://www.wikiwand.com/en/Indiana_Klan.

All ninety-two counties but two had a Klan chapter, Wade, *The Fiery Cross*, 215.

Indiana birthplace of recorded jazz, http://memory.loc.gov/diglib/legacies/loc.afc.afc-legacies.200003002/.

Klan in Anaheim, Jesse La Tour, "A Brief History of the KKK in Orange County," *Fullerton Observer*, January 7, 2019.

Klan on battleship, "Klan Is Formed on Board Battleship Tennessee," *Imperial Night-Hawk*, Aug. 29, 1923.

Fraternal orders; Odd Fellows, with 2 million members, second only to the Klan, https://odd-fellows.org/history/wildeys-odd-fellowship.

Gov. Morley of Colorado a Klansman. He made no secret of this, discussed at length in Cara Degette, "When Colorado Was Klan Country," *Colorado Independent*, January 9, 2009.

Morley quote, Elise Schmelzer, "The KKK Ruled Denver a Century Ago," *Denver Post*, June 9, 2021.

Indiana eugenics law, Lutz Kaelber, "Compulsory Sterilization in 50 American States," 2012, https://www.uvm.edu/~lkaelber/eugenics/.

Liquor restrictions, Daniel Okrent, *Last Call: The Rise and Fall of Prohibition* (New York: Scribner, 2010), 255.

Klan enforcing morals, Thomas R. Pegram, "Hoodwinked: The Anti-Saloon League and the Ku Klux Klan in 1920s Prohibition Reinforcement," *Journal of the Gilded Age and Progressive Era*, Jan. 2008.

Black disenfranchisement, Michael Perman, *Struggle for Mastery: Disenfranchisement in the South* (Chapel Hill: University of North Carolina Press, 2001).

Anti-immigrant quote, "Sparks from the Fiery Cross," *Fiery Cross*, June 29, 1923.

Governor Walker, "build a wall," https://www.snopes.com/fact-check/governor-of-georgia-kkk/.

Imperial Wizard Evans on cover of *Time*, June 23, 1924, "Kleveland Konvention."

Evans quote in Denver, ibid.

"I'm going to be the biggest man," "Murder Wasn't Very Pretty," *Smithsonian Magazine*, Aug. 30, 2012, https://www.smithsonianmag.com/history/murder-wasnt-very-pretty-the-rise-and-fall-of-dc-stephenson-18935042/.

Gov. Ed Jackson a Klansman, quote on terrorist, "Indiana Secretary of State!," *Tolerance*, April 15, 1923.

"I did not sell the Klan on hatreds," *Hoosiers and the American Story*, 201, https://indianahistory.org/wp-content/uploads/Hoosiers-and-the-American-Story-ch-08.pdf.

Madge Oberholtzer banquet details from testimony of Stanley C. Hill, "Stephenson Case Nears Close," *Indianapolis Star*, Nov. 12, 1925.

Madge's job on the line, Feightner oral history, ISL, and testimony in Stephenson trial.

Steve's self-inflated biography, "Stephenson Guilty; Aides Free," *Indianapolis Star*, Nov. 15, 1925.

Steve's cars, Feightner oral history, ISL.

Steve's wealth: by his own account he brought in nearly $2 million for the Klan, Leibowitz, *My Indiana*, 192–93. Adjusted for inflation, equal to about $29 million in contemporary dollars, of which he got at least 40 percent. He made millions more in robe fees. Also see Ralph D. Gray, *Indiana History: A Book of Readings* (Bloomington: Indiana University Press, 1995), 306.

Steve quotes on money, bio, "Stephenson's Life is Told in Press," *Indianapolis Star*, Aug. 13, 1924.

Steve's political ambitions, Feightner oral history, ISL.

They talked, danced, "dying declaration" of Madge A. Oberholtzer, March 28, 1925, reprinted in full, "Girl's Deathbed Story Bared," *Indianapolis Times*, June 16, 1925. Hereafter, dying declaration.

1. Birth and Death of the Klan

Forty acres and a mule, https://www.pbs.org/wnet/african-americans-many-rivers-to-cross/history/the-truth-behind-40-acres-and-a-mule/.

Klan founders, Elaine Frantz Parsons, *Ku-Klux: The Birth of the Klan During Reconstruction* (Chapel Hill: University of North Carolina Press, 2016), 3–34.

Crowe quote, ibid., 32.

Fort Pillow Massacre, https://www.britannica.com/event/Fort-Pillow-Massacre.

Forrest quote, "insolent," David W. Chalmers, *Hooded Americanism: The History of the Ku Klux Klan* (Durham, NC: Duke University Press, 1987), 20.

Early Klan violence, federal response, Eric Foner, *Reconstruction: America's Unfinished Revolution* (New York: Harper Perennial, 2014), chap. 9.

Nearly all teachers at Black schools driven out of state, ibid., 79.

Klan in California, Kevin Waite, "The Forgotten History of the Western Klan," *Atlantic*, April 6, 2021.

Forrest boast of power of Klan, Ron Chernow, *Grant* (New York: Penguin Press, 2017), 621.

Johnson on race, David Priess, "How a Difficult, Stubborn, Racist President Was Removed from Power," *Politico*, Nov. 13, 2018.

Thirty men drowned, Michael Newton, *The Ku Klux Klan in Mississippi* (Jefferson, NC: McFarland, 2010), as summarized at https://docu.tips/documents/the-ku-klux-klan-in-mississippi-a-history-5c11a41d8824c.

Johnson pardon, American Presidency Project, https://www.presidency.ucsb.edu/documents/proclamation-179-granting-full-pardon-and-amnesty-for-the-offense-treason-against-the.

Number of killings and "we are the law," Wade, *The Fiery Cross*, 64.

Reynolds quote, ibid., 79.

Sallie Adkins, from https://courses.lumenlearning.com/suny-ushistory1ay/chapter/racial-violence-in-reconstruction-2.

Douglass quote, Chernow, *Grant*, 746.

2. An Opening in Indiana

Scene at the church, "Ku Klux Klan Stages Public Demonstration," *Evansville Courier*, March 27, 1922.

Ethnic makeup of Evansville, 1920 Census, https://www.census-online.com/links/IN/1920.html.

Baptisttown, author visit to exhibits at the Evansville African American Museum, Evansville, Indiana.

Southerners in Indiana, racial attitudes, Emma Lou Thornbrough, *Indiana in the Civil War Era* (Bloomington: Indiana University Press, 1995).

Evansville life, Todd Gould, *For Gold and Glory: Charlie Wiggins and the African-American Racing Car Circuit* (Bloomington: Indiana University Press, 2007), 55–60.

No service to Black customers at gas station, William E. Wilson, "Long, Hot Summer in Indiana," *American Heritage*, Aug. 1965.

Blacks shouldn't mix, "The Negro Problem," *Indianapolis Times*, April 28, 1922.

Langston Hughes quote, "The Negro Artist and the Racial Mountain," as reprinted in *The Harlem Renaissance Reader* (New York: Viking, 1994), 91.

Johnson quote, James Weldon Johnson, *Along This Way* (New York: Penguin, 1990), 308.

Steve joined Klan in 1921, "Stephenson's Life Told in Press," *Indianapolis Star*, Aug. 13, 1924.

Attack in Dallas, sheriff quote on attack, Darwin Payne, "When Dallas Was the Most Racist City in America," *D* magazine, May 22, 2017.

Evans's views on race, Thomas R. Pegram, *One Hundred Percent American: The Rebirth and Decline of the Ku Klux Klan* (Lanham, MD: Rowman and Littlefield, 2011), 32.

Castration, other Texas attacks, Chalmers, *Hooded Americanism*, 41.

Evans on immigration, "The Klan's Fight for Americanism," *North American Review*, March 1926.

Disenfranchisement, Perman, *Struggle for Mastery*, 48–70.

Alabama vote, "Alabama Begins Removing Racist Language from Its Constitution," *New York Times*, Sept. 19, 2021.

Dixon comment to Woodrow Wilson, from https://wwplblog.wordpress.com/2017/09/01/birth-of-a-nation/.

Facts on film, "Writing History with Lightning: *The Birth of a Nation* at 100," *Time*, Feb. 8, 2015.

Simmons, Klan founding, "A Preacher Used Christianity to Revive the Ku Klux Klan," *Washington Post*, April 10, 2018.

Simmons statement on Klan principle, undated, on file at Bracken Library, Special Collections, Ball State University.

One in three Americans enemies of the Klan, from 1920 census: Blacks, 13 percent; Jews, 3 percent; Catholics, 17 percent.

Blacks at Harvard, "Attacks Harvard on Negro Question," *New York Times*, Jan. 13, 1923.

Clarke and Tyler hatreds and origins, Chalmers, *Hooded Americanism*, 31–36.

Klan membership growth, ibid.

40 percent of adult males belonged to fraternal order, Richard Hofstadter, "The Paranoid Style in American Politics," *Atlantic*, Nov. 1964.

Klan start in Evansville, "Indiana Reminds Everyone: State's KKK Charter Started in Evansville," *Evansville Courier & Press*, June 17, 2016.

Quote from preacher in Bloomington, monroehistory.org, April 22, 2019.

Steve's plan to use clergy, Edgar Allen Booth, *The Mad Mullah of America* (Columbus, OH: Legacy Reprints, 1997), 4.

Steve hires Blair, Lutholtz, *Grand Dragon*, 59–60.

Blair speech, "Rev. Blair Speaks of Ku Klux Klan," *Fiery Cross*, Feb. 9, 1923.

Steve cuts a deal, his own account in 1926 grand jury, D. C. Stephenson Collection, on file at Indiana Historical Society, hereafter IHS.

Steve making $12 a week from Klan, "Stephenson's Life Told in Press," *Indianapolis Star*, Aug. 13, 1924.

Klan charter in Evansville, on file at IHS.

Assault on Violet Stephenson, details in divorce granted Feb. 28, 1924, Summit County, Ohio, IHS.

3. Men with Badges

Origin of Horse Thief organization, "The Ku Klux Klan in Indiana," *McClure's*, May 1924.

Declining power of HTDA, historicIndianapolis.com, Oct. 13, 2013, https://historicindianapolis.com/friday-favorites-the-national-horse-thief-detective-association/.

Steve's idea to co-opt HTDA, Wade, *The Fiery Cross*, 225.

Klan language, governing philosophy, *Klansman's Manual*, 1924, published by Knights of the Ku Klux Klan, https://archive.lib.msu.edu/DMC/AmRad/klansmansmanual.pdf.

Quote from Wilson on unlawful searches, etc., "Long, Hot Summer in Indiana," *American Heritage*, Aug. 1965.

Kern County torture, "The Kern County Local KKK Members, Including Bakersfield's Police Chief, Were Outed 90 Years Ago," *Bakersfield Californian*, May 7, 2012.

New York World exposé, "Secrets of the Ku Klux Klan Exposed by the *World*," three-week series, Sept. 6–26, 1921.

Simmons testimony, "Hearings Before the House Rules Committee," *Congressional Record*, 1921.

Klan growth after hearing, Simmons obituary, "William Simmons of Ku Klux Klan," *New York Times*, May 22, 1945.

"unofficial constabulary," and four recorded horse thefts, "Horse Thief Detectives," *Indianapolis News*, Oct. 9, 1922.

How Klan recruits and the oath, Ezra A. Cook, *Ku Klux Klan: Secrets Exposed* (Berlin, OH: TGS Publishing, 2009), 25–45.

Steve's winning combination, Asher quote, "Dragons in Indiana," *Chicago Tribune*, March 15, 1936.

Asher quote on hiring ministers, "Court Asher Tells How Stephenson Ruled State," *Richmond Palladium*, Oct. 13, 1926.

Average factory worker salary in 1920, from Internal Revenue Service tables, https://www.irs.gov/pub/irs-soi/20soirepar.pdf.

Steve's profits, a study by Roland G. Fryer, Jr., and Steven D. Levitt, "Hatred and Profits: Getting Under the Hood of the Ku Klux Klan," National Bureau of Economic Research, Sept. 2007.

Campaign against film, Melvyn Stokes, *D. W. Griffith's* The Birth of a Nation: *A History of the Most Controversial Motion Picture of All Time* (New York: Oxford University Press, 2008), 129–40.

"as inhuman," Derek Hickerson, "The Relic of a Barbarous Age: James Matthew Townsend and Indiana's Black Laws," *Black History News and Notes*, Winter 2009, a newsletter of the IHS.

William Stern, "W. H. Stern Makes Pleas for Colored Race: Thinks They Should Be Recognized Same as White People," *Noblesville Ledger*, Sept. 24, 1927.

Steve's Machine, dossiers, field command, Richard K. Tucker, *The Dragon and the Cross* (Hamden, CT: Archon Books, 1991), 88–100.

Mecklin quote, Klan attraction, John Moffatt Mecklin, *The Ku Klux Klan: A Study of the American Mind* (New York: Russell & Russell, 1963), 95–98.

4. A Coup and a Clash

"foremost mass psychologist," Wade, *The Fiery Cross*, 229.

Steve and Mussolini, "What the Klan Did in Indiana," *New Republic*, Nov. 16, 1927.

Evans on immigration, a pamphlet, "Attitude of Knights of the Ku Klux Klan toward Immigration," published in 1923, https://books.google.com/books/about/Attitude _of_the_Knights_of_the_Ku_Klux_K.html?id=uNMNSwAACAAJ.

More than fifty beatings in Dallas, Chalmers, *Hooded Americanism*, 41–42.

Majority of Dallas police officers Klan, Dallas history site, www.hometownbyhandlebar .com.

Quote from Malcolm X, Adam Fletcher Sasse, "A Biography of Malcolm X in Omaha," https://northomahahistory.com/2019/03/13/a-biography-of-malcolm-x-in-omaha/.

Steve works to defeat Beveridge, Wade, *The Fiery Cross*, 230.

"the damn Ku Klux Klan," Feightner's oral history, ISL.

Steve sends questionnaire, Joseph M. White, "The Ku Klux Klan in Indiana in the 1920s as Viewed by the *Indiana Catholic and Record*," graduate thesis, Butler University, 1974.

Background of George Dale, column quotes, George R. Dale Collection, Ball State University Digital Media Repository, https://archivessearch.bsu.edu/repositories /5/resources/651.

Dale sometimes exaggerated, Ron F. Smith, "The Klan's Retribution against an Indiana Editor," *Indiana Magazine of History*, Dec. 2010.

Steve v. Dale, "The Grand Dragon," *Muncie Post-Democrat*, Nov. 12, 1925.

More on attack, "George Dale Dies; Ku Klux Klan Foe," *New York Times*, March 28, 1936.

Blacks segregated in Muncie, Robert S. Lynd and Helen Merrell Lynd, *Middletown* (New York: Harcourt, Brace, 1929), 479.

Judge Dearth sentencing, "It Is Somebody's Business," *Muncie Post-Democrat*, June 1, 1923.

Klan wanted to gain control of America, Booth, *Mad Mullah*, 45.

Sandal, "Clarke and Tyler Arrested," *New York World*, Sept. 19, 1921.

Coup, Simmons's own account, "The Fiery Double Cross," *Collier's Weekly*, July 28, 1928; Wade, *The Fiery Cross*, 186–91; and Kenneth T. Jackson, *The Ku Klux Klan in the City* (New York: Oxford University Press, 1967), 14.

"nobody from nowhere," Karen Abbott, "'Murder Wasn't Very Pretty': The Rise and Fall of D. C. Stephenson," *Smithsonian Magazine*, Aug. 30, 2012.

5. Woman of the Year

Daisy Douglas Barr, Stephen J. Taylor, "A Ku Klux Quaker?," Sept. 28, 2015, https://historicindianapolis.com/a-ku-klux-quaker/.

Alcohol consumption, National Institute on Alcohol Abuse and Alcoholism, https://pubs.niaaa.nih.gov/publications/surveillance113/tab1_17.htm.

Billy Sunday quote, Okrent, *Last Call*, 2.

"father and mother of the Ku Klux Klan," etc., Thomas R. Pegram, "Hoodwinked: The Anti-Saloon League and the Ku Klux Klan in 1920s Prohibition Enforcement," *Journal of the Gilded Age and Progressive Era*, Jan. 2008.

No lobby more powerful than ASL, Okrent, *Last Call*, 2, 34–42.

Steve's deal with Barr, Dwight W. Hoover, "Daisy Douglas Barr: From Quaker to Klan 'Kluckeress,'" *Indiana Magazine of History*, June 1991.

Barr speech in Rushville, "Urges Women to Join Klan Body," *Rushville Republican*, March 2, 1923.

Barr quote on whites and Jews, ibid.

Madison Grant's book, *The Passing of the Great Race* (New York: Scribner, 1916).

"What a thrill," Kathleen M. Blee, *Women of the Klan* (Berkeley: University of California Press, 1991), 101.

Ideals of women's Klan, Kelli R. Kerbawy, "Knights in White Satin: Women of the Ku Klux Klan," master's thesis, Marshall University, 2007.

Creed of Klanswomen of America, Primary Sources: The 1920s: Ku Klux Klan, Christopher Newport University, https://cnu.libguides.com/1920s/kukluxklan.

Women's state convention, Madison, *The Ku Klux Klan in the Heartland*.

Run the Jews out of the state, Blee, *Women of the Klan*, 147.

"Intolerance was everywhere," Leibowitz, *My Indiana*, 208.

Number of Jews, Blacks, and Catholics in Indiana, U.S. Census, 1920.

Germans and Vonnegut, a talk by Ray Boomhower, reprinted in *Traces*, Spring 1999.

Shapiro's Kosher Foods, Madison, *The Ku Klux Klan in the Heartland*, 143.

Rabbi Fink, his obit, "Dr. Joseph L. Fink, Rabbi, 69, Is Dead," *New York Times*, Nov. 27, 1964.

Leo Frank hanging, Steve Oney, *And the Dead Shall Rise: The Murder of Mary Phagan and the Lynching of Leo Frank* (New York: Vintage, 2004), 3–17.

Dearborn headline, "The International Jew: The World's Problem," *Dearborn Independent*, May 22, 1920.

Ford candy bar comment, Gordon Thomas and Max Morgan-Witts, *The Day the Bubble Burst* (Open Road Integrated Media, 1979).

Rabbi Morris M. Feuerlicht, *A Hoosier Rabbinate* (Fort Wayne: Indiana Jewish Historical Society, 1974), 46.

Steve quote on White House, "Stephenson's Fall Blots Out Dreams of U.S. Presidency," *Indianapolis Star*, Nov. 16, 1925.

Court Asher background, "Ex-Klansman Tells His Story," *Indianapolis News*, Aug. 6, 1965.

Steve's armed associates, from a typescript, William H. Remy, unpublished memoir, undated, IHS.

Quote, "godsend," "Junior Klan News Brings Enthusiasm," *Fiery Cross*, Aug. 10, 1923.

Klan in high school, Charlotte Halsema Ottinger, *Madge: The Life and Times of Madge Oberholtzer* (Indianapolis: Indiana Historical Society, 2021), 108.

Poison squads, Blee, *Women of the Klan*, 148.

Poison travels statewide in six hours, "The Fiery Double Cross," *Collier's*, July 21, 1928.

Steve's quote on Jesus, letter he wrote to Ed Jackson, Jan. 17, 1925, IHS.

Steve's abuse of Violet Stephenson, her reaction, infection from sexually transmitted disease—all from her divorce case, Feb. 28, 1924, on file at IHS.

Three million Klan members nationwide, Chalmers, *Hooded Americanism*, 109.

Evans predicts 20 million Klansmen, Christine M. Erickson, "Boys in Butte: The Ku Klux Klan Confronts the Catholics, 1923–1929," graduate thesis, University of Montana, 1991.

Barr's poem, "A Ku Klux Quaker?"

6. The Other Indiana

Details of recording session, Rick Kennedy, *Jelly Roll, Bix, and Hoagy: Gennett Records and the Rise of America's Musical Grass Roots* (Bloomington: Indiana University Press, 2013), xix.

Number of Klansmen in attendance, "Local Cross-Burnings Recalled," *Richmond Palladium-Item*, Nov. 6, 1979.

Louis Armstrong background, Nat Shapiro and Nat Hentoff, *Hear Me Talkin' to Ya: The Story of Jazz As Told by the Men Who Made It* (New York: Dover, 1966), 128–38.

First jazz recording, white musicians, https://www.smithsonianmag.com/smithsonian-institution/was-first-jazz-recording-made-group-white-guys-180962246/.

Players and songs recorded on Oct. 5, 1923, *The Syncopated Times*, https://syncopatedtimes.com/king-olivers-creole-jazz-band/.

Hoagy Carmichael, https://riverwalkjazz.stanford.edu/?q=program/gennett-records-little-studio-could.

Studio recording logistics, thanks to IHS, which re-created the Gennett studio during a 2021 exhibition.

Particulars of the studio, from historical signage at the old studio site, Richmond, Indiana, "Walk of Fame."

Richmond parade, quotes, "Dense Crowds at Richmond Meeting," *Fiery Cross*, Oct. 19, 1923.

Madam Walker, from IHS exhibit, 2020.

Bios of Madam Walker, Emma Lou Thornbrough, *Indiana Blacks in the Twentieth Century* (Bloomington: Indiana University Press, 2000), 14–15.

Madam Walker, from IHS exhibit, spring 2021.

Blacks forced out, "All Negroes Driven from Indiana Town, *New York Times*, January 21, 1923.

Fifteen Black physicians, *Indianapolis Colored Directory and Yearbook*, 1923.

Dr. Meriwether and the fence, Paul Mullins, "Racist Spite and Residential Segregation," *Invisible Indianapolis*, Jan. 20, 2019, https://invisibleindianapolis.wordpress.com/2019/01/20/racist-spite-and-residential-segregation-housing-and-the-color-line-in-inter-war-indianapolis/.

Dr. Meriwether's life, "Dr. Lucian Meriwether, Leading Dentist, Dies," *Indianapolis Recorder*, Jan. 30, 1982.

Quote from handbill, Richard B. Pierce, *Polite Protest: The Political Economy of Race in Indianapolis* (Bloomington: Indiana University Press, 2005), 59.

Great Migration, Blacks to Indianapolis, Thornbrough, *Indiana Blacks*, 33–46.

More than two hundred sundown towns, http://sundown.tougaloo.edu/sundowntownsshow.php?state=IN.

Sundown laws, "Sundown Towns: Midwest Confronts Its Complicated Racial Legacy," *Christian Science Monitor*, March 27, 2017.

"Klan Is My Friend If I Live Right, Says Negro," *Fiery Cross*, Aug. 10, 1923.

Elwood (Indiana) headline, "All Black Coons," *Elwood Call Leader*, Oct. 12, 1922.

Tulsa massacre, "What to Know about the Tulsa Greenwood Massacre," *New York Times*, June 20, 2020, and report of the official commission, published in 2001, https://www.okhistory.org/research/forms/freport.pdf.

Klan membership in Tulsa, quotes on "best thing," ibid.

Klan horse-whipping in Tulsa, "Bares Terrorism of Tulsa Floggers," *New York Times*, Sept. 7, 1923.

7. The Unmasking

O'Donnell speech, "St. Patrick's Day Speakers Advocate Church Tolerance," *Indianapolis Star*, March 17, 1923.

Klan manual on secrecy, "Why We Wear the Hood," undated, IHS.

Chicago reaction, Chicago History Museum blog, Fall 2006, https://issuu.com/chicagohistorymuseum/docs/2006fall-chm-chicagohistory-vol34-no3/s/11440616.

Klan in South Bend, "Notre Dame Students Stage a Riot" and "Mayor of South Bend Gives Orders," *Fiery Cross*, March 16 and March 23, 1923.

Klan members revealed, "Never Mind the Minnows: Get the Whales!," *Tolerance*, April 1, 1923.

Green Gabbard raid, an affidavit on file in *Cummins v. State of Indiana*, State Court of Appeals, April 26, 1929.

Helen Jackson, ex-nun, White, "The Ku Klux Klan in Indiana in the 1920s as Viewed by the *Indiana Catholic and Record*."

"Join the Klan" exchange, Niblack, *Life and Times*, 192.

8. Creating D. C. Stephenson

Steve's early years, Harold Zink, "A Case Study of a Political Boss," *Psychiatry*, Nov. 1938.

Steve stiffs creditors, lies to wife, prosecutor's biography assembled in advance of his trial, Feightner, ISL.

Nettie Hamilton's story, "I Wouldn't Do Anything to Harm Him," *Indianapolis Star*, June 17, 1927.

Steve's military background, Zink, "A Case Study of a Political Boss."

Steve lies about never being married, Ohio Marriage License, Jan. 6, 1920, IHS.

Valparaiso University, Stephen Taylor, "Ku Klux U: How the Klan Almost Bought a University," *Indiana History Blog*, Indiana Historical Bureau, Indiana State Library, Dec. 8, 2021, https://blog.history.in.gov/ku-klux-u-how-the-klan-almost -bought-a-university/.

Steve's wealth, "How Klan Dragon Flew to Power in Indiana upon Gold-Tipped Wings," *St. Louis Post-Dispatch*, Oct. 10, 1926.

Headline, "Klan Will Take Over Poor Man's Harvard," *Rushville Daily Republican*, Aug. 16, 1923.

Klan baseball teams, Gordon, *The Second Coming of the KKK*, 85.

Klan violence in Muncie, Dale's account, "Outrages in Muncie Saturday Night Arouse Citizens," *Muncie Post-Democrat*, June 8, 1923.

Dale spit on by women of Klan, W. A. S. Douglas, "The Mayor of Middletown," *American Mercury*, Aug. 1930.

Morality campaigns, "Hammond Sounds Call of Crusaders," *Fiery Cross*, March 30, 1923.

Steve and sheriff's deputies in Ohio, June 11, 1923, testimony of the two officers who confronted him on June 10, 1923, Klan tribunal, June 23, 1924, ISL.

9. A Master Race in the Midwest

Steve eugenics speech, "Immigration Is Periling America," *Fiery Cross*, Sept. 21, 1923.

Better babies, Alexandra Minna Stern, "We Cannot Make a Silk Purse Out of a Sow's Ear: Eugenics in the Hoosier Heartland," *Indiana Magazine of History*, March 2007.

Number of sterilizations, eugenics law, https://eugenicsarchive.ca/discover/timeline/53234888132156674b00024e.

70,000 sterilized across the U.S., "'You Just Feel Like Nothing,'" *New York Times*, July 12, 2021.

Praising Hitler, Andrea DenHoed, "The Forgotten Lessons of the American Eugenics Movement," *New Yorker*, April 27, 2016.

Davenport, as quoted in Daniel Okrent, *The Guarded Gate: Bigotry, Eugenics and the Law That Kept Two Generations of Jews, Italians, and Other European Immigrants out of America* (New York: Scribner, 2019), 147.

Johnson speech in Indianapolis, "J. W. Johnson to Speak at Monster Meeting," *Indianapolis Star*, Nov. 24, 1923.

Johnson on culture, *Along This Way*, 328.

Stanford's David S. Jordan and eugenics, Stanford Eugenics History Project, https://www.stanfordeugenics.com/.

Stoddard a Klansman, Chalmer, *Hooded Americanism*, 270.

Calvin Coolidge, "Whose Country Is This?," *Good Housekeeping*, Feb. 1921.

Colorado's push for sterilization, https://coloradoencyclopedia.org/article/eugenics-colorado.

"on a raft," as quoted in Blee, *Women of the Klan*, 172.

10. Independence Day

The opening scene is from several eyewitness descriptions, among them Robert Coughlan's "Konklave in Kokomo," reprinted in *The Aspirin Age: 1919–1941* (New York: Simon & Schuster, 1949), 105–49, and Niblack, *Life and Times*, 194–95.

Half of Kokomo belonged to the Klan, "City Has Long History as a Hotbed for Klan Activity," *Kokomo Tribune*, Feb. 28, 2017.

Crowd size, "200,000 Klansmen Meet," *Fiery Cross*, July 13, 1923, and "Kokomo Site of Largest Gathering in KKK History," *Kokomo Tribune*, May 2, 1999.

Asher quote, "How Klan Dragon Flew to Power in Indiana upon Gold-Tipped Wings," *St. Louis Post-Dispatch*, Oct. 10, 1926.

Largest Klan gathering ever, and reporter pledges of secrecy, "Monster Throng at Klan Meeting," *Indianapolis Star*, July 5, 1923.

Steve's speech, "Back to the Constitution," *Fiery Cross*, July 6, 1923.

Klan size, "Indiana Entirely Swayed by Klan," *New York Times*, Nov. 7, 1923.

Ford dealership's "100 percent American" ad in *Fiery Cross*, Feb. 23, 1923.

Bus company denied service to Black customers, "Discrimination by Motor Bus Company Denied," *Indianapolis Star*, May 25, 1925.

Interview with Steve, Niblack, *Life and Times*, 196.

Steve tries to rape woman, from her statement, undated, IHS, and transcript of Klan tribunal, June 23, 1924, ISL.

Klan tribute to women, "An Ode to the Women Organizers," *Fiery Cross*, July 6, 1923.

Fiery Cross account, including Evans quotes, "200,000 Klansmen Meet," July 13, 1924.

Coughlan quotes, "Konklave in Kokomo."

Asher quote on church, "Dragons in Indiana," *Chicago Tribune*, March 15, 1936.

Asher quote on "slip into the robes," "Dragons in Indiana," *Chicago Tribune*, March 15, 1936.

Asher quote on "hicks," "The Printer Who Turned Indiana Over to the KKK," *St. Louis Post-Dispatch*, Nov. 14, 1926.

11. Governors, Guns, and God

Steve's yacht, and attendees, Asher's grand jury testimony, Oct. 13, 1926, IHS, and Booth, *Mad Mullah*, 108.

Harding, Howard Markel, "The 'Strange' Death of Warren G. Harding," *PBS NewsHour*, Aug. 2, 2015, https://www.pbs.org/newshour/health/strange-death-warren-harding.

Harding's affair with woman thirty-one years his junior, Nan Britton, *The President's Daughter*, first published 1927 (New York: Ishi Press, 2008). DNA evidence later proved that he had a child with her.

Klan reacts to Harding's death, "President Harding Is Laid to Rest at Cemetery in Marion," *Fiery Cross*, Aug. 17, 1923.

Sen. Watson letter to Steve, May 5, 1924, IHS.

Size of Summit County Klan, and mayor, "Ku Klux Klan," Ohio History Central, https://ohiohistorycentral.org/w/Ku_Klux_Klan.

Klan numbers in Ohio, 195,000, Jackson, *The Ku Klux Klan in the City*, 237.

Bombings in Dayton, Battalion of Death, Pennsylvania, "Burnings at Stake at Behest of Evans," *New York Times*, April 11, 1928.

Tension between Steve and Evans, Booth, *Mad Mullah*, 70–72.

Minister kidnapped, branded, Leibowitz, *My Indiana*, 209.

Riot, rocks thrown in Indianapolis, "Stoning of Firemen Arouses Police Chief," *Indianapolis News*, July 19, 1923.

Buckeye Lake scene, "Ohio State Konklave Is Attended by 75,000," *Fiery Cross*, July 20, 1923.

Attempted rape at Buckeye Lake, Klan tribunal, June 23, 1924, ISL.

Oklahoma governor martial law, Chalmers, *Hooded Americanism*, 52.

Oregon Klan, most per capita outside Indiana, Gordon, *The Second Coming of the KKK*, 139.

Klan in Astoria, Knute Berger, "The Chilling Threads of Our Racist Past," *Crosscut*, April 23, 2018.

Klan violence, political activity in Colorado, Robert Alan Goldberg, *Hooded Empire: The Ku Klux Klan in Colorado* (Urbana: University of Illinois Press, 1981), 68–96.

Evans quote "millions," "The Fight for Americanism," *North American Review*, March 1926.

McAdoo segregates workforce, Dylan Mathews, "Woodrow Wilson Was Extremely Racist—Even by the Standards of His Time," *Vox*, Nov. 20, 2015.

Riot in Carnegie, John M. Craig, "There Is Hell Going On Up There: The Carnegie Klan Riot of 1923," *Pennsylvania History*, Summer 2005.

"Message from the Old Man," *Fiery Cross*, Sept. 19, 1923.

Asher quote, "Court Asher Tells How Stephenson Ruled State," *Richmond Palladium*, Oct. 8, 1926.

12. Lord of the Manor

Irvington details, homes, author visit, and National Register of Historic Places form, https://npgallery.nps.gov/GetAsset/296a0687-0bb1-4dd4-8246-7ceca12fbb7b/.

Madge background, "Mrs. Oberholtzer Weeps on Stand," *Indianapolis Times*, Oct. 29, 1925.

Additional background, Ottinger, *Madge*, 39–79.

Quote on Madge in college, *The Drift*, Butler yearbook, 1917, 65.

Steve's bio, "Stephenson's Life Told in Press," *Indianapolis Star*, Aug. 13, 1924.

Madge plan to meet Steve, "Hill Tells of Governor's Ball," *Noblesville Ledger*, Nov. 11, 1925.

Stephenson house and history, from historicindianapolis.com, Sept. 24, 2013, and author visit to the home.

The house, "Stephenson's Life Told in Press," *Indianapolis Star*, Aug. 13, 1924.

Parties, orgies, including cake and satyr, Asher, "Court Asher Tells How Stephenson Ruled State," *Richmond Palladium*, Oct. 8, 1926, and "Dragons in Indiana," *Chicago Tribune*, May 15, 1936.

Steve's vision of "a great revolution," letter from him to John Rutledge, April 14, 1924, ISL.

Quote of partygoer, Zink, "Case Study of a Political Boss."

"shamed Nero," Asher, "Stephenson Rule of Indiana Exposed by Court Asher," *Richmond Palladium*, Oct. 8, 1926.

Bernice Glass, her oral history, June 1978, on file through Digital Indy, a service of the Indianapolis Public Library.

Butler College and Blacks, "Life on the Irvington Campus," digitalcommons .butler.edu.

Cross burning at Our Lady of Lourdes, oral history of Edwin K. Steers, Jan. 5, 1977, ISL.

Steve and Klan benign claim, "Stephenson's Life Told in Press," *Indianapolis Star*, Aug. 13, 1924.

Letter, from "Mary," broken engagement, April 24, 1924, IHS.

Steve treated for alcoholism, "Suicide, Stephenson's Opening Gun," *Indianapolis Times*, Nov. 5, 1925.

Clela Hull letter to Steve, May 11, 1924, IHS.

Woman, Marion Darr, drugged, possibly raped, her 1925 deposition, April 1925, IHS.

Deshler Hotel assault, Klan tribunal, June 23, 1924, ISL.

Press on assault, "Three Men Held after Brawl at Deshler," *Ohio State Journal,* Jan. 6, 1924.

13. Rage of the Resistance

O'Donnell letters to Reverend Walsh, May 26, 1923, and Dec. 20, 1923, University of Notre Dame archives, UKKK.

O'Donnell and Wrigley, Aaron Gordon, "Doxing Racists Is a 100-Year-Old American Tradition," *Vox,* Jan. 12, 2021, and "Tolerance Hooks a Bear," *Fiery Cross,* Feb. 9, 1923.

Opposition, "Indiana Swayed Entirely by Klan," *New York Times,* Nov. 7, 1923.

Riot details, Todd Tucker, *Notre Dame vs. the Klan: How the Fighting Irish Defeated the Ku Klux Klan* (Chicago: Loyola Press, 2004), 145–62.

Father Walsh memo from archives of the Klan at Notre Dame, UKKK.

Wilson exchange with son, Wilson, "Long, Hot Summer in Indiana," *American Heritage,* Aug. 1965.

NAACP letter to Coolidge, William. W. Giffin, "The Political Realignment of Black Voters in Indianapolis, 1924," *Indiana Magazine of History,* June 1983.

Johnson meeting Grant, Johnson, *Along the Way,* 43; close to Roosevelt, 239; despises Wilson, 306; hinge moment, 308; meeting with Coolidge, 374.

Muncie, Constitution ceased to function, "Editor, Victim of Klan Justice, Loses His All," *Chicago Tribune,* July 9, 1926.

Growth of women, Gordon, *The Second Coming of the KKK,* 127–28.

Dale poem, "Daisy Kept the Nighty Money," *Muncie Post-Democrat,* June 6, 1924.

Rabbi Feuerlicht quote, *A Hoosier Rabbinate,* 51.

Jewish boycott, "How the Kleagles Collected the Cash," *Independent,* Dec. 13, 1924.

Bribe attempt and quotes, "Stephenson Stubborn on Stand," *Indianapolis Times,* Feb. 14, 1928, and Niblack, *Life and Times,* 227.

Remy as prosecutor, his unpublished memoir, IHS.

14. The Klan on Top

Denver, 30,000 Klansmen, a ledger compiled in 2021 by History Colorado, https://www.historycolorado.org/kkkledgers.

Quote from Denver judge, Klan control, John C. Ensslin, "Former Denver Mayor Stapleton and His Involvement with the KKK," *Colorado Politics*, July 29, 2019.

More Colorado, Chalmers, *Hooded Americanism*, 126–34.

Kansas, Kansaspedia, Kansas Historical Society, https://www.kshs.org/kansapedia /ku-klux-klan-in-kansas/15612.

Steve files and dossiers on voters and pols, Niblack, *Life and Times*, 200.

Voters' choice, "Ku Klux Issue Pushed," *Indianapolis Times*, May 7, 1924.

1924 Immigration Act, Okrent, *The Guarded Gate*, 328–30.

"America of the Melting Pot Comes to End," *New York Times*, April 27, 1924.

Anne Frank, "Anne Frank's Family Was Thwarted by U.S. Immigration Rules," *New York Times*, July 6, 2018.

"Immigration Bill Passes," *Fiery Cross*, April 25, 1924.

"Kleveland Konvention," *Time*, June 23, 1924.

Blacks not allowed at DNC until 1924, "Blacks and the Democratic Party," factcheck .org, April 18, 2008.

Democrats, longest political convention, "G.O.P. Path Recalls Democrats' Convention Disaster, in 1924," *New York Times*, March 15, 2016.

Convention details, Robert K. Murray, *The 103rd Ballot* (1976; New York: Harper Paperbacks, 2016), 175–273.

Evans tour of West, Chalmers, *Hooded Americanism*, 283–84.

Klan and Evans in Pacific Northwest, Trevor Griffey, "Citizen Klan: Electoral Politics and the KKK in WA," Seattle Civil Rights and Labor History Project, https://depts.washington.edu/civilr/kkk_politicians.htm.

Quote from Evans, Klan and the West, a speech from 1924, "American Tide Turns to the Klan," *Fiery Cross*, Feb. 13, 1925.

Evans comments at national convention in Kansas City, "Ku Klux Klan at Klansas City," *Time*, Oct. 6, 1924.

Steve's new Klan, "Stephenson Heads Defiant Klansmen," *Indianapolis Star*, May 13, 1924.

Blacks react to Klan, Giffin, "The Political Realignment of Black Voters in Indianapolis, 1924."

Johnson urges vote against Republicans, "Asks Negro Voters to Cut Party Lines," *New York Times*, Sept. 21, 1924.

Johnson quote, "use a navy," "Launches Fight to Aid Negroes," *Indianapolis Star*, June 28, 1926.

Knox urges vote against Republicans, *Slave and Freeman: The Autobiography of George L. Knox* (Lexington: University Press of Kentucky, 1979), 31.

Steve election eve prediction, Feightner oral history, ISL.

Klan victories in Colorado, Cara Degette, "When Colorado Was Klan Country," *Colorado Independent*, Jan. 9, 2009.

Colorado governor tries to outlaw Mass, "The Crazy, True Story of How the Church Helped to Take Down the Ku Klux Klan," *Denver Catholic*, April 22, 2021.

Illinois Grand Dragon quote, Tara McClellan McAndrew, "History: The 1920s Saw the KKK's Rise in Illinois," NPR Illinois, Feb. 28, 2017.

Evans controls the Senate, Pegram, *One Hundred Percent American*, 199.

Wilson, "Long, Hot Summer in Indiana," *American Heritage*, Aug. 1965.

Only 48.9 percent voted, all-time low, Jamelle Bouie, "Republicans Now Have Two Ways to Threaten Elections," *New York Times*, July 16, 2021.

Election headline, "Protestant Ticket Sweeps State," *Fiery Cross*, Nov. 7, 1924.

Steve's attack on Lucille Fuller, her deposition, April 6, 1925, IHS.

Inaugural party details, Leibowitz, *My Indiana*, 196.

15. Hoosier Hysteria

Jefferson Davis monument, "Is There a Place for the President of the Confederacy?," *New York Times*, Oct. 8, 2020.

Number of slaves owned by Davis, "The Anti-Secessionist Jefferson Davis," National Park Service, https://www.nps.gov/bost/the-anti-secessionist-jefferson-davis.htm#:~:text=He%20graduated%20from%20West%20Point,in%20the%20Mexican%2DAmerican%20War.

Quote from Confederate vice president Stephens, https://thehill.com/homenews/house/502521-here-are-the-confederate-statues-in-the-capitol.

Makeup of the "Klan Legislature," Lutholtz, *Grand Dragon*, 153.

Democrat and Klansman in Indiana legislature, oral history of Edward B. Bender, recorded Oct. 31, 1968, ISL.

"We cleaned up," "Court Asher Tells How Stephenson Ruled State," *Richmond Palladium*, Oct. 8, 1926.

Letter from David Hoover to Stephenson, March 7, 1925, ISL.

"There was no argument," "Court Asher Tells How Stephenson Ruled State."

Klansman sat next to senate majority leader, Feightner oral history, ISL.

Wright "Bone Dry" Law, Thomas R. Pegram, "Hoodwinked: The Anti-Saloon League and the Ku Klux Klan in 1920s Prohibition Enforcement," *Journal of the Gilded Age and Progressive Era*, Jan. 2008.

Walgreen's fortune, Okrent, *Last Call*, 197.

Madge at Steve's office, dying declaration.

Nutrition book, Asher testimony, Oct. 13, 1926, IHS.

Madge, two dates, quoting Steve, dying declaration.

"Vice cleanup" squads run by Steve, testimony of Stephenson employee Joseph S. Bell, on file at Ball State University's Bracken Library.

Fuller follow-up, her testimony, IHS.

Ritual, Steve quotes at orgy, "Court Asher Tells How Stephenson Ruled State," *Richmond Palladium*, Oct. 8, 1926.

16. The Last Train to Chicago

Phone call, "Mrs. Oberholtzer Weeps on Stand," *Indianapolis Times*, Oct. 29, 1925.

Extortion, Indianapolis streetcars hiring Klan, police, from "How the Kleagles Collected the Cash," *Independent*, Dec. 13, 1924.

Madge's day on March 15, 1925, and her call to Steve, "Girl's Story Is Told at Trial," *Indianapolis Star*, Oct. 30, 1925.

Blacks turned away from buses, "Contest Evidence to Show Buses Lawful Carriers," *Indianapolis Star*, May 25, 1925.

The assault, her wounds, all dialogue, dying declaration, and Dr. Kingsbury testimony, "Girl's Story Is Told at Trial."

Klan opens hospital, "Study Identifies Kokomo as Home of KKK Hate Group," *Kokomo Tribune*, Feb. 28, 2017.

Steve to Madge at garage, dying declaration.

Shultz on seeing Madge, Asa Smith contacted, Mrs. Oberholtzer looking for her daughter, "Mrs. Oberholtzer Weeps on Stand."

17. A Vigil in Irvington

Smith summoned, trip to Steve house, his testimony, "Girl's Story Is Told at Trial," *Indianapolis Star*, Oct. 30, 1925.

Smith background, his oral history, March 20, 1969, ISL.

Dr. Kingsbury dialogue with Madge, "Oberholtzer Doctor Is Witness," *Indianapolis Times*, June 17, 1925.

Nettie Brehm child support, "Inman Lawyer for Stephenson," *Indianapolis Times*, April 4, 1925.

Father and daughter, his court testimony, "Mrs. Oberholtzer Weeps on Stand," *Indianapolis Times*, Oct. 29, 1925.

Smith in Steve's office, negotiations over settlement, "Facts Concerning Evidence," undated, IHS.

Steve quote, "blackmail," testimony of Griffith Dean, "Mrs. Oberholtzer Weeps on Stand."

Remy background, Steve dinner at Severin Hotel, Remy's unpublished memoir, IHS.

Steve's arrest, quotes, "Stephenson Indicted on Charge of Assault with Intent to Kill Girl," *Indianapolis Times*, April 3, 1925.

18. The Witness

Madge says goodbye to the doctor, his testimony, "Girl's Story Is Told at Trial," *Indianapolis Star*, Oct. 30, 1925.

Quote from doctor on Madge condition, "Reindictment of Stephenson Is Discussed," *Indianapolis Times*, April 8, 1925.

Joe Huffington on Klan banishing Steve, "D. C. Stephenson Hires Attorney Inman," *Indianapolis Times*, April 4, 1925.

Nebraska Klan terrorizes home of Malcolm X, Adam Fletcher Sasse, "A Biography of Malcolm X in Omaha," https://northomahahistory.com/2019/03/13/a-biography -of-malcolm-x-in-omaha/.

"Death Takes Madge Oberholtzer," *Indianapolis Times*, April 14, 1925.

Madge's funeral and Steve's plea, "Friends Lay Madge Oberholtzer to Rest," *Indianapolis Times*, April 16, 1925.

George's prior losses, Ottinger, *Madge*, 22.

Pact between Steve and Duvall, "Stephenson Influence Described," *Indianapolis Times*, April 21, 1925.

"no mean city," *Encyclopedia of Indianapolis*, https://indyencyclopedia.org.

40,000 Klansmen in Indianapolis, Jackson, *The Ku Klux Klan in the City*, 154.

"Klanopolis," "How the Kleagles Collected the Cash," *Independent*, Dec. 13, 1924.

Fire, "Stephenson's House Set on Fire," *Indianapolis Times*, April 17, 1925.

Rug removed, "Oriental Rug from Stephenson Home Is Taken to House of Official in Charge," *Indianapolis Times*, May 8, 1925.

Remy death threats, his unpublished memoir, IHS.

Beautician's story, Smith oral history, ISL.

Sorority girl, Chicago, ibid.

Protests by women, Ottinger, *Madge*, 224–25, and "Stephenson Is Still in Jail," *Indianapolis Times*, April 21, 1925.

Resolution from Butler, "Stephenson Is behind Bars," *Indianapolis Times*, April 20, 1925.

Duvall and Klan ticket win, "Duvall's Lead Mounts over 7,000," *Indianapolis Times*, May 6, 1925.

Mayor and Klan in Evansville, "1920s Evansville Mayor Was in KKK," *Evansville Courier & Press*, Sept. 24, 2018.

19. Big Man in a Small Town

Church scene, "Moore Discusses the Ku Klux Klan," *Noblesville Ledger*, Jan. 8, 1923.

Noblesville Klan, Allen Safianow, "You Can't Burn History," *Indiana Magazine of History*, June 2004.

Klan parade largest in town history, "Klansmen in a Monster Parade Saturday Night," *Noblesville Ledger*, July 2, 1923.

William Stern, quotes and feelings, "W. H. Stern Makes Plea for Colored Race," *Noblesville Ledger*, Sept. 24, 1927.

Stern recounts war, "Anniversary of Battle of Shiloh," *Noblesville Ledger*, April 7, 1925.

W. E. B. Du Bois, "The Shape of Fear," *North American Review*, June 1926.

Change of venue, "Stephenson Trial in Noblesville," *Indianapolis Times*, May 23, 1925.

Matilda wanted to kill Steve with her hands, Ottinger, *Madge*, 196.

Ruling on declaration, quotes from Steve and his lawyers, "Stephenson Wins State Evidence," *Indianapolis Times*, June 16, 1925.

Dale quotes from his column, "'I am the Law,' Stephenson," *Muncie Post-Democrat*, June 26, 1925.

Klan failing in Muncie, "Disgraced," *Muncie Post-Democrat*, May 8, 1925, and "The Ku Klux Klan," *Muncie Post-Democrat*, May 15, 1925.

"Hicks," "Klan Delegates Are Taught All of the New Songs of the Day," *Muncie Post-Democrat*, June 19, 1925.

Caleb Ridley arrested, "Seizes Klan Chaplain as Intoxicated in Car," *New York Times*, Oct. 18, 1923.

Quote from *Chicago Defender*, Jill Lepore, "Why the School Wars Still Rage," *New Yorker*, March 21, 2022.

Scopes Monkey Trial, Noah Adams, "Timeline: Remembering the Scopes Monkey Trial," NPR, July 5, 2005, https://www.npr.org/2005/07/05/4723956/timeline -remembering-the-scopes-monkey-trial.

20. One Nation under a Shroud

Parade description and quotes, "Sight Astonishes Capital," *New York Times*, Aug. 9, 1925.

"one of the greatest demonstrations," "Klan's 1925 Rally: 'A Great Parade,'" *Washington Post*, Aug. 29, 1982.

Nearly 90 percent from Northern states, "Sight Astonishes Capital."

W. E. B. Du Bois quote, "The Shape of Fear," *North American Review*, June 1926.

Coolidge work habits, Irving Stone, "Calvin Coolidge: A Study in Inertia," reprinted in *The Aspirin Age: 1919–1941* (New York: Simon & Schuster, 1949), 144.

Coolidge quote, ibid.

Mencken quote, "The Klan Walks in Washington," *Literary Digest*, Aug. 22, 1925.

Steve's gifts in jail, Niblack, *Life and Times*, 212.

Attempt to bribe reporters, ibid., 213.

Steve felt threatened by Evans men, Lutholtz, *Grand Dragon*, 228.

Klan pressure in Noblesville, "Klan Komment," *Noblesville Ledger*, July 20, 1925.

"Klan Komment," *Noblesville Ledger*, July 8, 1925.

Evans, "Imperial Wizard of Klan Spoke at Chautauqua," *Noblesville Ledger*, Aug. 10, 1925.

New judge, delay of trial, "Judge Sparks to Try Stephenson," *Indianapolis Times*, Aug. 11, 1925.

21. To Slay a Dragon

Remy weight loss and fears, his unpublished memoir, HIS.

Remy, quotes and strategy, ibid.

Remy notebook on strategy, on file at IHS.

Charles Cox bio, "Charles E. Cox Sr., Former Judge, Dies," *Indianapolis Star*, Feb. 4, 1936.

Stern bio, thoughts on Klan, "W. H. Stern Makes Plea for Colored Race," *Noblesville Ledger*, Sept. 24, 1927.

Threats to Oberholtzers, Ottinger, *Madge*, 266–67.

Makeup of jury, "Men Who Hold Trio's Fate," *Indianapolis Times*, Oct. 29, 1925.

Cox opening statement, "Stephenson Branded Dr. Jekyll-Mr. Hyde," *Indianapolis Times*, Oct. 29, 1925.

Opening testimony, ibid.

promise of "startling revelation," "Evidence of State Concluded in Murder Trial," *Indianapolis Star*, Nov. 7, 1925.

"which crowd are you in," "Klan Komment," *Noblesville Ledger*, July 20, 1925.

Dale note passed to Steve in courtroom, W. A. S. Douglas, "The Mayor of Middletown," *American Mercury*, Aug. 1930.

Kingsbury testimony, "Oberholtzer Lawyer Denies Bribe," *Indianapolis Times*, Oct. 30, 1925.

Smith, Battle of Belleau Wood, "More Stephenson Case Testimony," *Indianapolis Times*, Oct. 29, 1925.

Steve's dress, diamond on display, "D. C. Stephenson's Greatest Love Was of 'The Old Man,'" *Indianapolis News*, Oct. 9, 1950.

Judge statement in ruling, "D. C. Stephenson Trial: An Account," assembled by Professor Douglas O. Linder, University of Missouri-Kansas School of Law, https://www.famous-trials.com/stephenson/74-home.

22. She Said

Rally for Klan ticket, "G.O.P. Backs Klan School Board Slate," *Indianapolis Times*, Nov. 2, 1925.

Madge's dying declaration read in court, "Poison Room in Hotel Is Pictured," *Indianapolis Times*, Oct. 31, 1925.

Testimony of hotel employees, "Stephenson Charges Mistrial," *Indianapolis Star*, Nov. 1, 1925.

Testimony of Levi Thomas, porter, ibid.

Steve bribe attempt, oral history of Walter D. Meyers, 1970–71, ISL.

23. Inside and Outside

Steve quote, "cold, hard cash," "The Printer Who Turned Indiana Over to the KKK," *St. Louis Post-Dispatch*, Nov. 14, 1926.

Steve bribes the jailer, women visitors, etc., Court Asher testimony, Marion County Grand Jury, IHS, and Niblack, *Life and Times*, 212–13.

Carl Losey and Steve's "witnesses," "Defense Tries Attack on Girl's Statement," *Indianapolis News*, Nov. 7, 1925.

Niblack on bribes, *Life and Times*, 213.

Feightner hears rumors of attempts to bribe jurors, his oral history, ISL.

Evans plea to Grand Dragons, "Klan Official Urges Secrecy," *Dayton Daily News*, Aug. 26, 1925.

Evans, "The Klan: Defender of Americanism," *Forum* 74 (Dec. 1925).

"the greatest organization ever," Steve message, Sept. 19, 1923, ISL.

Letter to "Mildred," undated, on file at IHS.

Asher and $17,000, his testimony to Marion County Grand Jury, IHS.

Testimony of MacDonald and Moon, "State Bolsters New Blood Poison Theory," *Indianapolis Times*, Nov. 3, 1925.

Election results, Klan statement, "John L. Duvall Wins by 8,991," *Indianapolis Star*, Nov. 4, 1925.

City Hall to the Klan, "Klan Scores Heavily in Political Plum Passing," *Indianapolis Times*, Nov. 9, 1925.

24. He Said

Smiley on the stand, "Suicide, Stephenson's Opening Gun," *Indianapolis Times*, Nov. 5, 1925.

Steve "affable," "Evidence in State Concluded in Murder Trial," *Noblesville Ledger*, Nov. 5, 1925.

Steve lunges for Niblack, "Suicide, Stephenson's Opening Gun."

Cora Householder and Chester Clawson testimony, "Evidence in State Concluded in Murder Trial." Householder "affair" story, Lutholtz, *Grand Dragon*, 271–73.

Remy cross of Clawson, "Stephenson Defense Outline," *Indianapolis Star*, Nov. 7, 1925.

Hotel employee testimony, ibid.

A-Y-A-K letters on roadside, Remy's unpublished memoir, IHS.

Steve going through political pledges, "Lawyer Insists He Saw Papers," *Indianapolis Times*, Oct. 14, 1926.

Steve's gunman in court, "Steve Was the Terrorist instead of the Terrified," *Indianapolis News*, Oct. 5, 1950.

Rigdon testimony, "Witness Invites Kane Out on the Street for Fight," *Noblesville Ledger*, Nov. 9, 1925.

Whereabouts of Shorty DeFriese, Ottinger, *Madge*, 440.

Final defense witnesses, Red Cross donation, "Hill Tells of Governor's Ball," *Noblesville Ledger*, Nov. 11, 1925.

25. The Closers

First four Remy quotes in closing argument, "Facts Back Up Dying Story—Remy," *Indianapolis Times*, Nov. 12, 1925.

Plan to kill Remy, his unpublished memoir, IHS.

Remy quote after lunch, "Facts Back Up Dying Story—Remy."

Holmes quotes, ibid.

First Cox quotes, "Inman Assails Blood Cry of Mob," *Indianapolis Times*, Nov. 13, 1925.

Cox on medieval times, "Jury Retires to Deliberate Case," *Indianapolis News*, Nov. 14, 1925.

Cox on doing right by Oberholtzer parents, ibid.

Floyd Christian, "Inman Assails Blood Cry of Mob," *Indianapolis Times*, Nov. 13, 1925.

More Inman, ibid.

Kane, on whole nation looking to verdict, "Jury Retires to Deliberate Case," *Indianapolis News*, Nov. 14, 1925.

26. Verdict

Details while awaiting verdict, Niblack, *Life and Times*, 215.

Attempt to bribe two jurors, Feightner oral history, ISL.

Reaction of Stephenson to verdict, number of Indiana Klansmen, "Finds Ex-Klan Head Murdered Woman," *New York Times*, Nov. 15, 1925.

Verdict details, "Stephenson Is Sentenced," *Indianapolis Times*, Nov. 16, 1925.

New charges, arson etc., "Stephenson to See Prison by This Weekend," *Indianapolis Times*, Nov. 17, 1925.

Remy nearly forced off road, his unpublished memoir, IHS.

Steve checks into penitentiary, "Prison Door Closes upon Stephenson," *Indianapolis Times*, Nov. 21, 1925.

Contents of his pockets, request for cigars, measurements of the Bertillon system, "Stephenson to Be Assigned to Work in Prison Soon," *Noblesville Ledger*, Nov. 23, 1925.

One of the jurors a Catholic, "Steve Was the Terrorist instead of the Terrified," *Indianapolis News*, Oct. 5, 1950.

27. Dirt from the Dragon

Steve in prison, his plan for a pardon, Niblack, *Life and Times*, 217.

Steve's motion, "Plans to Ask for New Trial," *Indianapolis Star*, Dec. 10, 1925.

Evans, "The Klan's Fight for Americanism," *North American Review*, March 1926.

Oregon dentist and collapse of Klan there, Ben Bruce, "The Rise and Fall of the Ku Klux Klan in Oregon during the 1920s," *Voces Novae* 11 (2019).

Colorado, Elise Schmelzer, "The KKK Ruled Denver a Century Ago," *Denver Post*, June 6, 2021.

Klan records found, "Two Bags of Klan Records Floating down River," *Noblesville Ledger*, Aug. 21, 1925.

Dale comments, "Stephenson before Starting for Prison Says Courtroom Crowd Was Hostile," *Muncie Post-Democrat*, Nov. 18, 1925.

"Democrats Flay Klan in Meeting," *Indianapolis Times*, Nov. 19, 1925.

Editorials, *Indianapolis Times*, Nov. 16, 1925.

Paper lost 5,000 subscribers, Leibowitz, *My Indiana*, 214.

Correspondence with San Francisco woman Verna Green, undated, IHS.

Letter from woman in South Bend, Dec. 15, 1925, signee unclear, ISL.

Martha L. Dickinson, from her letters, undated, IHS.

Adams report, "Outraged Editorial Conscience Tore Mask from Indiana Politics," *Editor & Publisher*, Oct. 16, 1926.

Adams bio, "T. H. Adams Dies; Foe of Ku Klux Klan," *New York Times*, Nov. 23, 1930.

Republican reaction to press accounts, "Stephenson Here, Talks to Jury," *Indianapolis Times*, Oct. 13, 1926.

Racial zoning law, "Segregation Measure Passes amid Cheers," *Indianapolis News*, March 16, 1926.

Whiteman's quote, Paul Mullins, "Racist Spite and Residential Segregation," *Invisible Indianapolis* (blog), Jan. 20, 2019, https://invisibleindianapolis.wordpress.com/2019/01/20/racist-spite-and-residential-segregation-housing-and-the-color-line-in-inter-war-indianapolis/.

Women of the KKK meeting, "Klan Women of Nation in Session Here," *Indianapolis Times*, Aug. 5, 1927.

Klan march on Washington, "Klan Ranks Thinner in Capital Parade," *New York Times*, Sept. 13, 1926.

Evans speech, "Women of Klan End Convention," *Indianapolis Star*, Aug. 7, 1927.

Steve quote, "I purchased," Libby Cierzniak, "D. C Stephenson's Revenge," historicindianapolis.com, Aug. 8, 2015.

Remy in Lick Skillet, Niblack, *Life and Times*, 221.

Steve's testimony against Jackson, Feb. 13 and 14, 1928, IHS.

Steve testimony on guns and violence, "$1,800,000 Harvested by Steve from Klan Office during His Dizzy Regime," *Indianapolis Times*, Oct. 15, 1928.

"Isn't it strange," "*New York Times* Analyzes Ku Klux Klan Complex," *Catholic Transcript*, Nov. 11, 1926.

Klan atrocities, "Steve Reveals Klan's Power," *Indianapolis Times*, April 2, 1928; "Burnings at Stake at Behest of Evans Told at Klan Trial," *New York Times*, April 11, 1928.

Judge comments in Pennsylvania case, *Knights of the Ku Klux Klan Inc. vs. Strayer*, 1928.

Chicago Tribune summary, "Indiana in the Dark Age," April 3, 1927.

Priest comes to Noblesville, "Father Holand Discussed Good Fellowship," *Noblesville Ledger*, Oct. 3, 1928.

Commencement speech, "Immense Crowd at Commencement," *Tipton Daily Tribune*, May 22, 1926.

Klan membership down 90 percent, Chalmers, *Hooded Americanism*, 291.

Feightner quote, oral history, ISL.

Lynching, "Marion Mob Storms Jail, Hangs Two," *Indianapolis Star*, Aug. 8, 1930.

Klan at lynching, atmosphere like a "picnic," "Old List of Klan Members Recalls Racist Past in an Indiana City," *New York Times*, Aug. 2, 1995.

Cameron's story of lynching, his book, *A Time of Terror: A Survivor's Account* (Lancaster, PA: LifeWrites Press, 2016).

Epilogue

Discovery of secrets, "Trunk Opens Up Indiana Town's Secret Past," *Los Angeles Times*, July 15, 1995.

Allen Safianow, "You Can't Burn History," *Indiana Magazine of History*, June 1, 2004.

"most talented psychopath," Wade, *The Fiery Cross*, 221.

Ritchie Boys, Bruce Henderson, *Sons and Soldiers: The Untold Story of the Jews Who Escaped the Nazis and Returned with the U.S. Army to Fight Hitler* (New York: William Morrow, 2017).

Supreme Court on sterilization, "Is Forced Contraception Alleged by Britney Spears Legal?," *New York Times*, June 27, 2021.

Effect of eugenics ruling, Adam Cohen, *Imbeciles* (New York: Penguin, 2017), 160–282.

Repeal of Horse Thieves, "Votes to Cut Out Horse Thief Law," *Indianapolis Star*, March 7, 1933.

Repeal of Prohibition, "U.S. Wet Again," *Indianapolis Star*, Dec. 6, 1933.

Consumption rose, Mark Thornton, "Alcohol Prohibition Was a Failure," Cato Institute, July 17, 1991.

"Manning Making Calls about His Bourbon," *Indianapolis Star*, Sept. 22, 2021.

State Supreme Court quote, from its ruling, *Stephenson v. State*, 1932, IHS.

Steve's release, "Stephenson Wins Commutation," *Indianapolis Times*, March 4, 1950.

Kicked out by daughter, "Death of a Klansman," *Louisville Courier-Journal*, Sept. 17, 1978.

Steve disappears, "Stephenson Seized on Murder Parole," *New York Times*, Nov. 16, 1950.

Steve's assault of teenager, "Death of a Klansman."

Reporters discover his death, ibid.

Steve never a war veteran, report of the adjutant general, "no overseas service," undated, on file at ISL.

Steve and presidency, Remy, his unpublished memoir, IHS.

Klan falls to less than 100,000, Chalmers, *Hooded Americanism*, 291.

Evans's later years, sale of Imperial headquarters, "Dr. Colescott Dies; Ex-Chief of Klan," *New York Times*, Jan. 13, 1950, and "Dr. Hiram W. Evans," Texas State Historical Association, June 2, 2016.

Colescott, Klan disbanding, "Dr. Colescott Dies; Ex-Chief of Klan."

Court Asher, his paper, sedition, death, "Court Asher, Controversial Muncie Figure, Dead," *Muncie Star Press*, Dec. 30, 1967.

Gentry death, "Who Murdered Earl Gentry?" *Milwaukee Journal*, April 25 and 26, 1938.

Dale, elected mayor, "George Dale Dies; Ku Klux Klan Foe," *New York Times*, March 28, 1936.

Feightner quote, oral history, ISL.

"The air of America," "The Crazy, True Story of How the Church Helped Take Down the Klan in Colorado," *Denver Catholic*, April 22, 2021.

Dr. Meriwether, "Dr. Lucian Meriwether, Leading Dentist, Dies," *Indianapolis Recorder*, Jan. 30, 1982.

Cameron key to city, "A Night of Lynching, a Life of Remembering," *Los Angeles Times*, Feb. 23, 2003.

Passage of anti-lynching bill, "Congress Gives Final Approval to Make Lynching a Hate Crime," *New York Times*, March 8, 2022.

Death of Remy, "William H. Remy, Retired Attorney," *Indianapolis Star*, Sept. 2, 1968.

Death of Niblack, "John L. Niblack, Ex-Senator, Judge," *Indianapolis News*, June 17, 1986.

Niblack quote, dedication, his *Life and Times*.

INDEX

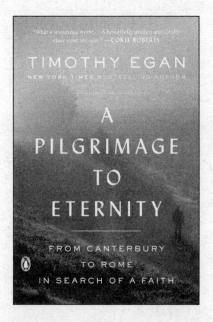